THE ROTATION DIET

THE ROTATION DIET

Martin Katahn, Ph.D.

BANTAM PRESS

NEW YORK · LONDON · TORONTO · SYDNEY · AUCKLAND

TRANSWORLD PUBLISHERS LTD
61–63 Uxbridge Road, London W5 5SA

TRANSWORLD PUBLISHERS (AUSTRALIA) PTY LTD
15-23 Helles Avenue, Moorebank NSW 2170

TRANSWORLD PUBLISHERS (NZ) LTD
Cnr Moselle and Waipareira Aves,
Henderson, Auckland

Published 1987 by Bantam Press,
a division of Transworld Publishers Ltd
Copyright © Katahn Associates Inc. 1986

British Library Cataloguing in Publication Data

Katahn, Martin
    The rotation diet.
    1. Reducing diets   2. Physical fitness
    I. Title
    613.2'5   RM222.2

    ISBN 0 593 01248 8

Typeset by Phoenix Photosetting, Chatham
Printed and bound in Great Britain by
Mackays of Chatham, Kent

Contents

STANDARD MEASURES FOR THE BRITISH EDITION

Since Dr Katahn's Rotation Diet originated in Nashville, Tennessee, many of the measurements for servings (and some in the recipes) are given by volume using the American cup. Measurement by volume is often the most sensible way, for dry rice, for example, and to give an idea of the appropriate quantity of fruit or vegetables. To be accurate, measure a 'cup' up to the 8-fluid-ounce (225-ml) mark in a standard measuring jug; you will soon be able to judge the proper amounts. As a rough guide, 3 stalks of raw celery (sliced), 2 medium carrots (sliced) or 3 ounces (80 g) of raw sliced mushrooms all approximate 1 cup. Again as a rough guide, 1 piece of fruit – a small apple or orange, half a large banana, 3 ounces (80 g) of grapes (about 20), a small slice of melon or a ¾-inch (1½-cm) slice of pineapple each approximates half a cup. A normal serving of any cooked vegetable approximates one cup; a small serving or 3 rounded tablespoons half a cup. In the menus that follow men are often allowed vegetable servings half as big again. These approximate the 'average' and 'small' helpings that a man could expect in a restaurant or at home. Accurately the greens or marrow would come up to the 12-fluid-ounce (330-ml) level in your measuring jug (for 1½ cups), the peas or carrots to the 6-fluid-ounce (180-ml) level (for ¾ cup).

Rice and pasta such as macaroni will roughly double in volume on cooking; for porridge, use the volume of water that you require and add the appropriate quantities of oatmeal or rolled oats according to the instructions for your usual brand – i.e. for one cup of porridge use 8 fluid ounces (225 ml) of water and 3 to 4 level tablespoons of rolled oats.

In the recipes most of the American cup measurements have been converted to British Imperial and Metric weights on the scales given below, the criterion being in each case: which is the easiest measurement to use? Spoonfuls are always level unless 'rounded' or 'heaped' is specified; and please remember that all teaspoons, including ½ and ¼ teaspoons, should be scant measures – just a little less than level.

Weights

1 kg = 2 lbs 3 oz
450 g = 1 lb
350 g = 12 oz
300 g = 10 oz
225 g = 8 oz
175 g = 6 oz
145 g = 5 oz
110 g = 4 oz
 80 g = 3 oz
 56 g = 2 oz
 40 g = 1½ oz
 28 g = 1 oz

Volume/Liquids

1 litre = 1¾ pints/35 fluid oz
700 ml = 1¼ pints/24 fluid oz
         (3 American cups)
570 ml = 1 pint/20 fluid oz
450 ml = 16 fluid oz
         (2 American cups)
330 ml = 12 fluid oz
         (1½ American cups)
225 ml = 8 fluid oz
         (1 American cup)
180 ml = 6 fluid oz
         (¾ American cup)
110 ml = 4 fluid oz
         (½ American cup)
 25 ml = 1 fluid oz
 15 ml = 1 tablespoon
 10 ml = 1 dessertspoon
  5 ml = 1 teaspoon

Acknowledgements

I am greatly indebted to my many colleagues and students in Nashville, Tennessee, who, from the start of the Vanderbilt Weight Management Program ten years ago, have contributed so much to the advances we have made in helping overweight people. Without their help, the Rotation Diet would never have been created.

To begin with, it was my former student Dr Gordon Kaplan who named the programme when he recruited participants for his dissertation study on the factors that lead to long-term success in weight management. At that time, Dr Kenneth Wallston joined us and assumed primary responsibility for the research component of the programme. More recently, Dr David Schlundt has collaborated in the development of our analysis of eating and activity problem areas, and in the design of our steps to weight-management mastery that form the basis for Chapters 9, 10 and 11 of *The Rotation Diet*. Dr Craig Heim, director of the Center for Health Promotion in the Vanderbilt Medical School, supervised the medical research that disclosed some of the health benefits associated with the Rotation Diet.

Another former student, Dr Mark McMinn, contributed greatly with his studies of the biochemical factors that underlie the problem of obesity. Three of my present graduate students, Ruth Daby, Tracy Sbrocco, and Crystal Sulyma, are all involved in implementing the Rotation Diet in the Vanderbilt Program and they have all contributed to the development of the material in Chapters 9, 10 and 11.

Our nutrition consultant, Rachel Willis, RD, helped in the design of the Alternative Menus for the Rotation Diet that appear in Chapter 12. Her menus and recipes help me illustrate that eating nutritiously on a weight-reduction and weight-maintenance diet does not have to be boring, nor does it require an intolerable amount of deprivation. And thanks to our master baker, Joyce Weingartner, for creating the unique bread recipes that you will find in Chapter 6.

I want to express my special appreciation to the one person who keeps the entire Vanderbilt Weight Management Program on track by coordinating all of our efforts: my associate director, Summer Davis. In addition to her administrative skills, her own personal experience and understanding of the special problems that women face in managing their weight and her knowledge of how those problems are intertwined with other aspects of their lives enrich us all and contribute to our ability as leaders.

I don't know what I did to deserve them, but I have a very special family. Words can do little to express my love and appreciation, first, for being such a support when I lost over 5 stone (34 kg) twenty-two years ago, second, for helping me maintain an environment that keeps it all off and, third, for the joy they take in helping me create and test the interesting and delicious recipes for this and my other books. This time, in particular, my daughter, Terri, provided the first review of everything I wrote, and helped design and write the recipes.

Once again, just as he has in my two previous books, my editor at W. W. Norton, Starling Lawrence, provided invaluable critical advice in helping me write comprehensibly. In this instance, it was the difficult job of translating the clinically supervised Rotation Diet, just as we use it in the Vanderbilt Program, into book form. In addition, many others at W. W. Norton, and their friends, jumped in to test the diet as it was presented in the manuscript, to make sure we had succeeded. These included Iva Ashner, Linda Corrente, Dierdre Dolan, Jeannie Luciano, Fran Rosencrantz, and Bill Rusin, among many others. They provided the first, long-distance, daily reports of people trying the Rotation Diet on their own, and they gave us invaluable advice on how to present the programme as simply and understandably as possible. Their efforts have helped make *The Rotation Diet* easy to use. And their reward was the loss of an average of 11½ pounds each.

As always – and I hope it goes on for ever – my super agents, Arthur and Richard Pine, have taken charge of every possible detail that could make an author's life more complicated. From the very beginning, when I first tried to tell the truth about the problems that overweight people face and to explain what it really takes to manage your weight, the Pines, together with Starling Lawrence, have believed in the value of my work when others did not think the truth had 'commercial value'. Their support and boundless enthusiasm are truly appreciated.

And thanks again to my friends at Tandy for making sure that my computer, the Tandy 1200HD, never left me in the lurch during the writing of this book. The only time that I had a problem, when my keyboard decided it no longer wished to communicate with my computer, it took but one phone call and I had a replacement keyboard in my hands within twenty minutes, loaned to me while my own was sent in for repairs. I wish that every manufacturer and retailer of every mechanical and electronic device were as concerned about the needs of their customers as the folks at Tandy have been for mine throughout the many years that I have used their products.

THE ROTATION DIET

1

Introduction

HOW FAST WILL YOU LOSE?

'How fast can I lose weight on your diet?'

'Will I ever be able to eat like a normal human being and not gain weight?'

These are easily the most frequently asked questions on the lips of persons about to enter the Vanderbilt Weight Management Program, and they are among the first questions I am asked as I go around the country speaking on the topic of weight management.

Finally, after twenty-two years of personal experience maintaining my own weight loss of 75 pounds (more than 5 stone or 34 kg) and ten years of work helping others lose weight in the Vanderbilt Program, I am able to give answers that will satisfy everyone who has 10, 20, 50, even 75 pounds of weight to lose:

Research results with participants in the Vanderbilt Program show that women will average a loss of approximately *two-thirds of a pound per day for twenty-one days on the Rotation Diet*. Some women, especially heavier women, will lose as much as a pound per day. Men may lose even more. But these are just the averages.

If you have a tendency to retain water, as many over-

weight persons do, you may lose as much as 2 or even 3 pounds a day during the first three days of the Rotation Diet. Many individuals lose two to three inches around the waist and buttocks in just three days and, as you will see from the comments made by participants in our programme (Chapter 3), you can be one or two dress or trouser sizes smaller in three weeks or less. Thus, while the Rotation Diet is designed to help individuals who are significantly overweight, it is also the perfect diet for anyone who has struggled with the last 5 or 10 pounds (2 to 4½ kg) that stand between them and their most desirable weight.

WHAT IS THE ROTATION DIET?

When you use the Rotation Diet you alternate your caloric intake over a three-week period in order to achieve a dramatic, quick weight loss without predisposing yourself to that frustrating rebound weight gain that tends to follow the use of every other low-calorie diet.

Women use a mixed diet consisting of a wide variety of foods and approximately 600 calories per day for three days, followed by 900 calories per day for four days, and then a week on 1200 calories per day. You then do the 600/900-calorie rotation once again.

Men use a mixed diet of approximately 1200 calories per day for three days, followed by 1500 calories per day for four days, followed by a week on 1800 calories per day. The 1200/1500 rotation is repeated once again.

Then, *you STOP dieting.* Weight loss has been so easy and so successful that you will want to continue if you have more weight to lose. But it is very important to the success of the Rotation Diet that you take at least a brief break from dieting. This brief break not only increases your motivation to succeed, *it helps guarantee that you do not regain any weight when you reach your goal weight.* I will explain why in just a moment.

After a week's or a month's break from dieting (it's up to you) you go on the Rotation Diet for another 10-, 15- or

2

20-pound weight loss. Your motivation to succeed will never be greater. After all, how many times have you had to FORCE yourself to STOP dieting in order to ensure your success? With other diets, you soon begin to feel so deprived, and weight loss becomes so frustratingly slow you give up in disgust. Not so with the Rotation Diet. You will be itching to get going once again. The rotation is the key to your success. Even if you have more than 5 stone (34 kg) to lose, the Rotation Diet is the surest way to get that weight off easily and quickly, *and keep it off.*

WILL YOU BE ABLE TO EAT LIKE A NORMAL HUMAN BEING AND NOT GAIN WEIGHT AFTER THE ROTATION DIET?

Yes! And that is the answer that we have all been searching for. For most of us, hard as it might be to lose weight, it is even harder to keep weight off once lost than to get it off in the first place.

In order for you to appreciate the true significance of the Rotation Diet you need to understand why it is so easy to regain weight after a diet, especially quick-weight-loss diets other than the Rotation Diet. One of the reasons for that rebound weight gain is that when you go on a low-calorie diet (800 calories or less) for as few as three weeks, *your metabolic rate can slow down rather drastically.* This means that when you finish dieting you cannot eat anywhere near what you did before you began to diet without gaining weight. The process works in the following way.

The term *metabolic rate* refers to the speed with which your body burns calories. Your resting metabolic rate is the speed with which your body burns calories at rest, just doing the job of keeping itself alive – circulating blood, nourishing and rebuilding your body cells, thinking and problem solving and so forth. Your total

3

daily need for calories is determined primarily by your resting metabolic rate, plus the amount of physical activity you add to your life each day.

Although there is a great deal of variability, the average woman needs a total of between 1800 and 2000 calories per day in order to maintain her weight. The average man needs between 2400 and 2700. This total includes the number of calories it takes to maintain the body at rest, plus the amount needed for movement.

THE STARVATION RESPONSE

When somebody goes on a low-calorie diet (especially a diet that ignores physical activity) a marvellous thing happens. It's called metabolic adaptation or, simply, the 'starvation response'. As a result of millions of years of evolution in which the human race faced periodic famine, our bodies have developed an automatic, built-in ability to cut back on our need for calories if we reduce our food intake. In some ways it's like turning down a thermostat to lower the heat in a house. Your body temperature falls, your heart rate slows, other body functions slow down, all in an effort to conserve energy. This ability to slow down is very important in case we have to face a famine, as many hundreds of millions of people in the world still do each year.

However, the body's ability to slow down and cut back on its metabolic needs is not very helpful for an overweight person trying to maintain a weight loss after a low-calorie diet. Our research, and that of many others, shows that after a low-calorie diet, if you eat any more than 60 per cent of what you used to eat before you began the diet, *you will start to gain weight.*

This will have a great deal more meaning for you if you think of what it takes to stay alive for an hour, just sitting still. The average non-dieting woman might need 60 or so calories; the man, about 80. But after a low-calorie diet, the woman may only need 35 or 40; the man, 45 or 50. And even the caloric cost of activity will have been reduced. Before a diet, you normally burn up about 100 calories per mile of walking. After a diet, you may burn up only 60 calories per mile. So, if you are a victim of the starvation response and have reduced your metabolic rate through unwise dieting, you can't even get the normal weight-management benefits of exercise.

If you have tried a low-calorie diet plan for as long as three weeks you will now understand one reason why it was so easy to gain weight when you finished. Your body doesn't need as many calories; that's why it may have become more difficult for you to lose weight after you have regained it following a low-calorie diet.

The main point of all of this is that you should not do anything to lower your metabolic rate while dieting. In fact, you should be doing every healthy thing you can to increase your metabolic rate. The higher your metabolic rate, the better off you are, because that means you are burning up those calories that would otherwise turn to fat.

And now for the good news! REALLY good news.

The Rotation Diet does not slow metabolic rates.

I know you are going to be happy with the speed of weight loss on the Rotation Diet. But you are going to be even happier when you discover that the Rotation Diet will not predispose you to that rebound weight gain you may have experienced after using other fast-weight-loss plans, whenever you have tried to stabilize your weight.

Research using the Rotation Diet with participants in the Vanderbilt Weight Management Program shows that in spite of a significantly increased rate of weight loss compared with the best non-rotation, strict 1200-calorie diet plan we had been able to devise, *there is no reduction in metabolic rate*. In fact, most participants using the Rotation Diet showed an *increase* in metabolic rate. This means that instead of training their bodies to get along on less food while they were dieting, they were *increasing* their ability to eat after the diet without regaining weight.

The Rotation Diet short-circuits the starvation response for several reasons. First, you use a mixed diet

5

containing a wide variety of foods (high-protein diets that cut out carbohydrates, such as bread, potatoes, fruits and vegetables, are more likely to slow metabolic rate). Second, you don't stay on a calorie intake below 1200 calories for more than a week. And third, if you are a sedentary person, you get more active.

Your final objective is, of course, to be able to eat like a normal healthy person without gaining weight. As part of the Rotation Diet maintenance plan, I will show you which foods and which exercises can increase your metabolic rate. Most people, with a wise choice of foods, can eat a good 20 per cent more calories per day than they are presently eating and not gain weight!

HERE'S WHAT THIS BOOK CONTAINS

In the next two chapters I am going to tell you how the Rotation Diet came into being. First I'll tell you how I, personally, lost over 5 stone (34 kg) twenty-two years ago, cured my hypertension and helped prevent a recurrence of the heart attack that started me on the road to creating the programme I am going to describe in this book. Then I want to tell you about the research that demonstrated how effective the Rotation Diet could be without lowering your metabolic rate.

In Chapters 4 and 5 I will explain what you will need to do to be as successful as the participants in the Vanderbilt Weight Management Program when you use the Rotation Diet. I want to tell you exactly what we tell them when they meet us for weekly supervision and guidance. Successful weight loss requires that you anticipate events, pressures and temptations that might interfere with your resolve to follow the Rotation Diet. If you follow my advice I think you will be prepared for anything and everything and end up having the most successful weight-management experience of your life.

Then we get down to the nitty-gritty. Chapters 6 and 7 lay out the Rotation Diet and the exercise plan that can give you that average of two-thirds of a pound of weight loss per day, without increasing the likelihood of gaining weight in the future.

Chapter 8 will show you how to maintain your weight loss as you take a break from dieting. In Chapters 9, 10 and 11 I will continue with a section on how to achieve Weight-Management Mastery. If you are over-fond of those rich foods we generally call 'junk food' (sweets, puddings, high-fat snack foods), I'd like to show you how to manage junk food in your diet, since there is no way in the world that you are going to succeed in giving up for life every single thing you like best. And, if you have been over-hard on yourself, kicking yourself because of your past inability to control your weight, you may have been feeding yourself a lot of 'mental junk food'. I'd like to show you how to deal with the rubbish in the mental part of your diet as well, so that you, too, can become a weight-management champion. You *can* manage your weight successfully.

Finally, just to keep your menus interesting and to illustrate how well you can eat on a healthful weight-reducing and weight-maintenance diet, I include in Chapter 12 a list of alternative menus and recipes for the Rotation Diet that were designed by our nutrition consultant, Ms Rachel Willis.

SPECIAL HEALTH BENEFITS OF THE ROTATION DIET

The Rotation Diet will not only lead to rapid weight loss. It has many other significant health benefits.

On average, there is a 10 per cent reduction in serum cholesterol levels and a 15 per cent reduction in circulating triglycerides, even in people who do not have abnormally high levels to begin with. Of course, the more elevated your cholesterol and triglyceride levels, the more benefit you can expect. (A high cholesterol level is a significant factor in cardiovascular disease, and high triglycerides have also been implicated.) Fasting glucose levels* tend to return to normal, if high, so that if your doctor has said that you have 'high blood sugar', there is every likelihood that it will normalize and stay normal if you follow my maintenance suggestions. And, by the way, we have not seen a single case of low fasting blood sugar in people using the Rotation Diet.

If you are hypertensive, about 50 per cent of all people with mild essential hypertension will eliminate their need for medication with the loss of only about 10 per cent of their body weight. Thus, you don't even have to reach ideal weight before you can obtain significant health benefits from the Rotation Diet.

A final word of advice before you begin. One of the first rules of good practice in the health field requires that my advice does not hurt anyone. We have a *perfect* record in the Vanderbilt Weight Management Program and I want it to stay that way. While the Rotation Diet can be used in reasonable comfort by people in good health, no one should undertake this or any other fast-weight-loss programme without consulting his or her doctor. The 600/900-calorie week in the Rotation Diet is not appropriate for diabetics. (If you are diabetic, the 1200-calorie plan – 1800 calories for men – is appropriate, and can be repeated indefinitely. Discuss it with your doctor.) If you are on any blood pressure medication, including a diuretic, your need for medication may be reduced *or entirely eliminated in just a few weeks*. That's a fantastic health benefit of the Rotation Diet. However, your medication must be monitored during a diet. *Do not make any changes in your medication without your doctor's supervision.*

Since this is a new diet, your doctor may not be aware of its details. The diet has been carefully designed with the Recommended Dietary Allowances of known vitamins and minerals in mind. One of our primary goals was to select foods that would maintain electrolyte balance

---

* All of our blood chemistry work must be done after a twelve-hour fast, that is, first thing in the morning before breakfast, in order to be accurate and not reflect nutrients that are being absorbed into the bloodstream after a meal. This is standard medical practice.

(the correct ratio of potassium, for example, to other minerals) over the entire period in which you would use the Rotation Diet. In this, we have been entirely successful. Because many health professionals are concerned about the effects of any fast-weight-loss programme, free copies of the daily plans, together with a summary report of the medical tests, which showed beneficial changes in serum cholesterol, triglycerides and fasting glucose without any harmful changes in electrolyte balance, will be sent to all physicians and other health professionals who write, on their letterheads, to the Vanderbilt Weight Management Program, 134 Wesley Hall, Vanderbilt University, Nashville, TN 37240, USA, enclosing international reply coupons to the value of 55 pence.

2

How the Rotation Diet Came into Being: A Personal Success Story

Twenty-two years ago I weighed over 5 stone (34 kg) more than I do today. The way that I lost that weight and kept it off for all these years forms the personal basis for the Rotation Diet. Perhaps because I really know from my own experience what it's like to be severely overweight and to have finally won my own battle, I have been able to inspire and help other individuals who have joined the Vanderbilt Weight Management Program to be more successful than they might otherwise have been. I'm proud of what I have accomplished and I think you can do just as well, so, I'd like to tell you something about myself and how I did it.

I was one of those fat kids who had no memory of ever being thin. Instead, I have memories such as not being able to run fast enough to keep up with my playmates, being chosen last for all games that required physical movement, and being so fat by the age of four or five that I couldn't even bend over in my snowsuit to make snowballs and join in the snowball fights that filled the winter afternoons with excitement for children in the upper New York State city where I grew up. I found some small consolation in comparing myself with another 'little' fat boy. I used to keep repeating to myself, 'I'm not the fattest boy in the class. Albert Rosenberg [that's not his real name] is fatter than I am.' Perhaps poor Albert was consoling himself in a similar way, using me for comparison.

By the time I was twelve years old I was 3½ stone (23 kg) overweight. My parents became so concerned that they took me to the paediatrician for a visit that I will never forget. The doctor measured my body frame and, in my mind's eye, I can see him clearly this very moment, standing before me, running his finger along the diagonal of a chart, reaching the corner, looking down at me, emitting a surprised little chuckle, and saying, 'You aren't even on the chart!'

I have fond memories of my childhood doctor even though I did not lose weight as a result of any of his efforts. I always had the feeling that he was trying to help me. After the appropriate tests, he determined that I was low in thyroid and had a slow metabolic rate. He placed me on thyroid medication and gradually increased the dosage up to 4 grains as I gradually upped my consumption of potato salad. He told my parents that they should encourage me to restrict my food intake, which they always did, but only after reminding me of the starving kids in Armenia (my parents were lucky enough to have left Russia at the turn of the century). I paid more heed to the needs of the starving kids in Armenia while I was eating than to my parents' admonitions to restrain myself, which always seemed to follow after I had finished. In the end, I began to have heart palpitations; the thyroid medication had to be discontinued, and my parents gave up on their efforts to control my eating.

By the time I reached thirty-five I was 5 stone (34 kg) overweight and hypertensive. I remember the day that I had to lie down on a couch for an hour in order to bring my blood pressure down to 140/90 so that the examining physician would OK me for an insurance policy to cover the new house I had just purchased on moving to Nashville. And I certainly know the effort that is involved in lugging an extra 5 stone of fat around! I would get out of breath just going across the street from my office and walking up one flight of stairs to the library. I remember putting off library visits until I had several tasks to do because of the effort involved in getting there and going up and down in the stacks.

My weight, inactivity and genetic predisposition also blessed me with varicose veins by the time I was twelve. At that early age, I had my first attack of thrombophleb- itis, which led to the injection treatment that was popular forty-five years ago and which resulted in permanent injury and disfigurement to one of my legs. Every two or three years I would suffer another attack, at times requir- ing me to spend as long as a month in bed, and two months more on crutches. Unfortunately, no physician was able to prescribe the treatment that finally ended this plague of inflammations and clotting in both my legs – I had to discover it for myself at the age of fifty. Because so many people suffer from similar problems with their veins, I'll have more to say about this problem later.

Of course I tried many diets during these years. I tried grapefruit diets and egg diets. I tried fasting and even devised my own version of a powdered, high-protein diet. I would stuff gigantic capsules with gelatin and swallow a package worth of capsules with two glasses of water for breakfast and another package worth of capsules for lunch, with yet another two glasses of water. (You can imagine what I did for the rest of the day.) I could lose weight as fast as anyone. And put it back just as fast.

It finally happened while I was playing a game of Ping-Pong outside my office in the hallway of the Psy- chology Department where we had set up a makeshift table. I began to get dizzy and nauseated, I broke out in a cold sweat, I could not catch my breath, and my knees began to quiver. Somehow I made it back to the chair in my office, but I did not want to face it: I was having a heart attack. I did not want to face it even though I had been having chest pains periodically for several years. I did not want to face it even though I had once actually

12

been knocked off my feet by the pain and unable to lift my arm.

I gradually returned to near normal in about forty-five minutes. I called my wife first, to tell her what had happened and to assure her that I felt all right but that I was about to get to a doctor. The cardiograms did indeed suggest that I had had a heart attack, and I am forever grateful to Dr Ed Tarpley for the treatment he prescribed. It was 1963, just before the time that physicians began to do coronary bypass operations, so I was spared that operation, and my doctor tended to use medication as a last resort. Ed said simply, 'You've got to lose that weight. I don't care what diet you use as long as it's a healthy one, but you *have got* to get active. That is the only way you will keep the weight off and possibly prevent another occurrence.'

The clearest thing in my memory of the days that followed is the recurring thought that I wanted to stay alive as my children grew up. My daughter was eight and my son ten. And it was no time to leave my wife – our love and friendship have always been very special and then, as always, we had so much to look forward to together. Would I finally find a way to take the weight off in spite of all of my past failures? Would I be able to keep it off? I had no successful past behaviour to guide me since there never was a time in my life when I had been thin. And could I find an activity that wouldn't hurt my legs and put me in bed with thrombophlebitis every other year? At that time, too much walking or the slightest bruise could do it. I knew no active games. I didn't even know what the inside of a gym might look like, and I certainly was not going to get inside one and undress so that everyone could see how fat and ugly I was.

Back in 1963 I did not know as much about the design of a diet for weight loss as I do now. (I was researching other areas of psychology having to do with the effects of anxiety on learning. The Vanderbilt Weight Management Program did not come into existence until 1976.) I did know one thing at that time, however, and that was – *something had to change!* You can't eat fatty foods, a lot of sweets, and consume large quantities of alcohol and lose weight easily.

So, I cut them all out. *All.* For periods of three weeks I was absolutely perfect. Then I would *stop* dieting and return to a normal eating pattern, which included those things we all seem to prefer in our diets. I never regained any of the weight I had lost. Without my realizing it, the principles that would form the basis of the Rotation Diet twenty-two years later were born.

What exactly was I doing and what had I learned? Here are a few of the main things:

First, I was following a quick-weight-loss plan that resulted in 15 to 20 pounds (7 to 9 kg) of weight loss each time I dieted.

Second, I never planned to diet more than three weeks at a time.

Third, I gradually increased my activity level, playing tennis every day (you will find an activity of your choice).

Fourth, by being active and not dieting for more than three weeks at a time, I evidently did not lower my metabolic rate, nor increase the fat storage ability that seems to follow prolonged use of a low-calorie diet, *because I never regained any weight after each period of weight loss.*

Fifth, before going on each weight-loss rotation, I would get really motivated to be perfect, knowing that 15 to 20 pounds was about to come off and that I intended to stop after three weeks. (I must admit that I once continued to diet for four weeks because I found it very hard to stop at three when I was being so successful in losing weight.)

I learned much, much more about successful weight loss as I began to implement my plan. The insights I gained made it relatively easy — much easier than I ever expected. Many things occurred to help me lose just over 5 stone in a little over a year that I did not actually plan or anticipate. I will tell you all about these things later in the book as I go along, showing step by step how I and other successful people actually implement the Rotation Diet. What I learned by chance, and trial and error, you can do intentionally.

14

As I write these introductory words, I am celebrating my fifty-seventh birthday. I can report that my blood pressure hovers around 120/80, I have kept that 5 stone (34 kg) off for twenty-two years: I was even able to stop smoking and keep the weight off. I have never had another heart attack (for which I also thank the good Lord). I love to get on the treadmill and watch that steady heartbeat on the polygraph as I approach maximum exertion, and I have not spent a single day in bed with either an inflammation or a blood clot in my legs after discovering what it takes to prevent their occurrence.

And I'm very, very glad to have stayed around, alive and healthy, to keep company with my wife and family, because as I reread and edit what I have written, I am looking forward to a special occasion. Tonight (19 October, 1985) the whole family will be together to celebrate my wife's fiftieth anniversary as a pianist when she performs Ravel's Piano Concerto in G Major with the Nashville Symphony Orchestra.

So mine has been a rewarding story. Now my hope is that what I have to say will be of help to you and add to the pleasure of your life.

3

How the Rotation Diet Came into Being: The Research

In spite of my own success with a fast-weight-loss programme twenty-two years ago, I began our formal experiments on a quick-weight-loss diet in the Vanderbilt Weight Management Program with a number of misgivings.

First and foremost among my reasons for being reluctant to experiment with a quick-loss plan was that in the past such plans have not been in accord with generally accepted practice in medicine and nutrition while I have always wanted to advise overweight people to use an approach to weight loss that was as safe as any programme could possibly be, for everyone. But finally, after many years, I simply had to face reality. Although we had achieved outstanding success in the Vanderbilt Weight Management Program in comparison with other weight-loss programmes, by following standard practice in our dietary recommendations we were not helping a majority of the participants to reach their desired weight.

Second, and I feel sure you will appreciate this if you are overweight, I wanted to be sure that, once you had lost the weight you wanted to lose, you would not have done anything to yourself through unwise dieting that would make it especially easy to regain that weight. Before we developed the Rotation Diet, the evidence against the long-term use of a low-calorie diet was quite clear. You might lose weight quickly but, in part because of the slowdown in your metabolic rate (the starvation response), you would be unable to eat more than a fraction of your former intake without regaining that weight.

Third, I was sensitive to the desire of overweight people to get their weight off 'as of yesterday'. At least at the outset, most people don't want to consider losing their weight as I did, in blocks of 15 to 20 pounds at a time, with a break period between their stretches of caloric restriction. No matter how much you have to lose, most overweight people are likely to want to take it all off in one massive, prolonged assault. Although I always told our participants in the Vanderbilt Program about my own methods, I would advise them to follow a moderate diet (1200 calories per day for women, 1800 for men), and, in weekly counselling sessions, all of the group leaders in the Vanderbilt Program would attempt to help our participants stick with their diets for anything from ten to twenty weeks.

In other words, I was (and am) concerned with safety and long-term maintenance. But although in the past my colleagues and I thought it best to go along with everyone's initial desire to stick with a single prolonged attempt to lose every single pound of excess weight in one fell swoop, no matter how much they had to lose or how long it took, we no longer think that this is the best way to go about it.

It's not that the results with our old approach were turning out badly in the long run for people with a modest amount of weight to lose. In comparison with the weight-loss and *weight-maintenance* records of most weight-control programmes, we were doing very well. But we were not at all as successful with this old, moderate approach as we and our participants would have liked.

Let me give you a brief summary.

17

PAST RESULTS: A REPORT ON THE OLD VANDERBILT PROGRAM

On the good side, 32.5 per cent of all participants in the old (pre-Rotation Diet) Vanderbilt Program are in the desirable weight range as long as three years after their participation. Twenty per cent of those who had 3 stone (18 kg) or more to lose did lose that much weight, and are keeping it off. Looking at our group averages, 85 per cent of the weight that was lost during the programme is being kept off. Compared with any other results of which we are aware, these achievements are outstanding.

We were, and, of course, still are, especially pleased with these weight-maintenance results. When we look at the follow-up questionnaires to determine why we have been so successful in maintenance, we see that people who have been through the Vanderbilt Weight Management Program tend to put the sound nutritional principles they learn in the program *and* an increase in their daily activity *together* in their permanent programmes for weight management. I am going to take special pains to show you how to be as successful in maintenance as they are.

On the bad side, however, when we looked at the weight-loss records of thousands of people (in our old programme as well as reports in the literature for programmes like it), we saw that the average weight loss on any moderate weight-reducing diet recommended for women is only about 1 to 1½ pounds per week. The average weight loss for programmes all around the United States lasting ten weeks is only about 10 pounds (4½ kg)! In intensive (and expensive) programmes lasting twenty or more weeks, for people who are 3½ to 9 stone (23 to 57 kg) overweight, the average loss is just over two stone (13½ kg). This is simply not good enough.

IT IS NOW MY OPINION THAT NO SLOW, MODERATE APPROACH TO WEIGHT REDUCTION WILL EVER WORK FOR A MAJORITY OF OVERWEIGHT PEOPLE. This is especially true for women, who lose weight so much more slowly than men.

The problem is that most people find it difficult, if not impossible, to follow the slow, moderate approach for very long. There are too many choices to make; we are surrounded by tempting high-calorie foods, and our family and outside social lives continually expose us to temptations that are hard to resist for more than a short time. Most of us can be 'pretty good' for short periods, but in a matter of weeks, say even three or four, we begin to make those tiny deviations, followed by larger deviations, that bring our weight losses to a virtual standstill.

All this means that the true focus of our past success, and of all programmes that use moderate approaches, has been, and will continue to be, with a small percentage of people who do not have very much weight to lose. Ten pounds (4½ kg) – good. Twenty or twenty-five pounds (9 to 11 kg) – still pretty good. But even in these instances, with relatively small amounts of weight to lose, only a few can actually expect to make it all the way into the desirable weight range if they use a slow, moderate approach to weight loss.

So, although we are proud of our past success in helping participants keep off whatever weight they did lose, with that 85 per cent weight-maintenance figure, as we looked at our less-than-perfect results we realized that *we had to keep prodding ourselves to find a way to help everyone lose ALL the weight they need to lose IN THE FIRST PLACE*. Then we could put our existing expertise to work in maintenance.

Considerations such as these kept me looking for ways to help people lose *more* weight and lose it *faster*, so that they would remain motivated for whatever period it would take to be perfectly successful.

THE ROTATION DIET IS BORN

As I pondered different approaches to increasing the rate and total amount of weight our participants would lose, I kept returning to the method I had used myself twenty-two years before – quick losses for three-week periods, and then a break. My daily activity kept me from regaining weight. Then, when the spirit moved me, another rotation. It's true that 'my way' of losing weight did not follow the guidelines that are part of standard practice in nutrition and 'my way' was not what we had been encouraging our participants in the Vanderbilt Weight Management Program to follow, but I had lost over 5 stone (34 kg) and kept them off for twenty-two years. How can you argue with such results? Had 'my way' hurt me? On the contrary, I had been more successful than all but a handful of the people I had been trying to help with 'standard practice' and I am in excellent health.

What about my metabolic rate? It had been so low as a child that the paediatrician had me on 4 grains of thyroid medication. Now, however, my metabolic rate is actually about 15 per cent higher than that of the average man of my age. I eat almost 3000 calories per day, which is about 15 per cent more than the average man of fifty-seven years. And I don't gain weight. Whatever I did to lose weight, and whatever I am doing to keep it off, have not interfered with my metabolism. Instead, I am healthier than ever before, and my body has responded to my present healthy diet and active life-style by actually *increasing*, rather than decreasing, its daily need for food. At the personal level, I certainly know the secret of weight loss and weight maintenance. So I kept asking myself, 'If my way of rotating my diet worked so well for me, why don't I break down and at least give it a shot? Why don't I at least try to adapt it for everyone who wants to try it?'

My major fear was that the beneficial results that I had experienced would not occur for everyone. However, many respected professionals all over the country were coming to the same realization: traditional dietary means, even when combined with the best that behavioural psychology had to offer, were not getting very much weight off the people who needed to lose more than 10 or 15 pounds. Many of these professional health

20

workers were beginning to experiment with very-low-calorie diets, including powdered formula diets of as low as 400 to 600 calories a day for periods of up to two months, in an effort to find more effective weight-loss strategies. I did not want to use such diets because of the possibly serious metabolic consequences. (They also can have serious effects on cardiac function and require constant medical supervision.) And I have personally seen the rapid gain in weight that almost invariably follows the use of such diets.

Several things finally changed my mind about trying to design a quick-weight-loss diet.

First, with respect to the data on changes in metabolic rate that take place when someone begins to diet, it seems that little if any reduction occurs for several days. In fact, when some people start a diet, they seem to get excited. They experience a sort of 'high' that might elevate the metabolic rate to a small extent temporarily.

Second, we and other researchers around the country had obtained evidence showing that, when a sedentary person increases physical activity, metabolic rates do not decrease, and may even increase, during moderate caloric restriction. Would activity also work to prevent the decrease if the diet were more severe?

Third, we were halfway through one of our ten-week programmes during the autumn/winter of 1984/85 when four of the eighteen women in one of my groups became dissatisfied with their rate of weight loss on our usual 1200-calorie diet. They were doing fine with their physical activity but they were having trouble making choices from the wide variety of foods we recommended and they were finding it difficult to maintain their motivation to continue to avoid the desserts and alcoholic beverages that have to be avoided *if someone wants to lose weight quickly*.

So, I laid out my plan to rotate a quick-weight-loss diet with a period of rest, then start the quick loss again, similar to my own practice many years before. The women were extremely eager to try it. We would monitor their metabolic rates on a weekly basis, to determine

21

whether or not a dramatic, but temporary, decrease in calories would lower their metabolic rates, which until that time had not suffered any decline.

The results caused a great deal of excitement. Although weight loss speeded up significantly, we could detect no decrease in metabolic rate. Morale skyrocketed and the women's motivation to continue with their weight-loss programme was restored. These results encouraged me to plan a much larger trial in the spring and summer of 1985.

We recruited twenty women who wanted to participate in a test of the Rotation Diet right from the start of their weight-loss efforts. They began with three days on a 600-calorie diet, upped it to 900 for four days, then increased to 1200 for a week. Then they repeated the 600/900 rotation. Physical activity (walking or its equivalent in terms of energy expenditure) was gradually increased, with a goal of fifteen minutes per day the first week, up to forty-five minutes per day during the third week. We also set a target of a minimum of five days per week for activity, with six or seven preferred, provided it felt good! We obtained pre-programme baseline resting metabolic rates and then monitored these rates on a weekly basis. We also obtained answers to a set of questions that measured the ease of sticking with the plan and satisfaction with progress. Of course, we were eager to compare the speed of weight loss with the 1- to 1½-pound weekly loss that is usually obtained with the 1200-calorie diets.

RESULTS WITH THE FIRST CLINICAL TRIAL USING THE ROTATION DIET

In a nutshell, the results were fantastic. The average weight loss was 12½ pounds (5½ kg) in twenty-one days. That's about two-thirds of a pound a day. The heaviest women lost as much as a pound a day. There was no reduction in resting metabolic rate; in fact, there was a small (but statistically insignificant) metabolic increase. Ninety per cent of the women said they preferred the Rotation Diet to the slower, more moderate diets they had tried in the past, and I had a great deal of difficulty persuading them to take that break from dieting (for at least one week) that is an essential part of the plan.

SOME PERSONAL REACTIONS TO THE ROTATION DIET

To monitor formally reactions to the diet each week, we asked participants to fill out a questionnaire. Here are some of the comments in our written records:

'It's so clear. You can't make a mistake!'

'It works!'

'The 600/900 is easy to stay on — fewer choices, fewer temptations.'

'Very happy with this diet plan. Can't think of anything bad to say about it.'

'The best thing about this diet is that I feel thinner (and better).'

'I am really having a good time on my walks. When I've lost weight before I've found it difficult to lose in my hips and thighs, but because of the walking this is the first place I'm losing. I've already gone down one entire dress size, and two in pant size [after one rotation]. I love it.'

'The best — plenty to eat and pleasant variety of foods [on the 1200 part of the rotation].'

'When I reach the 1200 calories per day I really feel rewarded for having been so good on the 600/900.'

'I feel better and have more energy.'

'It works, and I'm really building self-esteem.'

'I see the results I started out to accomplish.'

'The 600/900 part is even easier than I thought it could possibly be.'

Obviously, with such outstanding results, we had to make the Rotation Diet a part of our regular weight-loss programme for participants who have no physical condition that might make its use unwise.

NOW IT'S YOUR TURN!

And when you finish, I want you to write to me to tell me how well the Rotation Diet has worked for you. (Follow the instructions for writing given in Appendix B.) First, study the plan and put it into practice, exactly as I tell you, for those three weeks that can result in an average weight loss of two-thirds of a pound to a pound a day. Then write to me because I want to find out if a significant number of overweight people can lose weight with the help of a book like this just as well as they can in our programme. You see, the only way that I can be successful as a professional trying to help people lose weight is if *you* are successful! There is no way of finding that out unless you tell me.

If you write to me, enclosing international reply coupons to the value of £1.10, I'll put you on my follow-up maintenance list. Then you will hear from me periodically to find out how you are doing. Being on our follow-up list will help you stay motivated until your new thin life-style becomes so rewarding you will never go back to being fat, and your responses will give us needed information on long-term success in dealing with overweight. So, it will be of great benefit to both of us if you write, and I am encouraging you to do so.

4

Gearing Up for the Rotation Diet

Timing, planning, commitment. These are the keys to success. Let me explain what I mean.

I realize that there is no perfect time to start a diet, but some times are better than others. Don't pick a time to start the Rotation Diet when everything in your life will conspire to make you deviate from your plans. If you are a woman, you would have to be a masochist to begin Week 1 of the Rotation Diet, in which you will be adhering to a 600-calorie diet for three days, followed by a 900-calorie diet for four days, if that week coincides with a festive period such as a holiday, an anniversary or some other celebration. Right before and right after a holiday is just fine, since this is the rotation in which you will approximate a pound a day of weight loss. Thus, the week after the Christmas holidays is a great time to use Week 1 of the Rotation Diet and take off 5 or more pounds, and some women use Week 1 right before Christmas to lose 5 lbs (2 kg), since this promotes the relative freedom of a 1200-calorie diet during the holiday week itself. But you should never punish yourself by trying to exercise anything more than modest restraint *during* festive periods.

25

It just creates tension that can, in the end, lead to greater overeating than if you had not tried to be so extreme in the first place.

So, survey the weeks ahead. The best time for your first rotation will be when you can see three coming weeks in which you can plan to follow the Rotation Diet without anticipating a whole array of circumstances likely to encourage failure. You want three weeks in which the temptations to deviate will be about as low as you can expect them to be, considering your life situation.

Then, you must make a decision to be absolutely perfect in following the Rotation Diet.

PERFECT?

That word frightens you, doesn't it? If you could be perfect when it came to your eating habits, you wouldn't need to go on a diet!

Your feelings indicate that you don't have confidence in your ability to get the job done. You can't even *imagine* yourself being successful, and if you can't imagine yourself being successful, how in the world will you ever be able to do it in reality? I suspect that you may have had too many failures in the past to trust yourself on any plan that calls, from the start, for perfection.

If you have feelings such as these, then, at this point, *I have more faith in you than you have in yourself!* And I think I can show you how to develop all the confidence that you will need to succeed.

I have faith in you and in the plan because the Rotation Diet is, first of all, so easy to follow. Second, the steps to mastery that I will show you in Chapters 9, 10 and 11 will help you achieve perfection, or near-perfection, with just a little bit of practice and enough initial commitment to start. And when I speak of that two-thirds of a pound per day of weight loss that you can expect with the Rotation Diet, I include in the data even those who make it to *nearly* perfect, using a couple of insurance policies that I explain in Chapter 6, as well as those who follow it perfectly. Finally, I also know from experience that people who aim for perfection from the start end up doing the very best.

The reason I ask you to demand perfection of yourself, and to develop the frame of mind that keeps you striving for it, is that changing your weight is, in the beginning stages, one of the hardest things you may ever undertake in your life. It takes fantastic commitment. The secret of success lies partly in the attitude with which you approach the task, and partly in having a strategy that yields a payoff worthy of your efforts. Then, once you see and feel the payoff, weight-management difficulties will be reduced considerably and you will wonder why it seemed so hard at first.

After you see what the diet requires, as well as the exercise programme (Chapters 6 and 7), *you must take about half an hour to sit down and plan how to be perfect.* In those two chapters I'll show you, in detail, how to make your plans.

Here is the way I put the issue to participants in my groups in the meeting before we begin the Rotation Diet:

Three weeks of perfection is not too long to ask from anyone who is serious about weight loss. Think about it – I am not asking you to start a diet and stick with it for an indefinite period. You are not going to force yourself to stick with it until any set amount of weight is lost. You are going to plan for a limited time – *three weeks* – and in these three weeks you will actually have one week that demands relatively little of you. Upping your calories to 1200 per day, after the 600/900 rotation, feels like a tremendous reward. If you feel any pressure to deviate during the 600/900 rotation, simply look ahead to the 1200-calorie week, and wait with anticipation. Follow my advice and the results will be superb. Is it worth it to you to lose an average of two-thirds of a pound a day over that twenty-one-day period – maybe even a pound a day?

Okay – you are only human. Suppose something happens that is so overwhelming you cannot resist deviating from your plans. Never interpret this kind of event as ultimate defeat – you have only lost a skirmish. Aim for the best you can do; accept your humanness, and aim once again for perfection. You will get better at it – I'll show you how. If you have more than 15 or 20 pounds

27

(7 or 9 kg) to lose, your second twenty-one-day rotation on the diet will be even better than the first.

After this preamble, I go on to tell my group participants in the Vanderbilt Program about some of my personal experiences.

I learned a great deal about attitude, commitment, and strategy when I set out to lose those 5 stone (34 kg) twenty-two years ago. In view of my health, weight loss had finally become a very important goal. Weight loss has to be an important goal for you, too, because I cannot supply the initial motivation for you to begin – I can show you how to reach your goal quickly and easily, reinforcing your motivation to succeed, but you have to have enough motivation to put the whole plan into action.

As I thought about the kind of diet I would follow in my own efforts to lose weight, I realized that I must find a way to cut out *all* things that are considered 'dense-calorie' foods if I didn't want to dilly-dally around and take for ever. That is, cakes, pies, biscuits, ice cream, sweets and chocolate, alcohol, fried foods – in fact, everything that has fat or sugar as the primary source of calories had to go. I knew, from many past failures, that when I included such foods while trying to lose weight I could play around with the same 5 or 10 pounds (2 to 4 kg) for ever, losing and gaining, losing and gaining, and I would never make permanent progress. I'm sure that this comes as no surprise to you!

But I also knew that I, like most other people who love best the very foods we have to give up in order to lose weight efficiently, could not ask myself to exercise perfect restraint for ever. I needed a goal; it had to be attainable, and it had to be explicit.

So I asked myself how long I thought I could be perfect if I had a good diet and a good plan for sticking with it. There were three weeks left of the summer vacation before classes resumed at Vanderbilt, so I arbitrarily decided on three weeks. As for the diet, it was going to be plenty of fruits and vegetables, together with lean meat, fish, poultry and low-fat cheeses (I don't care much for milk, except with chocolate cake, apple pie, biscuits and peanut butter sandwiches). I decided to go light on bread (something I would not do today) because I could not imagine myself eating bread in those days unless it was hidden under a slab of butter.

So I had a time limit and the principles on which to build my diet. Now the question was, 'Will I be able to stick it out for the full three weeks?'

My family was a great help and I'll talk more about how they came to help me when I discuss the steps you need to take to prepare your environment and other people for success. There is no way that I could have been as successful as I have without the complete support I received, and continue to receive, from my wife and children.

With my family strongly behind me, my major fear was how to deal with lunches out each day, five days a week, in restaurants near my office, and the once- or twice-a-week dinner out or other social situation that had so often led me astray in my previous efforts to lose weight.

My fears were soon dispelled in a way that I did not fully appreciate until I reflected on it some years later. We were out to dinner with some good friends at a steak house, where I started off with a shrimp cocktail, foll-owed by steak and a salad. My companions remarked on my 'control' – I had declined the roll and butter and had been sipping my glass of iced water as they enjoyed their cocktails. They asked me what diet I was using and it just popped out, without much planning, because I had noticed that everything I had been eating began with the letter 's' – 'It's my own diet. I call it the 4S-Diet, and it's unlimited indulgence in shrimp, steak, salad and sex.'

The name got a few laughs and, since everyone began to notice that I was losing weight so quickly, I began to respond to all questions about what diet I was on with 'The 4S-Diet'. My description was always worth a chuckle or two, but I soon discovered that it was worth much, much more than a little laugh. It disarmed potential tempters. *No one, ever, at any party, dinner, or other social engagement, ever pushed me to deviate from my diet once I made my statement.* So I found it easy

29

to adhere to it, sticking, in reality, not just to the four S's, but to a wide variety of fruits, vegetables, lean meats, fish and poultry.

I had started my three weeks of dieting with commitment, and each time I announced and described the diet to someone else, that commitment grew. No matter what the temptation, I communicated unequivocally in all situations that I meant it when I said I was on a diet. Furthermore, talking about it in public whenever the occasion arose, as it almost always did on social occasions because so many people are interested in diets, was especially reinforcing. I lost between 15 and 20 pounds (7 and 9 kg) each time I went on my three-week diet. That amount of weight loss was always dramatic. All together – the quick loss, the humorous name, the public statement and the reactions, with no one even unconsciously making any effort to sabotage my endeavour – all of these factors combined to produce a snowball effect. It was almost more fun to be on the diet and get these reactions and reinforcements than it was to be off it.

The Vanderbilt Weight Management Program did not come into being until thirteen years after I had lost all of my weight. It was only then, when I began to analyse the reasons for my success in sticking to a diet and to compare them with the reasons so many others seem to fail, that I appreciated the value of each component that I had in part planned and in part chanced upon. Let me summarize:

A reachable, time-limited goal – three weeks of dieting, and then a break

A very reinforcing rate of weight loss

A bit of humour (which always helps to keep your spirits up while working on a difficult task)

An unequivocal public statement, made in such a way that it reflected my complete commitment and received complete respect

Public appreciation and reinforcement

Self-reinforcement ('bragging' about my diet, which is

something you can start to do with the Rotation Diet; a bit of bragging will help you, too)

The support of my family

In the next chapter I will show you some specific ways to apply all my personal experience, together with all the professional experience I have gained in helping others, to your own weight-management efforts.

5

Getting Started on the Right Foot

In the previous chapter I gave you some general principles that will assure your success on the Rotation Diet. Now I want to give you three important specific suggestions.

First, take charge of your social environment. Make sure your family, friends and co-workers know what you are about to do. If the people in your environment can have an impact on your behaviour (and they usually can and do) you will do better with their complete co-operation.

Second, take charge of your physical environment. Make sure the physical aspects of your home and place of work will support your efforts in every way possible.

Third, make sure you have exactly the foods you plan to eat during the Rotation Diet already available when you start the diet, and plan your menus according to the directions I give you in the next chapter. If you plan to eat any meals in restaurants during the three weeks of the Rotation Diet, you will need to follow my special recommendations for dining out. I was able to eat lunches in a restaurant five days a week, and go out to dinner occasionally, too, and still succeed. So can you.

SETTING UP YOUR WORLD TO SUPPORT SUCCESS

I don't think I could possibly have succeeded as easily as I did in losing weight and keeping it off without getting complete support from my family and setting up my daily schedule to facilitate weight loss.

I announced my intentions to my wife and requested that, for three weeks, we should not bring any foods into the house that would tempt me to eat something that was not on my plan. After all, it was only for three weeks. Everyone wanted me to succeed, so I had no problem doing this. We brought no ice cream into the house during this period, and we baked no cheesecakes, both of which happen to be among my favourite high-calorie foods.

You may wonder why I decided to remove temptation completely, right from day one, rather than learn to deal with my appetites and change my eating habits gradually. The answer is quite simple: I wanted to lose weight quickly. I had no time to wait while I learned which behaviour change strategies would work and which would not when it came to resisting temptation. That could wait for the periods when I experimented with *maintenance*, not weight loss. Besides, I really like ice cream and cheesecake. There was no way in the world I could fool myself into disliking my favourite foods or keep them around the house for the entire period in which I was going to be losing weight and not end up eating them.

Fortunately I discovered as I went through my rotation diet that I didn't need to change my attitudes about food — I love to cook and I love to eat a wide variety of foods that include some dishes that nutritional 'purists' would do away with entirely. I discovered a strategy that lets me live with and enjoy all these foods once again in amounts that bear no danger for my weight, and I plan to show you how I and other successful participants from the Vanderbilt Weight Management Program do it.

However, when it comes to implementing the very best strategy for weight loss – *removing all temptation temporarily from your home* – you, unfortunately, may find that your family is not as co-operative as mine, especially if you are a woman! Even for that brief three-week period that I am suggesting, you may meet with almost insurmountable resistance. You are likely to hear 'Why do we have to go on a diet because you are trying to lose weight?' This response, generally received by women, makes me very angry. In fact, after working to help almost three thousand women in the Vanderbilt Weight Management Program lose weight, I can't express just how angry I am at my fellow males when it comes to helping the women they say they love to lose weight. In comparison with women, men with families usually have no problems when they announce they are ready to diet. Everyone rallies round, out goes the junk food. Mum makes low-calorie main dishes, and everyone falls in line to take care of things when Dad goes out to exercise. When Dad makes an unequivocal statement about what he wants, most families seem ready to co-operate.

In part because of the family co-operation that males receive, they find it much easier to lose weight. They also find it much easier to stay active after weight loss. But I can't find words to tell you how frustrated I am with the mates of the women in my groups. I am embarrassed and ashamed of male insensitivity to the problems that women face. Even today, when we are so much more likely to preach 'equality' and co-operation in our marriages than was the case twenty-two years ago when I lost my weight, it still seems to be more talk than action: men still get more support and encouragement for the decision to lose weight than women do. Husbands seem to expect their wives to maintain the status quo, and so do the children. You (woman, wife and mother) are expected to keep all the tempting foods in the house and will be made to feel like an ogre if you don't want to supply daily doses of sweets and biscuits for the children. You will be expected to continue to prepare all the high-fat and high-sugar dishes to which the family has been accustomed, continue to be both mum, wife and possibly career woman, and certainly not inconvenience anyone with a change in your diet or physical activities because you would like to be healthier, happier and more pleased with yourself.

Watch out, however, for something very subtle in your own attitudes about what you feed the family. As the saying goes, you may be caught 'between a rock and a hard place'. You, like an amazing number of women, may not feel like a 'good mother' or a 'good wife' unless you provide your family with junk food. You may obtain a great deal of satisfaction from the joy your family derives from eating these foods and, as a woman, wife and mother who cares for her family, may not feel that you are showing that love, or are, yourself, fully loved or lovable, unless you see your brood relishing those high-fat and high-sugar foods that are not particularly good for anyone's health on a daily basis. You may be equating love and caring with the food you feed the family! Watch out! If you share any of the feelings I am talking about, you should stop and think – and realize that equating love and caring with the biscuit tin does no one any good. You are not doing anyone a favour with a *daily* diet of junk food.

WEIGHT LOSS AND WEIGHT MAINTENANCE REQUIRE DIFFERENT STRATEGIES

Before going on with the recommendations for ensuring success while using the Rotation Diet for the next three weeks, I want to make some contrasts between what leads to the very best and most efficient weight loss and what I think works best for maintenance. Weight loss and weight maintenance are very different matters.

During each three weeks on the Rotation Diet, you aim for perfection, and the closer you get, the better you will do. After all, you can't lose two-thirds of a pound a day without sticking to the plan very closely. Removing temptation from your home environment and avoiding it elsewhere are the easiest ways to come close to perfection.

As for the long term, *it's balance and moderation, NOT striving for perfection*, that will ensure success in maintenance. Some of our successful participants call their approach to incorporating high-calorie foods into their diets 'controlled bingeing'! They intentionally plan to include some every week. They avoid being over-restrained because they find that trying to be too perfect for too long can actually set them up for long-term failure. If you are at all like them, you, too, may have found that constant denial only increases your drive for dense-calorie foods. Then, the moment you indulge in a single bite, the floodgates open and you are overwhelmed by the appetite that has been building up. Thus, in maintenance, you control the appearance of temptations, having periodic indulgences that never let your drive to eat sweet and fatty foods build up to the point where you will overeat and put on weight.

In Chapters 9, 10 and 11, you will learn the strategies for self-mastery and environmental control that allow for 'controlled bingeing' without regaining any weight after you have reached your goal. Just as ice cream and cheese-cake are back in my present maintenance diet (together with a couple of beers after a nice jog in the park), your favourite high-calorie foods will return to your diet. But you will be in control, deciding just how many and how much of these foods you want to eat, and when.

So, to repeat, during the Rotation Diet you will find the task far easier if you remove temptations from your home environment. I hope you will be able to do this. If you are a woman, talk it over with your husband, and make plans for him and the rest of the family to have their ice cream, biscuits, cakes and sweets as special treats away from home. It will be good for Dad to go out with the kids – they'll love him for it and it will give you a chance to go for a walk alone!

36

(If you are one of those persons who cannot, or doesn't want to, remove temptations from home, or who knows that temptations will be unavoidable in your social situation, read Chapters 9, 10 and 11 before you begin. There I describe a strategy that yields a 95 per cent success rate among participants in the Vanderbilt Program when they need special help in developing their resistance for the three weeks of the Rotation Diet.)

WHAT ABOUT EATING OUT?

I had lunches out, five days a week, all during my periods of quick weight loss. Here's how.

I found a small restaurant near my office that would serve me one of three dishes that I had on my diet plan. The first was the dieter's special, a 6-ounce (175-g) lean hamburger patty with a selection of two side dishes from the following list: small mixed salad, sliced tomato and lettuce, coleslaw or cottage cheese. The second dish was 'soup of the day', usually either vegetable, tomato, cream of mushroom or split pea, which I would have with five water biscuits or crispbread. The third was a large mixed salad which I would have with one dessertspoon of dressing. For three weeks, I ate every single lunch at this restaurant. Thus I exposed myself to no special temptations. The waitresses, as well as the owner, got to know me very well and supported my diet plans. They greeted me with, 'What's it going to be today, Doc – salad, soup or the hamburger?'

I have already explained how I used my '4S-Diet' label to ward off 'well-intentioned' friends who might tempt me to deviate on social occasions. If invited out to dinner at someone's home, I always let them know when I was in my 'diet cycle'. For me, it was skip the drinks, no dessert (other than fruit and a piece of cheese), don't pass the bread, and scrape off the sauce if my host had the audacity to prepare something especially rich for the main course.

I used similar strategies for eating out at restaurants. I

always suggested that we go somewhere I would have no difficulty sticking to my diet. Selfish? Hell, no! That 15-pound loss was really worth it, and I had more at stake with that one meal out than anyone else in the crowd. For me, it was my life.

We never failed to find a place where everyone could be satisfied.

If you must eat out socially, think about your plan of action in advance, just as I did. Talk it over with your dinner companions and set up your support system. Just remember – most dieters fail on their diets because they are in conflict. They want to eat the foods they must temporarily deny themselves, so they find themselves 'co-operating with circumstances' and setting themselves up for failure. You must make an unequivocal statement about your intentions, to yourself and to others, once you have made up your mind to follow the Rotation Diet. And the more you repeat the statement, publicly as well as silently to yourself, the more you will reinforce your intentions and assure your success.

If you work outside the home, it's a good idea to think about how you will face the temptations that will occur during work breaks as well as at lunchtime. Your place of work will probably not offer a perfect environment for weight control. The cafeteria and snack machines will still have their fried and junk foods, even when they also offer healthful alternatives.

So what are you going to do?

Here's how I did it. I didn't want to be caught unprepared when I felt like a snack. To this day I take bread and fruit to the office. I eat what I have brought for snacks, even if I join someone else. And for lunch, if I eat out, my colleagues and I always go where we can choose healthful dishes. We also go where we are served, not where we must choose from a buffet. I do not like to submit myself to the temptations of a buffet – I find myself in conflict, fighting my desire to eat all my money's worth and then some (I still remember the starving children in Armenia), knowing that if I do I will probably feel sleepy afterwards, or uncomfortable when

38

I go out for a jog or play tennis at the end of the day.

If you are a woman about to begin the Rotation Diet, during the week that you are on the 600/900-calorie phase you will do best if you provide your own lunch and avoid eating out. The lunches are easy to prepare and there is no problem preserving them until time to eat. When you are in the 1200-calorie week, there is more leeway for eating out. Men will have little trouble finding a way to eat out since they never drop below 1200 calories a day.

A FINAL WORD OF ADVICE

The Rotation Diet is the best quick-weight-loss plan that I know of – if you can be close to perfect, you can expect to average an enviable two-thirds of a pound of weight loss per day over the next three weeks. But I know the unexpected is to be expected. By that I mean, you may feel an almost irresistible urge to eat something not on the plan simply because someone puts it right in front of your nose and catches you off guard. A party occurs at work, for example. Or, you find yourself dying for a little something before going to bed, which is likely to happen to people who are accustomed to one large, continuous meal from the time they get home from work until they go to sleep at night.

Of course, things such as I have just described happened to me while I was losing weight. Because I did not want to feel deprived, and did not want to go to bed hungry, I decided I needed to have a 'safe food' that I liked reasonably well and of which I could eat almost unlimited quantities without doing much damage to my weight-loss efforts.

However, choosing a 'safe food' presented me with a problem. I just don't care much for the so-called 'free foods' that anyone (you included) can always eat in unlimited quantities. (Free foods include lettuce, parsley, watercress, cucumber, celery – I'll give you a complete list in the next chapter.) I needed something that was

39

more satisfying than the free foods, but still healthful and filling while containing relatively few calories.

I decided that my safe food would be a fruit (and I now call it a *safe fruit*). Compared with other foods, fruit provides the most satisfaction in taste and bulk for the least amount of calories. And, in addition, I wanted something I liked so that it would be a reasonable substitution for foods that are much higher in calories.

I selected grapefruit as my safe fruit. A whole grapefruit has only about 110 calories. I carried one to the office in my briefcase and made a vow that I would have to eat that grapefruit instead of any high-calorie snack that happened my way. At least, I would say to myself that I had to eat it first, and then, if I wanted to, I could eat something else. But I never did. All the while that I peeled the grapefruit, I thought about how well I was losing weight, and how the high-calorie snack would slow me down. I would then break the grapefruit up into sections, and eat them, one at a time, as slowly as I could. If I was still hungry when I finished, I would drink a large glass of water.

I did the same at night at home whenever I felt hungry before going to bed. Sometimes I ate two grapefruit, peeled and sectioned. It is hard to be hungry after two whole grapefruit!

I don't want you to feel deprived, either, on the Rotation Diet, so I want you to choose a *safe fruit* just in case you, too, don't care very much for the free foods. I want you, too, to take a vow that your safe fruit is the only extra food you will eat while you are following the plan, no matter what temptations present themselves. In this way, you may end up losing only 10 pounds (4½ kg) rather than 15 or 20 (7 or 9 kg) during the next three weeks, but you will be prepared to resist the worst the world has to offer and you will not end up 'blowing it all' and feeling frustrated.

I will give you a list of safe fruits in the next chapter, which describes the Rotation Diet. Choose one from the list. Have plenty at home and have some with you at all times. Your safe fruit will soon begin to act like a charm,

40

protecting you from your old fat self as well as from the temptations in your environment. In just two or three days, your friends will become accustomed to seeing you dip into your bag or briefcase for your healthful snack, and they will no longer encourage you to deviate. You, too, will be surprised at your own demonstration of willpower. Reaching for your safe fruit becomes a very simple thing to do – almost automatic, in fact. When you begin to feel a bit proud, even smug, over your ability to say 'No, thanks' to temptation as you reach for your safe fruit, you can be sure that you are securely on your way.

And you can give any odds you like to anyone silly enough to bet against you that you will end up considerably thinner and stay that way.

6

The Rotation Diet
for Women and Men

I want to emphasize once again, before you begin the Rotation Diet, why you need to follow the suggestions I am making very closely.

The Rotation Diet, followed exactly as described in this chapter, does not lead to a reduction in your metabolic rate. I mean by this that you will need just as many calories to maintain yourself at a lower weight after you finish the diet and follow my instructions for maintenance as you did before you began the diet. Unlike other quick-weight-loss diets, the Rotation Diet does not make it easier for you to get fat all over again, after the diet is over.

In this chapter I will lay out the complete dietary plan for women and men. *Do not start on the Rotation Diet until you have read Chapter 7, which describes the Rotation Diet activity programme.* If you are interested in permanent weight control, you must implement the entire plan.

GENERAL INSTRUCTIONS

For Women

Women follow a rotation plan during Week 1 that includes approximately 600 calories a day for three days, followed by 900 calories a day for the next four days. In Week 2, you eat approximately 1200 calories a day for the entire week. In Week 3, you repeat the 600/900-calorie rotation. You can repeat the menus of Week 1 during Week 3 or, for more variety, you can use the Alternative Menus for the Rotation Diet in Chapter 12.

It is very important for women to follow the Week 2 menus, which call for an increase in food intake to around 1200 calories. If you do not, you may reduce your metabolic rate. In addition, the increase feels like a feast and does wonders for your motivation. After what feels like a week of hardly being on a diet, you will be eager to get back on the 600/900-calorie rotation once again for another quick weight loss. Your weight loss in Week 2 will, of course, be less than in Weeks 1 and 3, but the increase in calories helps prevent your regaining weight after you finish your diet. This protection is worth the temporary slow down.

For Men

Men follow a rotation plan during Week 1 that includes approximately 1200 calories a day for three days, followed by 1500 calories a day for the next four days. In Week 2, you eat approximately 1800 calories a day for the entire week. In Week 3, you repeat the 1200/1500-calorie rotation. You can repeat the menus of Week 1 during Week 3 or, if you desire more variety, you can use the Alternative Menus for the Rotation Diet in Chapter 12.

It is very important for men to follow the Week 2 menus, which call for an increase in food intake to around 1800 calories. If you do not, you may reduce your metabolic rate. Eighteen hundred calories a day will

43

hardly feel like a diet and the break it gives you will add to your motivation to return to the 1200/1500 rotation for another quick weight loss. Your weight loss in Week 2 will be less than in Weeks 1 and 3, but the increase in calories helps prevent your regaining weight after you finish your diet. This protection is worth the temporary slowdown.

Expected Weight Loss

On average, people who follow the Rotation Diet exactly as printed will lose over 5 pounds the first week, around 2½ pounds the second week, and up to around 5 pounds again the third week (just over 2, 1 and 2 kg). The heavier you are to begin with, the more you can expect to lose, up to an average of about a pound a day for the twenty-one days. And even though the calorie intake for men is higher, men will tend to lose faster than women. Men need more calories than women to maintain their initial weight and they burn more calories in physical activity because they are heavier.

PERMISSIBLE VARIATIONS ON THE ROTATION DIET

The Rotation Diet permits some variations that make it possible for people who have trouble sticking with low-calorie diets to use it and still be very successful. I include these variations because some women may need to have a little more food than the basic 600/900-calorie rotation allows in order to avoid feeling empty at certain times of the day. The same goes for men who may find it difficult to stick exactly to 1200 calories. If you are such a person, you need to know what you can do without appreciable damage to your efforts. Other people, such as nervous nibblers or those who find themselves on a food expedition the moment they have nothing particularly demanding to do and begin to feel a little bored, also need to have

44

something to fall back on as a snack that will not hurt the overall effectiveness of the diet.

Here are the permissible deviations that still make the diet effective. These deviations include the use of *free vegetables* and a *safe fruit*. Together they constitute your insurance policy. Our research shows that women who include some of the permitted deviations may lose, on the average, only half a pound a day, but they still end up with a loss of 10½ pounds (4¾ kg) in twenty-one days. Be sure to follow these directions so that you can adhere to the plan for the full three weeks with the least damaging deviations, no matter what happens!

DIRECTIONS FOR USING FREE VEGETABLES

Certain foods have so few calories that you can eat them in unlimited quantities. They are called *free vegetables*. Because of their water and fibre content, relative to the number of calories they contain, you cannot eat enough of them to prevent yourself from losing weight provided you follow my other suggestions exactly. Thus, whenever you see 'unlimited free vegetables' on my menus, you can eat from the following list of vegetables until you feel satisfied (if you add salad dressing, use only my No-Cal Dressing, page 83 or a no-calorie commercial variety).

You are also permitted to add free vegetables to any meal and to nibble on them as snacks. Because they contain so many vitamins and minerals (plus fibre) in relation to their caloric content, you will be increasing the nutritional value of your diet tremendously if you do so. (Free vegetables have fewer than 10 calories per serving. If you are interested in more exact caloric values, see Appendix A.)

asparagus
celery
chicory
Chinese cabbage
courgette

cucumber
endive
lettuce
parsley
radish
spinach (raw)
watercress

DIRECTIONS FOR CHOOSING
A SAFE FRUIT

The free vegetables that I recommend above will help round out your meals so that you never have to feel hungry when you have finished the prescribed lunch or dinner. But if you are at all like me, free vegetables are not always satisfying – they don't have much flavour eaten alone and, perhaps more important, they have so few calories that they don't give you any lift when you may really need one. That's why I think you should choose a *safe fruit* to fall back on whenever you feel hungry *between* meals or are tempted by some rich dessert. That's what I did twenty-two years ago when I decided that whenever I felt like a bedtime snack, or felt hungry between meals, I would peel and eat a whole grapefruit, *but only grapefruit and nothing else*, for the entire three weeks of my diet. By sticking with this vow I never failed to lose at least 15 pounds (7 kg) over any three-week period, and I never had to feel hungry!

Safe fruits do contain calories. From 40 calories for a small apple to 110 calories for a whole grapefruit. For this reason, they can give you a lift when you feel low on energy. The lift (and the bulk provided by the water and fibre) helps you stick with your diet until the next regular meal. The fruit sugar that they contain makes a safe fruit taste pretty good – not as good as your favourite high-calorie foods, perhaps, because safe fruits don't contain any fat, but good enough to get you by at a pinch. You must keep reminding yourself that every time you choose a safe fruit you are avoiding a choice of food that would prevent you from losing weight.

Choosing a safe fruit is very important from a psychological standpoint. It becomes symbolic of your weight-loss effort. You carry it with you to work and it's always available at home. Every time you get the urge to deviate from the Rotation Diet you reach for your safe fruit. Believe me, it's a charm! It's your absolute guarantee of success. Even if you have two or three servings a day during the 600/900-calorie rotations – a mid-morning snack, a mid-afternoon snack, a bedtime snack – you cannot add much more than 150 to 200 calories to your intake. Should you go farther and add three whole grapefruit, which is considered to be six servings of a fruit, you will add only 330 calories, and *YOU WILL STILL LOSE WEIGHT*. It may be only 8 or 10 pounds (3½ to 4½ kg) in three weeks instead of 12 or 15 (5½ to 7), but even that is a success. It beats the complete failure that occurs when you allow yourself to dip into the sweet jar or biscuit tin, begin to feel disgusted with yourself for having blown your diet and then let all hell break loose. (Safe fruits are built into the diet at levels of 1200 calories and above, without exceeding calorie limits.)

It is very important, however, that you choose only ONE safe fruit to be your ally during the Rotation Diet. Be sure, of course, to eat the different fruits that are included in the basic diet plan for each day's menu because they have been selected to provide you with adequate vitamins and minerals. However, if you add variety in your safe fruits, which you can eat at any time, you may stimulate your appetite. So, follow my advice: choose just one safe fruit from the following list. Use it as your snack food when it is called for at calorie levels of 1200 and above, and as an insurance or 'fallback' food to be used whenever it is needed to prevent dangerous deviations from the Rotation Diet.

Be sure to think of your safe fruit as your ally. Pick one of the fruits in the short list below that you really do like. Have 'friendly' feelings toward it! I think of fruit as one of Mother Nature's most enjoyable gifts to mankind – the word *fruit* comes from a Latin word meaning 'enjoyment' or 'to enjoy'. I know that I am going to stay slim and

47

healthy every time I substitute a piece of fruit for one of man's enticing, but less healthful, junk-food creations! (If you are interested in determining more exact calorie values for each of these fruits, see Appendix A. I have restricted my list to fruits that are more generally available, but almost any fresh fruit will do.)

apple
berries
grapefruit
melon
orange
peach
pineapple
tangerine

ALLOWABLE BEVERAGES

You must have eight 8-fluid-ounce (225-ml) glasses of water each day. Water facilitates weight loss and helps you to stay healthy and regular when you are on a diet. Use iced water with a piece of lemon or lime if you find it difficult to drink the required amount, or use mineral or soda water.

Avoid artificially sweetened beverages (see discussion on pages 108-11). Up to two cups of coffee or tea are permitted, black coffee preferred. If you can't drink it black, a teaspoon of low-fat milk powder will only add about 8 calories. You can also use herb teas in moderation, but I would avoid, for daily use, those that have laxative qualities. Try low-salt bouillon cubes for a change (or make your own bouillon with meat or vegetable stock and added vegetables; see one of my recipes on pages 78-9).

FOOD PREPARATION AND SIZE OF SERVINGS

Prepare your food simply without adding fat during the 600-calorie rotation, and use only the very small amounts of fat prescribed in the 900- and 1200-calorie rotations. Learn to use herbs and spices in place of salt (see discussion of salt below).

I have developed many recipes to illustrate delicious ways of preparing foods with few added fat calories. I have provided recipes, and serving suggestions, for all the items on the Rotation Diet that are followed by an asterisk. (Recipes for the basic Rotation Diet begin on page 70.)

The correct serving sizes in either weight or volume are given both with the menus and with my recipes, and the calories in each serving are given with the recipes.

However, if you dislike weighing and measuring, as well as counting calories, as much as I do, then, for convenience, all you need to remember when you prepare foods your own way, or when eating out, is that you will tend to be within the dietary guidelines when you choose standard restaurant portions such as you will find at a cafeteria.

If you do not have a good idea of serving sizes, it is worth weighing and measuring for a few days. Then you will have portion sizes stored in your memory and can discontinue the practice.

Standard Portions for Vegetables

Generally, a standard portion for vegetables (other than *free vegetables*) is measured up to 4 fluid ounces (110 ml) in an ordinary measuring jug, or 3 heaped tablespoons. Some vegetables have so few calories that standard portions are as large as 8 fluid ounces (225 ml), a full American cup. You will see which vegetables fall into this category as you follow the diet. And, of course, some vegetables are unlimited.

Standard Portions for Meat, Fish and Poultry

For meat, fish and poultry a standard portion to fit the Rotation Diet plans for women during the 600/900 rotations is generally 3 ounces (75 g) cooked weight

49

(about 4 ounces/110 g raw). (Exceptions are noted in the daily menus.) Portions for women go up to either 4½ ounces (125 g) or 6 ounces (175 g) cooked (about 6 to 8 ounces/175 to 225 g raw) on the 1200-calorie rotation.

Portions for men are 4½ or 6 ounces (125 or 175 g) cooked weight (6 to 8 ounces/175 to 225 g raw) on their 1200-calorie rotations, and 6 ounces (175 g) cooked (about 8 ounces/225 g raw) on the 1500-calorie and 1800-calorie rotations. (The variation in the recommended portions depends in part on what is on the rest of the day's menu, and the calories in the meat or fish itself.)

Standard Portions for Grain Foods

Among grains, 1 slice of bread = 1 ounce (28 g) of dry cereal = up to the 4-fluid-ounces (110-ml) measure of cooked rice (½ cup) = 5 crispbread

Standard Portions for Milk Products

Among milk products, 8 fluid ounces (225 ml) of milk = 1 ounce (28 g) of hard cheese = 4 ounces (110 g) of low-fat cottage cheese.

SNACKS

During the 600/900-calorie rotations for women, any snacks except for *free vegetables* will add enough calories to slow your weight loss slightly. However, should you feel uncomfortably hungry, I do urge you to use your *safe fruit* as a snack during this time. The slowdown in your rate of weight loss will be negligible compared to what will happen if you use anything other than your safe fruit. Remember, free vegetables and your safe fruit are your insurance policy. Use them and *guarantee* your weight loss.

Snacks *(safe fruits)* are included in all menus of 1200 calories and higher. It is not obligatory for you to eat all these snacks, but when you reach the level of 1200 calories or higher, you should experiment with having one at mid-morning, at mid-afternoon and at bedtime. As I indicated, I never went to bed hungry. And, after a grapefruit snack at bedtime, I always slept well, without waking up famished in the middle of the night.

Most people who learn to eat healthful snacks during the Rotation Diet and then continue to do so during maintenance (eating fruits, vegetables and low-calorie grains such as unbuttered Melba toast or Ryvita instead of junk food) find it easier to control their weight in the long run. I normally nibble on fruit throughout the day. To be sure that you are not tempted to overeat and interfere with your rate of loss during the three weeks of the Rotation Diet, I suggest that you stick with your safe fruit as your only snack during this time. This will ensure that you stay well within the calorie guidelines. We will add more variety in the maintenance diet.

SUBSTITUTIONS

Women will do best to make as few substitutions as possible during the week they use the 600/900-calorie rotations. Even at this low intake, the diet has been designed to supply Recommended Dietary Allowances of the major vitamins and minerals, and to preserve your electrolyte balance (which affects heart rhythm). You can, of course, add free vegetables and your safe fruit. Everyone can be somewhat freer during Week 2, provided you make substitutions in accordance with certain dietary principles. If you need to make substitutions in any of the menus, whether because certain foods are not available or because you don't like them, please read the section on making substitutions which begins on page 105.

AN IMPORTANT WORD ABOUT SALT

The use of salt will impede your weight loss. Either use no salt at all in food preparation or, as I suggest in my recipes, add only the smallest amount, to taste. Many people find they can cut back on salt considerably if they wait until after their food is cooked before adding any. Soy sauce is also somewhat high in sodium (about one-seventh the concentration of salt granules, or about 285 milligrams per teaspoon, compared with 2000 to 2200 milligrams for salt). Therefore, do not exceed the amounts called for when I suggest the use of soy sauce in my recipes. Also look for reduced-sodium soy sauces, which taste just as good.

If you generally use salt, by all means try my recipe for Herb Salt (page 105). Herb Salt has one-seventh the amount of sodium in plain salt, which means that it contains far less sodium than many commercially blended salt substitutes. Whereas just one-eighth teaspoon of salt has between 250 and 275 milligrams of sodium, that amount of Herb Salt has about 40 milligrams. Although Herb Salt has the same relative proportion of sodium to salt as does regular soy sauce, it is safer to use than soy sauce because you will tend to use much less of it. (Some salt substitutes completely replace the sodium component with potassium, but they tend not to taste nearly as good as Herb Salt.)

8 fluid ounces (225 ml) of commercially prepared soup, such as mushroom, may contain nearly 1000 milligrams of sodium – that's *less than half a pint*. The same goes for a single serving of a frozen diet-dinner main course or a helping of sauce or pickle; that much sodium can lead to pounds of water retention.

Since my menus often call for crackers or crispbreads, look for the low-salt or no-salt varieties. Nowadays many packages of foods (canned and frozen) have taken note of the new salt consciousness and now label some products 'no salt added'. You may wish to try some of these.

THE COUPLES ROTATION DIET

Although we designed separate menus for women and men, couples can use the Rotation Diet together. To do this, men use the basic Rotation Diet for women and add approximately 600 calories each day, throughout the twenty-one days.

Weeks 1 and 3

For best results, in Weeks 1 and 3 men use the Rotation Diet for women and add all of the following each day:

2 more grain servings (bread, cereal or crispbread)
50 per cent larger portions of meat, fish or poultry
⅓ ounce (10 g) of butter or 1 dessertspoon of oil or regular salad dressing
3 safe fruits

This is the healthiest way to add the 600-calorie difference required by men when they use the Rotation Diet for women during Weeks 1 and 3.

Week 2

In Week 2, when women are at approximately 1200 calories and men at 1800 calories, men have a tremendous amount of flexibility. Since the 1200-calorie diet for women has been designed to provide the RDAs of essential vitamins and minerals, a man could add 600 calories to the Rotation Diet for women in many different ways and still end up with a nutritious diet. For best results during Week 2, men should use the menu for women (which already includes three safe fruits and ⅓ ounce (10 g) or 1 dessertspoon of fat for spread or seasoning) and add all of the following each day:

2 more grain servings (bread, cereal, or crispbread)
50 per cent larger portions of vegetables and main dishes

This will bring men up to about 1700 calories a day. The shortfall is due to the recipes in the male diet for Week 2 having slightly more fat in their preparation than the Week 2 recipes for women. This results from our following the nutritional guidelines of the United States Senate

Committee on Nutrition and Human Needs in all daily menus of 1200 calories and over. In relation to total calories, these guidelines call for approximately 55 to 60 per cent from carbohydrate, 25 to 30 per cent from fat and about 15 per cent from protein. Thus, as calorie levels increase, men can have more of every nutrient. Including fat! But I wouldn't overdo it.

And women please note that the Week 2 menus and suggested recipes in the men's version of the Rotation Diet are very likely to be close to maintenance menus and recipes for you. I will be discussing the use of the men's menus in the transition to maintenance in Chapter 8.

ADVICE FOR SINGLE PEOPLE AND FOR THE DIETER WITH A FAMILY

For Single People

I know it is hard for single people to go on a diet and cook for themselves alone, perhaps even harder than eating nutritiously as a single person when not on a reducing diet. Every time my wife goes on the road to perform and I am alone at home for days or weeks at a time, I find myself not wishing to prepare well-rounded meals. But it can be done, and done easily, with just a little planning.

The best way, I think, is to cook servings for two (cut recipes for four in half) and refrigerate or freeze the unused portions. You will be using the same foods again later in the diet, so you will already have them on hand. Most foods will keep well for three to five days in the refrigerator, and for months, of course, in the freezer. Cover appropriately for the refrigerator, and with freezer wrap for the freezer. You may also do the recipe for four and then freeze the food in separate, serving-size packages. That will save you time and bother in the future. We do a good deal of this large-batch cooking at weekends, and the remains serve us well during the

54

coming week, when my wife and I both get home late from work and a bit too tired to cook a full meal from scratch.

For the Dieter with a Family

Whenever possible, use the basic menu in large enough amounts to feed everyone, adding any fattening seasonings later and separately for the family. Often this doesn't work, at first, because many members of the family are not accustomed to eating a nutritious diet! They will want different foods, turning up their noses at the vegetables and insisting on fried dishes or other foods not on the diet with lots of added fat or sugar. A microwave oven is a great gift on these occasions, since you can make your own vegetables in a couple of minutes. You may have to prepare your own menu separately – the plain-cooking style of the Rotation Diet will make it easier than if you try to follow elaborate methods of food preparation.

But if you plan in advance, I think you can reconcile the way you need to eat to lose weight quickly with the way your family likes the food prepared. Take a look at the menus and see if you can make each evening's meal with your main dish held to the side while you add whatever your family wants to make it more enticing (if less nutritious) for them. And, if necessary, make your meals, or even some of your family's meals, in advance, at the weekend. Divide into serving sizes that will get you through the coming week or weeks, and freeze them.

Remember once again my advice to sit down for half an hour before you begin the Rotation Diet and work out what it will take for you to approach perfection, given your particular life situation. If you talk it over with your family, explaining exactly what you will need to do for the next three weeks, I think you can get their help and co-operation. Lay the menus for the Rotation Diet before them, and discuss what it will take to keep everybody happy as you lose weight.

COPY (OR CUT OUT) YOUR PERSONAL
POCKET EDITION OF THE ROTATION DIET.
For your convenience in following the
Rotation Diet, I have designed a Pocket Edition
of the menus that I am about to give you. The
Pocket Edition for women will be found beginning on page 247, and the one for men on page 257.
You can Xerox the Pocket Edition and carry it
with you to help you select your foods
throughout each day. You can show it to your
friends when they begin to marvel at your
weight loss (but if your friends decide to go on
the Rotation Diet with you, make sure they
follow the instructions in the Pocket Edition). In
case a photocopier is not easily available to you,
the pages of the Pocket Edition are arranged so
that you can cut them out of the book without
damaging the other contents.

THE COMPLETE ROTATION DIET PLAN MENUS FOR WOMEN

Additional information on serving sizes, *with calorie
values*, will be found with the recipes that accompany all
items followed by an asterisk. Do check out these
excellent recipes. They illustrate that low-calorie
cooking does not have to mean boredom and
deprivation.

Week 1

For couples who wish to use the Rotation Diet together,
men may use the basic diet plan for women with the
addition of all of the following each day:

2 more grain servings (bread, cereal or crispbread)
50 per cent larger portions of meat, fish, or chicken

56

1 dessertspoon of oil or regular salad dressing (or ⅓
ounce/10 g butter or margarine)
3 safe fruits

The calorie goal for men is 1200 calories for the first three
days and 1500 calories for the next four.

DAY 1

Breakfast:	½ grapefruit, 1 slice of whole-wheat bread and 1 slice of cheese (1 ounce/28 g see Mexican Cheese Toast*), no-cal beverage
Lunch:	1 serving of salmon (2 ounces/56 g canned in water, see Salmon with Herbs*), unlimited free vegetables, 5 whole-wheat crispbread, no-cal beverage
Dinner:	Baked Chicken* (3 ounces/80 g cooked), 1 serving each of Cauliflower* (1 cup) and Gingered Beets* (½ cup), 1 apple, no-cal beverage

DAY 2

Breakfast:	½ banana, 1 ounce (28 g) of high-fibre cereal (see pages 73-4), 8 fluid ounces (225 ml) of skim or low-fat milk, no-cal beverage
Lunch:	1 serving of low-fat cottage cheese (4 ounces/110 g, see Cottage Cheese Plus*), unlimited free vegetables, 1 slice of whole-wheat bread, no-cal beverage
Dinner:	Poached Fish Fillets* (3 ounces/80 g, cooked), 1 serving each of Broccoli* (1 cup) and Carrots* (½ cup), ½ grapefruit, no-cal beverage

DAY 3

Breakfast:	1 slice of whole-wheat bread, 1 dessertspoon of peanut butter, 1 apple, no-cal beverage

Lunch: Luncheon Tuna Vinaigrette* (2 ounces/56 g packed in water or 3 small sardines from Sardines Vinaigrette*), 5 whole-wheat crispbread, unlimited free vegetables, no-cal beverage

Dinner: Beefsteak or hamburger patty (3 ounces/80 g cooked, see Steak and Hamburger Teriyaki-Style*), 6 stalks of Asparagus,* 1 cup of Dinner Salad,* No-Cal Salad Dressing,* 1 slice of cheese (1 ounce/28 g), 1 orange, no-cal beverage

DAY 4

Breakfast: ½ banana, 1 ounce (28 g) of high-fibre cereal (see pages 73-4), 8 fluid ounces (225 ml) of skim or low-fat milk, no-cal beverage

Lunch: Tuna Salad* (with 2 ounces/56 g of water-packed tuna), unlimited free vegetables, 2 slices of whole-wheat bread, 1 teaspoon of mayonnaise or Lo-Cal Salad Dressing,* ½ grapefruit, no-cal beverage

Dinner: Baked Chicken* (3 ounces/80 g cooked), ½ cup of Carrots,* 1 cup of Dinner Salad,* 1 slice of cheese (1 ounce/28 g), 1 apple, no-cal beverage

DAY 5

Breakfast: 1 cup of berries, 1 serving of low-fat cottage cheese (4 ounces/110 g, see Cottage Cheese Plus*), 5 whole-wheat crispbread, no-cal beverage

Lunch: Sardines Vinaigrette* (3 small; or Tuna Vinaigrette,* 2 ounces/56 g canned in water), unlimited free vegetables, 2 slices of whole-wheat bread, 1 teaspoon of mayonnaise or Lo-Cal Salad Dressing,* ½ grapefruit, no-cal beverage

Dinner: Beefsteak or hamburger patty (3 ounces/80 g cooked, see Steak and Hamburger Teriyaki-Style*), 1 serving each of french or runner beans (½ cup) and Broccoli* (1 cup), 1 slice of cheese (1 ounce/28 g), 1 apple, no-cal beverage

DAY 6

Breakfast: ½ cantaloupe, 1 slice of cheese (1 ounce/28 g) and 1 slice of whole-wheat bread (see Mexican Cheese Toast*), no-cal beverage

Lunch: 1 hard-boiled egg (see Curried Unstuffed Hard-boiled Egg*), unlimited free vegetables, 2 slices of whole-wheat bread, 1 teaspoon of mayonnaise or Lo-Cal Salad Dressing,* ½ grapefruit, no-cal beverage

Dinner: Poached (or Baked) Fish Fillets* (3 ounces/80 g), 6 stalks of Asparagus,* Peas* (½ cup), 1 apple, no-cal beverage

DAY 7

Breakfast: ½ banana, 1 ounce (28 g) of high-fibre cereal (see pages 73-4), 8 fluid ounces (225 ml) of skim or low-fat milk, no-cal beverage

Lunch: 1 cup of berries, 1 serving of low-fat cottage cheese (4 ounces/110 g see Cottage Cheese Plus*), 2 slices of whole-wheat bread, no-cal beverage

Dinner: Baked Chicken* (3 ounces/80 g cooked), 1 serving each of Cauliflower* (1 cup) and Carrots* (½ cup), 1 apple, no-cal beverage

Week 2

In Week 2 women may add a mid-morning, a mid-afternoon and an evening snack, intentionally incorporating three servings of your *safe fruit*. It is not obligatory to include all these snacks in addition to the menus below, but they are permitted within the 1200-calorie limits for this week. You may also add 1 dessertspoon of oil or regular salad dressing or ⅓ ounce (10 g) butter or margarine to your diet each day. Use it for cooking or as a spread.

For couples, men should add all of the following each day to the daily menus of the Rotation Diet for women below.

2 more grain servings (bread, cereal or crispbread)
50 per cent larger portions of vegetables and main courses

Optional for men: another dessertspoon of fat for spread or seasoning. The calorie goal for males is 1800 per day throughout Week 2. Additional information on serving sizes, *with calorie values*, will be found with the recipes.

DAY 8

Breakfast: ½ grapefruit, 1 slice of whole-wheat bread, 1 dessertspoon of peanut butter, 8 fluid ounces (225 ml) of skim or low-fat milk, no-cal beverage

Lunch: large fruit salad (about 16 fluid ounces/450 ml, see Creative Fruit Salad*), 1 slice of cheese (1 ounce/28 g), 5 whole-wheat crispbread, no-cal beverage

Dinner: salmon steaks (4½ ounces/125 g see Royal Indian Salmon*), 1 serving of Peas and Baby Onions* (½ cup), 1 cup of Dinner Salad,* no-cal beverage

DAY 9

Breakfast: ½ banana, 1 ounce (28 g) of high-fibre cereal (see pages 73-4), 8 fluid ounces (225 ml) of skim or low-fat milk, no-cal beverage

Lunch: large chef salad (1 ounce/28 g each of cheese and turkey plus any salad vegetables, see Creative Chef Salad*), 5 whole-wheat crispbread, Lo-Cal Salad Dressing,* no-cal beverage

Dinner: chicken (4½ ounces/125 g cooked, see Chicken Tomasi* for something special tonight), 1 small baked potato (3½ ounces/90 g), french or runner beans (1 cup, or try Green Beans Almondine*), 1 slice of cheese (1 ounce/28 g), 1 apple, no-cal beverage

DAY 10

Breakfast: sliced fresh fruit of your choice (1 cup), 1 serving of low-fat cottage cheese (4 ounces/110 g), 1 slice of whole-wheat bread, no-cal beverage

Lunch: sandwich (2 ounces/56 g of meat or cheese, or see Combination Sandwich*), unlimited free vegetables, 1 orange, no-cal beverage

Dinner: 1 serving of Stir-Fry Vegetables* (2 cups), Brown or Wild Rice* (½ cup, cooked), 2 dessertspoons of grated cheese, 1 apple, no-cal beverage

DAY 11

Breakfast: 2 slices of fresh pineapple (or 2 pieces of other fresh fruit), 1 slice of cheese (1 ounce/28 g), 1 slice of whole-wheat bread, no-cal beverage

Lunch: Spinach Salad* (large, 2–3 cups, with sliced mushrooms, green peppers, and chopped egg), Lo-Cal Salad Dressing,* 1 apple or pear, 1 slice of cheese (1 ounce/28 g), no-cal beverage

Dinner: steak (6 ounces/175 g, see Steak Flamed in Brandy* or Marinated Steak*), 1 small baked potato (3½ ounces/90 g), Braised Carrots and Celery* (1 cup), ½ grapefruit, no-cal beverage

DAY 12

Breakfast: sliced fruit for cereal (½ cup), 1 ounce (28 g) of high-fibre cereal (see pages 73-4), 8 fluid ounces (225 ml) of skim or low-fat milk, no-cal beverage

Lunch: Tuna Salad* or Sardines Vinaigrette* (with 3 ounces/80 g of water-packed tuna or 4–5 sardines), unlimited free vegetables plus sliced tomato and green peppers, Lo-Cal Salad Dressing,* 1 slice of whole-wheat bread, no-cal beverage

Dinner: Herbed Pork* (6 ounces/175 g), serving Baked Marrow or Courgette,* Broccoli with Black Olives* (1 cup of broccoli), ½ grapefruit, no-cal beverage

DAY 13

Breakfast: ½ melon, 1 hard- or soft-boiled egg, 1 slice of whole-wheat bread, no-cal beverage

Lunch: dieter's special: ground-beef patty (4½ ounces/125 g cooked), 1 serving of low-fat cottage cheese (4 ounces/110 g), sliced tomato and unlimited free vegetables, Lo-Cal Salad Dressing,* no-cal beverage

Dinner: My Favourite Pasta* (1 cup, plus sauce), 2 dessertspoons of Parmesan cheese, 1 cup of Dinner Salad,* choice of 1 fresh fruit for dessert, no-cal beverage

DAY 14

Breakfast: ½ grapefruit, 1 cup of porridge (see page 74), 2 dessertspoons of raisins, dash of cinnamon, 4 fluid ounces (110 ml) of skim or low-fat milk, no-cal beverage

Lunch: toasted open faced sandwich (try Mexican Bean Spread),* 1 slice of cheese (1 ounce/28 g), and sliced tomato, or see Day 10 for a regular sandwich), unlimited free vegetables, 1 cup of assorted sliced fresh fruit (2 pieces), no-cal beverage

Dinner: Pot Roast of Beef* (4 ounces/110 g of meat,
cooked, including vegetables), 1 cup of
Dinner Salad*, Lo-Cal Salad Dressing,*
1 slice of cheese (1 ounce/28 g), 1 apple,
no-cal beverage

Week 3

Repeat the menus of Week 1, or use the Alternative
Menus in Chapter 12 for the 600- and 900-calorie
rotations.

> When you finish your twenty-one days on the
> Rotation Diet, BE VERY SURE THAT YOU
> FOLLOW MY DIRECTIONS FOR MAKING A
> TRANSITION TO MAINTENANCE IN WEEK 4
> (CHAPTER 8).

THE COMPLETE ROTATION DIET PLAN MENUS FOR MEN

Week 1

Men may incorporate three *safe fruit* snacks each day
within calorie guidelines throughout the Rotation Diet,
but it is not obligatory. You may also add 1 dessertspoon
of regular salad dressing (in place of lo-cal) or ⅓ ounce
(10 g) of butter or margarine to each day's menu and
remain within the calorie limits.

DAY 1

Breakfast: ½ banana, 1 ounce (28 g) of high-fibre
cereal (see pages 73-4), 8 fluid ounces (225 ml)
of skim or low-fat milk, no-cal beverage

Lunch: large chef salad (1 ounce/28 g each of
cheese and turkey, plus any salad

vegetables, see Creative Chef Salad*),
Lo-Cal Salad Dressing,* 5 whole-wheat
crispbread, no-cal beverage

Dinner: Baked Chicken* (4½ ounces/125 g
cooked), 1 small baked potato (3½
ounces/90 g), 1 serving of french or runner
Beans (1 cup), 1 apple, 1 slice of cheese (1
ounce/28 g), no-cal beverage

DAY 2

Breakfast: ½ grapefruit, 1 slice of whole-wheat bread,
1 dessertspoon of peanut butter, 8 fluid
ounces (225 ml) of skim or low-fat milk,
no-cal beverage

Lunch: large fruit salad (about 2 cups, see Creative
Fruit Salad*), 1 slice of cheese (1
ounce/28 g), 5 whole-wheat crispbread,
no-cal beverage

Dinner: Poached (or Baked) Fish Fillets* (6
ounces/175 g cooked), 1 serving of Peas
and Baby Onions* (½ cup), Dinner Salad* (1
cup), Lo-Cal Salad Dressing,* no-cal
beverage

DAY 3

Breakfast: 1 cup of sliced fruit (your choice), 1 serving
of low-fat cottage cheese (4 ounces/110 g), 1
slice of whole-wheat bread, no-cal beverage

Lunch: Combination Sandwich* (2 ounces/56 g of
meat or cheese), unlimited free vegetables,
1 orange, no-cal beverage

Dinner: Stir-Fry Vegetables* (2 cups), brown or wild
rice* (½ cup, cooked), 2 dessertspoons of
grated cheese, 1 apple, no-cal beverage

DAY 4

Breakfast: 1 cup of berries, 1½ ounces (40 g) of
high-fibre cereal (see pages 73-4), 8 fluid

	ounces (225 ml) of skim or low-fat milk, 1 slice of whole-wheat bread, 1 teaspoon of jam or marmalade, no-cal beverage
Lunch:	Spinach Salad* (large, 2–3 cups, with sliced mushrooms, green peppers, chopped egg, and Lo-Cal Salad Dressing*), 5 whole-wheat crispbread, 1 apple or pear, no-cal beverage
Dinner:	½ grapefruit, steak (6 ounces/175 g cooked, see Steak Flamed in Brandy* or Marinated Steak*), 1 small baked potato (3½ ounces/90 g), Braised Carrots and Celery* (1 cup), no-cal beverage

DAY 5

Breakfast:	½ melon, 1 hard- or soft-boiled egg, 2 slices of whole-wheat bread, 1 teaspoon of jam or marmalade, no-cal beverage
Lunch:	ground-beef patty (4½ ounces/125 g cooked, see Steak and Hamburger Teriyaki-Style*), 1 serving of low-fat cottage cheese (4 ounces/110 g), unlimited free vegetables, 1 slice of whole-wheat bread, 1 serving of fruit (your choice), no-cal beverage
Dinner:	My Favourite Pasta* (1 cup, plus sauce), 3 tablespoons of grated Parmesan cheese, Dinner Salad* (1 cup), Lo-Cal Salad Dressing,* ½ grapefruit, no-cal beverage

DAY 6

Breakfast:	1 cup of sliced fruit for cereal, 1½ ounces (40 g) of high-fibre cereal (see pages 73-4), 1 slice of whole-wheat bread, 8 fluid ounces (225 ml) of skim or low-fat milk, no-cal beverage
Lunch:	Tuna Salad* or Sardines Vinaigrette* (3 ounces/80 g of water-packed tuna, or 4–5 small sardines), unlimited free vegetables

plus sliced tomato and green pepper, Lo-Cal Salad Dressing,* 2 slices of whole-wheat bread, no-cal beverage

Dinner: Herbed Pork* (6 ounces/175 g cooked), serving of Baked Marrow or Courgette,* Broccoli with Black Olives* (1 cup of broccoli), 1 slice of whole-wheat bread, ½ grapefruit, no-cal beverage

DAY 7

Breakfast: ½ grapefruit, 1 cup of porridge (see page 74), 2 dessertspoons of raisins, dash of cinnamon, 4 fluid ounces (110 ml) of skim or low-fat milk, no-cal beverage

Lunch: Open-faced sandwich (2 portions, see Mexican Bean Spread,* with 1 slice of cheese (1 ounce/28 g) and sliced tomato, or see day 3 for a regular sandwich), unlimited free vegetables, Lo-Cal Salad Dressing,* 1 cup of assorted fresh fruit (2 pieces), no-cal beverage

Dinner: Pot Roast of Beef* (4 ounces/110 g of meat, including vegetables), Dinner Salad* (1 cup), Lo-Cal Salad Dressing,* 1 apple, no-cal beverage

Week 2

During Week 2 you can add 1 dessertspoon of oil or regular salad dressing or ⅓ ounce (10 g) of butter or margarine to each day's menu, as well as the three *safe fruits*, and remain within the calorie limits.

DAY 8

Breakfast: ½ melon, 2 slices of whole-wheat bread, 2 slices of cheese (2 ounces/56 g), no-cal beverage

Lunch: Tuna-Salad Sandwich* (3 ounces/80 g of water-packed tuna), unlimited free vegetables, 1 serving of fruit (your choice), no-cal beverage

Dinner: Baked Chicken* (6 ounces/175 g cooked), Spinach and Broccoli Casserole* (½ cup, or 1 cup of broccoli plainly prepared), serving of Baked Marrow or Courgette,* 1 apple, 1 slice of cheese (1 ounce/28 g if casserole recipe is not used), no-cal beverage

DAY 9

Breakfast: 1 cup of porridge (see page 74), 2 dessertspoons of raisins, dash of cinnamon, 4 fluid ounces (110 ml) of skim or low-fat milk, 1 slice of whole-wheat bread, 1 teaspoon of jam or marmalade, no-cal beverage

Lunch: large fruit salad (2 cups, see Creative Fruit Salad*), 1 serving of low-fat cottage cheese (4 ounces/110 g), 5 whole-wheat crispbread, no-cal beverage

Dinner: Baked (or Poached) Fish Fillets* (6 ounces/175 g), Baked Tomato* (½ Tomato), 1 small baked potato (3½ ounces/90 g), Dinner Salad* (1 cup), 1 slice of cheese (1 ounce/28 g), 1 apple, no-cal beverage

DAY 10

Breakfast: 1 orange, 2 slices of whole-wheat bread, 2 slices of cheese (2 ounces/56 g), no-cal beverage

Lunch: Tuna Salad* (3 ounces/80 g of water-packed tuna) on salad greens with sliced tomatoes and green pepper, plus unlimited free vegetables, Lo-Cal Salad Dressing,* no-cal beverage

Dinner: Steak (6 ounces/175 g cooked, see Marinated Flank Steak* or Steak Flamed in Brandy*), Stir-Fry Spinach* (1 cup), 1 small baked potato (3½ ounces/90 g) with

Cottage-Cheese Dressing* (or 2
dessertspoons of sour cream), choice of 1
fruit, no-cal beverage

DAY 11

Breakfast: ½ melon, 1 serving of low-fat cottage cheese
(4 ounces/110 g), 1 slice of whole-wheat
bread, 1 teaspoon of jam or marmalade,
no-cal beverage

Lunch: sandwich (2 ounces/56 g of meat or cheese;
see Combination Sandwich*), unlimited
free vegetables, Lo-Cal Salad Dressing,*
no-cal beverage

Dinner: Baked Salmon* (6 ounces/175 g cooked, see
Royal Indian Salmon*), Peas and Baby
Onions* (½ cup), Dinner Salad* (1 cup),
Lo-Cal Salad Dressing,* choice of 1 fruit, 1
slice of cheese (1 ounce/28 g), no-cal
beverage

DAY 12

Breakfast: ½ grapefruit, 2 slices of whole-wheat bread,
1 dessertspoon of peanut butter, 1 teaspoon
of jam or marmalade, no-cal beverage

Lunch: 8 fluid ounces (225 ml) of soup (commercial
or see Soups*), 10 whole-wheat crispbread,
2 slices of cheese (2 ounces/56 g), unlimited
free vegetables, Lo-Cal Salad Dressing,*
no-cal beverage

Dinner: Veal Loaf* (or 6 ounces/175 g, cooked, of
lean meat of your choice), carrots* (½ cup),
Dinner Salad* (1 cup), Lo-Cal Salad
Dressing,* 1 apple, no-cal beverage

DAY 13

Breakfast: 1 cup of berries, 1½ ounces (40 g) of
high-fibre cereal (see pages 73-4), 1 slice of
whole-wheat bread, 1 teaspoon of jam or
marmalade, 8 fluid ounces (225 ml) of skim
or low-fat milk, no-cal beverage

Lunch: large chef salad (1 ounce/28 g each of cheese and turkey, plus any salad vegetables, see Creative Chef Salad*), Lo-Cal Salad Dressing,* 5 whole-wheat crispbread, no-cal beverage

Dinner: Baked Chicken* (6 ounces/175 g cooked, or try Almond Chicken*), 1 serving of Brown or Wild Rice* (½ cup), Broccoli* (1 cup), 1 slice of cheese (1 ounce/28 g), 1 apple, no-cal beverage

DAY 14

Breakfast: choice of sliced fruit (1 cup), 1 serving of low-fat cottage cheese (4 ounces/110 g), 1 slice of whole-wheat bread, 1 teaspoon of jam or marmalade, no-cal beverage

Lunch: sandwich (2 ounces/56 g of meat or cheese, see Combination Sandwich*), unlimited free vegetables, Lo-Cal Salad Dressing,* ½ grapefruit, no-cal beverage

Dinner: fish of your choice (6 ounces/175 g cooked, or try Baked or Broiled Rainbow Trout*), Baked Tomato* (½ tomato), Green Beans with Chives* (1 cup, or use mushroom variation), 1 slice of whole-wheat bread, 1 slice of cheese (1 ounce/28 g), 1 fruit of your choice, no-cal beverage

Week 3

Repeat the menus of Week 1, or use the Alternative Menus in Chapter 12 for the 1200- and 1500-calorie rotations.

When you finish your twenty-one days on the Rotation Diet, BE VERY SURE THAT YOU FOLLOW MY DIRECTIONS FOR MAKING A TRANSITION TO MAINTENANCE IN WEEK 4 (CHAPTER 8).

RECIPES

The recipes and serving suggestions for the Rotation Diet are meant to illustrate that low-calorie cooking need not be boring and without taste. However, for simplicity's sake, you may prepare everything plain, or according to your own favourite recipes, provided you do not add fat, sugar or anything else that will increase the calorie content.

To facilitate weight loss, do not use salt. However, if you must have a small amount of salt for flavouring, it is best to add it after cooking, at the table.

See my recipe for Herb Salt (page 105), which cuts out over 85 per cent of the sodium. It's a great blend.

Except for *free vegetables*, be sure to adhere to the serving sizes recommended. And, of course, remember that you have a *safe fruit* that you can use to make sure you do not feel hungry.

Grains, Breads, Crispbreads, Cereals

I advise you to use either 100 per cent whole-grain breads and crispbreads or those that have as their primary ingredient a whole grain. If the primary ingredient is a whole grain, it will be listed first on the label of a commercial product.

Breads and crackers that say '100 per cent whole wheat' and those listing 'whole-wheat or wholemeal flour' as the only grain ingredient will be made entirely of whole grains. Blends will list other grains or types of flour.

I like breads made from whole-grain products because they offer a wider array of vitamins and minerals than the refined-grain products and three or more times the dietary fibre.

Most commercial whole-wheat breads contain about 65–70 calories per slice, and the usual whole-wheat crispbread has about 17 calories (five whole-wheat crispbread will be about 85 calories).

70

BREADS

Here are two outstanding whole-wheat breads that were developed especially for the Rotation Diet by one of Nashville's outstanding bakers and teachers of baking, Ms Joyce Weingartner. As you will see when you try these recipes, blending a small amount of other flours with the primary whole-wheat flour provides a lighter, more attractive texture than can be obtained by using only whole-wheat flour. In addition, the use of other flours in small amounts increases the overall nutritional value of the bread since the other flours have a different array of nutrients. Both these breads are batter breads, which makes for quick and easy baking.

WHOLE-WHEAT BATTER BREAD

In a large warmed mixing bowl combine:

  1 pound 14 ounces (850 g) of whole-wheat flour
  3 ounces (80 g) of barley flour (white can be substituted)
  3 ounces (80 g) of soy flour
  3 ounces (80 g) of sugar (you may mix half white and half brown)
  1 dessertspoon of salt
  2 packages of fast action or easy blend dry yeast
    Pour in 1 pint 8 fluid ounces (800 ml) of hand hot water and stir 200 strong strokes until blended.

Mixing the ingredients should take at least 3 minutes until the flours are completely incorporated. This will yield a soft batter that is not to be kneaded.

With a wooden spoon, fill two 2 pound (1 kg) bread tins, which have been well greased. Push dough into the corners and smooth the top surface. A wet spoon helps this process.

Cover with a warm, wet towel and place in a warm draught-free area until the batter has doubled.

71

Preheat oven to 400°F (Gas Mark 6/200°C) and bake for 15 minutes.

Reduce heat to 350°F (Gas Mark 4/180°C) and continue baking for another 45 minutes.

To prevent the top of the bread from becoming too dark, you may cover it with foil for the last half-hour of baking.

Test the bread for a hollow sound when you remove it from the tins. If the bread is soft on the bottom, return it to the oven for about 10 additional minutes, either in the tins or directly on the oven shelf if you prefer a crusty bottom.

Remove bread and place on a metal rack to cool, with a cloth over the bread.

Cool before serving.

Storage: in a plastic bag in the refrigerator if you will use it immediately (in a week, for example), or in a plastic bag in the freezer for longer periods.

Note: If you wish to have a bread that is 100 per cent whole wheat, delete the barley and soy flours and use 2 pounds 4 ounces (1 kg) of whole-wheat flour in this recipe.

OATMEAL BATTER BREAD

Either prove 2 packages of yeast in 2 fluid ounces (50 ml) of warm water to which have been added ¼ teaspoon of sugar and ¼ teaspoon of ginger or mix 2 packages of fast action or easy blend dry yeast with the flour below.

Mix 16 fluid ounces (450 ml) of hand hot water with 3 ounces (80 g) of rolled oats, ⅓ ounce (10 g) of butter, 1½ teaspoons of salt, and 4 ounces (110 g) of molasses.

Add the yeast mixture to the oats and stir in 12 ounces (350 g) of whole-wheat flour. Stir 100 strong strokes to blend.

Add:

> 3 ounces (80 g) of soy flour
> 3 ounces (80 g) of white flour
> 2 rounded tablespoons of wheat germ
>> Stir well after each addition.
>> Add an additional 8 ounces (225 g) of
>> whole-wheat flour.

Stir well for 3 minutes so that all ingredients are completely blended. This will yield a soft, sticky batter which is not to be kneaded.

Cover with a warm, wet cloth and place in a draught-free warm place until the batter has doubled – about 1 to 1¼ hours.

Stir down and spoon into three 1 pound (500 g) greased bread tins, or two 2 pound (1 kg) bread tins for larger loaves.

Cover with a wet cloth and allow to double in bulk (around 45 minutes).

When spooning the batter in, it helps to use a wet spoon to fill the tins and push the batter into the corners. The top will look like a ploughed field, but this is not important to the taste.

Preheat oven to 350°F (Gas Mark 4/180°C) and bake for 55 minutes.

For a crusty bottom you may place the loaf on the rack of the oven for 5 minutes without the tin (optional).

Cool on a wire rack with a cloth over the bread before serving.

Storage: in a plastic bag in the refrigerator or for longer periods in the freezer.

CEREALS

With respect to cereals, I hope there is one you like from the following list because they are among the best that you can use in a calorie-restricted diet – they are the high-fibre cereals I refer to in my menus:

30% Bran Flakes	Bran Buds	Grape-Nuts
Shredded Wheat	Puffed Wheat	Weetabix
All Bran	Oat Bran	Porridge Oats

The calorie values of these cereals, per serving, will be found on the package. They tend to range between 70 and 110 calories per ounce.

To make 1 cup of porridge use 8 fluid ounces (225 ml) of water and 3 to 4 tablespoons of rolled oats.

CRISPBREADS

Many so-called plain biscuits contain a great deal of sodium, which will seriously slow your weight loss. Check labels, and if your store does not carry attractive crispbread that have a whole grain listed as their first or only ingredient, choose those that list a whole grain, or bran, as a second ingredient.

Milk and Milk Products

Skim milk has virtually no fat and contains about 80 calories per 8 fluid ounces (225 ml). Semi-skimmed will contain about 100 calories for 1 per cent butterfat content, and around 120 calories if it has a 2 per cent butterfat content. I use low-fat milk because its fat content satisfies hunger for a much longer time than does skim milk (and I prefer the flavour).

CHEESE

Many herbs, seeds, and spices can be used to advantage with cheese. My favourite herbs are dillweed, rosemary, sage and thyme. Seeds include caraway, celery and dill. Certain spices can be sprinkled over Cheddar, or havarti or other hard cheeses and then toasted on a slice of whole-wheat bread, in either a regular or microwave oven. This makes a tasty toasted open-faced sandwich for breakfast or lunch. The best spices for cheese toast include chilli powder, cumin or curry powder, plus a dash of cayenne pepper.

Be sure to control your serving size of cheese. Many varieties are high in sodium. Cheddar has about 200 milligrams per ounce, while blue has almost 400 milligrams per ounce. Cottage and cream cheeses are among the lowest, at around 100 milligrams per ounce, followed by Cheddar, Parmesan and Edam in that order. Camembert, processed cheese and cheese spreads all contain relatively high quantities of salt.

Try the following Mexican Cheese Toast when the diet calls for 1 slice (about 1 ounce/28 g) of cheese and 1 slice of whole-wheat bread.

MEXICAN CHEESE TOAST

1 ounce (28 g) of Cheddar or other hard cheese
chilli powder
1 slice of whole-wheat bread
Dash of cayenne (optional)

Slice the cheese thinly so that it covers the bread. Sprinkle generously with chilli powder and add a dash of cayenne if you like it hot. This takes less than a minute to melt in a microwave, or you can do it under the grill, in which case it will take a little longer and need watching.

Any time that the menus call for a slice of cheese and a slice of bread, you can combine them to make some form of cheese toast. Vary the recipe by using other herbs and spices.

The average slice of bread is about 70 calories, while a slice of cheese (about 1 ounce/28 g in weight) will generally contain 100 calories. Thus, cheese toast will have approximately 170 calories.

COTTAGE CHEESE PLUS

Of course the Rotation Diet recommends cottage cheese as one of the dairy staples in its menus. Cottage cheese is a very good source of protein, carbohydrate and calcium. I like cottage cheese with just about any fruit except citrus. If you don't care much for cottage cheese in its plain form, or soon get bored with it, try flavouring it with one or more of the herbs and spices I mentioned above to make Cottage Cheese Plus. Also, in addition to or instead of celery seed and fresh black pepper, I especially like to sprinkle my cottage cheese with either onion or garlic powder.

Serving size is 4 ounces (110 g), at about 90 calories per serving.

Eggs

CURRIED UNSTUFFED HARD-BOILED EGG

You can more than double the calories in devilled or stuffed eggs when you add those gobs of mayonnaise. It's unnecessary. Just sprinkle slices of hard-boiled egg with one or more of the following: curry or chili powder, cumin, onion powder, celery seeds, fresh ground black pepper. I find that any of these seasonings will satisfy my palate without adding mayonnaise or salt. The recipe is now called Curried Unstuffed Hard-boiled Egg.

Serving size is 1 egg, at about 80 calories per egg.

Sandwiches

COMBINATION SANDWICH

The label 'Combination Sandwich' refers to any combination of ingredients between 2 slices of bread, such as ham (or any slice of meat) and cheese, or spreads with vegetables or cheese.

The way to prepare sandwiches with limited calories is to use lean cuts of meat or chicken and only limited amounts of dressing. Two slices of bread, with 1 ounce (28 g) each of meat and cheese, will contain about 295 calories. Mayonnaise is about 33 calories a teaspoon, ketchup is 16 calories a dessertspoon, and mustard is negligible. Add *free vegetables* and you have a satisfying lunch for about 350 calories. (Compare the calorie content of this lunch with the 650 or so calories you obtain in the typical fast-food hamburger sandwich. The fast-food hamburger can have as much as five times the fat content of your lean slice of meat, and three to six times more mayonnaise or salad dressing will be used to enhance the flavour.)

For variety, try one of the following spreads. They make especially attractive open-faced sandwiches. Serve with beansprouts, or a slice of tomato or cheese, and grill or bake in the oven for a hot sandwich.

Meat Spread

8 ounces (225 g) of cooked meat or chicken
1 small onion, diced
2 rounded tablespoons of wheat germ (or cooked red beans)
2 level dessertspoons of soy flour
Herb Salt (p. 105)
Freshly ground black pepper

Blend all ingredients in a food processor. Moisten as needed with ketchup or low calorie salad dressing.

Serving size is about 2 ounces (50 g), or 2 rounded tablespoons, at about 95 calories per serving.

Crab-Meat Spread

8 ounces (225 g) crab meat
3 sticks of celery, diced
1 small onion, diced
Herb Salt to taste (p. 105)
½ green pepper, diced
8 fluid ounces (225 ml) of beansprouts
8 ounces (225 g) of low-fat cottage cheese

Blend with enough low calorie salad dressing to moisten. Makes about 3 cups; serving size is about 2 ounces (56 g) or 2 rounded tablespoons, at about 35 calories per serving.

Mexican Bean Spread

This is one of my favourites. It can be used as a dip and is great grilled or baked in the oven covered with a slice of cheese or tomato and sprinkled with oregano.

15½ ounce (440 g) tin of dark-red kidney beans
1 small onion
3 dessertspoons of ketchup
⅛ teaspoon of cayenne

pepper   Freshly ground black
Herb Salt (p. 105)   pepper

Blend in a food processor, adding more ketchup if
needed for desired consistency.

Serving size is about 2 ounces (56 g) or 2 rounded
tablespoons at about 90 calories per serving.

TUNA- OR SALMON-SALAD SANDWICH

See the recipe for tuna and salmon salad on page 81. With
2 slices of bread, lettuce and/or beansprouts, plus ¼ of
the salad recipe, a typical sandwich will contain between
260 and 325 calories, depending upon the amount of
mayonnaise used.

Soups

SOUP BASE

This is the basic stock that I use for making soup of
various kinds and for cooking rice and boiled potatoes. It
is excellent for soaking and cooking beans. By adding
only a minimal amount of salt, you can keep the sodium
content of your own stock at a fraction of what is contained in commercial soups and bouillons.

Save all chicken and turkey giblets (necks, hearts,
gizzards, but *not* livers) until you have accumulated the
parts of 4 to 6 birds. Freeze these parts immediately, first
trimming skin and any fat from the necks, and hold in
your freezer until you have enough of the makings, or
buy ready frozen giblets. Then:

Place giblets in a big saucepan with enough water to
cover – about 3 to 4 pints (2 to 2½ litres). Bring to a boil
and skim as necessary. When finally clear of scum, add:

1 large bay leaf   2 large stalks of celery, in
1 teaspoon each of   2 inch (5 cm) pieces
   rosemary, sage, thyme   (include leaves)
   and tarragon   Salt and pepper to taste

78

1 large onion, coarsely chopped	2 large carrots, in 2-inch (5-cm) pieces

Throw in any other wilted vegetables you have hanging out in your refrigerator (except for brussels sprouts, spinach, cabbage, broccoli or cauliflower).

Bring to the boil once again, then reduce heat and simmer for at least 2 hours.

Separate giblets and vegetables from water. Blend vegetables and return to stock.

Freeze the stock in plastic containers of various sizes and use as needed.

THURSDAY'S VEGETABLE SOUP

This soup bears this name because I made it for the first time on a Thursday, a day before I was about to do a television show on low-calorie cooking when the temperature was near zero outdoors. What could be better than a hot cup of soup on such a day?

To 8 fluid ounces (225 ml) of soup stock (or commercial low-salt bouillon), throw in a quartered onion, a sliced carrot and a sliced stalk of celery, plus anything else in the way of vegetables that you have left over in the refrigerator (red cabbage will give it a delightful red tint).

Add seasonings to taste – for example, thyme, a few sprigs of rosemary, a touch of parsley, etc.

Each 8 fluid ounce (225 ml) contains about 15 to 20 calories; depending on how many vegetables you throw in, you can end up with 2 or 3 servings at about 40 or 60 calories for the total.

This soup is another food that you can use almost as freely as a *free vegetable* (some of the vegetables that you use may make it more than 10 calories a serving).

You can make the soup a little heartier by using some potatoes, and I strongly suggest that you do occasionally. This will make the soup even more filling and satisfy your hunger for longer periods. A small (3½-ounce/90-g) potato will add only 90 calories to the entire recipe.

Salads

CREATIVE FRUIT SALAD

This is called Creative Fruit Salad because you use what-ever fruits you have on hand, cut them up into chunks, sprinkle with lemon juice to keep the fruit looking fresh and to add a bit of tang, and then add 1 dessertspoon of ONE of any of the following:

Grated coconut
Chopped unsalted nuts (of any kind)
Raisins or chopped dates

Add a sprinkle of any of the following spices:

Cinnamon   Ginger
Nutmeg   Anise
Allspice   Cardamom

A main-course serving is 16 fluid ounces (450 ml) of any combination of fresh fruits plus 1 dessertspoon of nuts or raisins. Average calories: about 200 per serving.

CREATIVE CHEF SALAD

Several large leaves of cos lettuce or chicory
¼ head of any soft round lettuce shredded
small wedge of red cabbage, shredded
2 rounded tablespoons of grated carrots
1 ounce (28 g) of hard cheese, cut in narrow strips
1 ounce (28 g) of white-meat turkey or chicken, in strips
Plus choice of *free vegetables*
1 egg quartered (optional)
1 tomato, quartered
1 slice of green pepper
Lo-Cal Dressing (p. 84)
Herb Salt (p. 105)
Freshly ground black pepper

Arrange your selections attractively on the cos or chicory and use 1 to 2 dessertspoons of dressing.

The calorie content of this salad will range from 300 to 400 depending on whether you include the egg, and the amount of dressing you use.

DINNER SALAD

For each portion, use:

½ carrot, thinly sliced
1 stalk of celery, thinly
sliced or
¼ green pepper, diced
lettuce or greens *(free
vegetables)*

small wedge of
shredded red cabbage
or
4 sliced mushrooms
2 thin slices of sweet red
onion

A dinner-size salad bowl of this mixture will contain about
40 calories. Use with No- or Lo-Cal Dressing (pp. 83-4)
and flavour with Herb Salt (p. 105) if you like.

TUNA OR SALMON SALAD

1 6½ ounce (185 g) tin of
water-pack tuna or
salmon

1 large carrot
2 stalks of celery

Blend in a food processor or blender, adding enough
salad dressing or mayonnaise for desired consistency. If
you prefer to do the blending by hand, the carrot and
celery should be sliced thin, or chopped. Serve with
lettuce and tomato, or with 2 slices of bread and beansprouts as a sandwich.

Blended with 1 dessertspoon of mayonnaise, this makes
3 tuna-salad portions at 136 calories each. If you leave out
the mayonnaise, the calories per serving are 103. For
salmon-salad portions of the same size, add 30 calories.

SALMON WITH HERBS

Even tinned salmon can be interesting when it's dressed
in its most complementary herbs. My favourites are
thyme, marjoram or sage – just a dash or two of each.
Celery seed goes well, too, and so does the mustard
vinaigrette dressing I suggest below for the sardines (a
bit of mustard and a drop of lemon juice or vinegar).
Serve with toast, whole-wheat crispbread and/or a loaf of
cos lettuce.

Serving size is 3 ounces (80 g), at 156 calories per serving.

SARDINES VINAIGRETTE

I include sardines, should you like them, because they are an excellent low-calorie source of protein and calcium, even when packed in oil. Their nutritional value makes them an excellent addition to the 600/900-calorie rotations. Just drain and top with a bit of Dijon mustard and a drop of lemon juice or vinegar. Serve on a leaf or two of lettuce, and garnish with any of your *free vegetables*.

Serving size is 2 ounces (56 g), or about 3 small sardines, at 88 calories per serving.

SPINACH SALAD

For each serving:

3 handfuls of fresh spinach, washed and dried

3 large mushrooms, sliced

½ hard-boiled egg, chopped

1 sweet red onion, sliced (optional)

3 slices of green pepper Lo-cal dressing of your choice (or see p. 84)

Arrange spinach on a large plate, and then arrange the other vegetables over it in an attractive manner – a spinach salad is one of the most pleasant salads to behold, especially if you do choose to add a few slices of red onion.

Contains about 115 calories per serving, including the egg. Add 33 calories per dessertspoon of Lo-Cal Salad Dressing (p. 84), or check the bottle of any lo-cal dressing of your own. If you wish to keep the calories down, use No-Cal Salad Dressing (p. 83)

LUNCHEON TUNA VINAIGRETTE

I prefer my tuna plain with a few drops of fresh lemon juice or wine vinegar. For extra zest, try water-packed tuna with tarragon vinegar (you can buy this commercially) or use my recipe for No-Cal Salad Dressing (see below) with the addition of tarragon. This dressing has no calories.

Serving size is 3 ounces (80 g) at 120 calories per serving.

Salad Dressings

COTTAGE-CHEESE DRESSING

4 ounces (110 g) of low-fat cottage cheese	4 radishes, sliced
4 fluid ounces (110 ml) of plain low-fat yogurt	2 dessertspoons of chives
½ green pepper, chopped	1 dessertspoon of poppy seeds
	Herb Salt to taste

Mix in a blender or food processor. It is excellent with salads and baked potatoes. For variety, add onions or 2 ounces (56 g) of blue cheese. (Blue cheese will add about 40 milligrams of sodium to each dessertspoonful of this dressing.)

About 12 calories per dessertspoon or 22 calories per dessertspoon when blue cheese is added.

NO-CAL SALAD DRESSING

4 fluid ounces (110 ml) of wine vinegar	1 dessertspoon of fresh chopped parsley
½ teaspoon of Herb Salt (see p. 105)	1 clove of garlic, crushed

Mix well. Use other herbs and vinegars for variety. Tarragon is one of the best herbs for salad dressings. And, if available, try the fruit vinegars (they are excellent) such as raspberry or strawberry. You may add 2 to 4 fluid ounces (50 to 110 ml) of water to this dressing if it is too vinegary for your taste.

LO-CAL SALAD DRESSING

2 fluid ounces (50 ml) of   1 clove of garlic, crushed
   fine olive oil   ½ teaspoon of salt
2 fluid ounces (50 ml) of   1 teaspoon of dried
   water   tarragon
2 fluid ounces (50 ml) of
   wine or fruit vinegar

Blend by shaking in a jar and let stand for several hours before its first use. Always shake before using.

Use different herbs for variety.

For extra tang, add 1 teaspoon of Dijon mustard.

About 33 calories per dessertspoon. (Don't be concerned about the water in this recipe – it helps spread the flavours and saves calories. Many commercial recipes use water to save calories, just as this one does.)

Meats: Beef, Pork and Veal

You probably have some favourite ways of preparing meat, and you should feel free to use them if the recipes call for lean cuts and no added fat or oil.

Here are three quick ways of flavouring steak or lean beef patties. Similar seasonings can be used with other cuts of beef.

STEAK AND HAMBURGER TERIYAKI-STYLE

Sprinkle a 4 ounce (110 g) – raw weight – lean beef patty with ground ginger, fresh ground pepper, just a touch of garlic powder and onion powder and a teaspoon of soy sauce. Try a low-salt variety of soy sauce if you wish to be more moderate in your salt intake. Fry or grill without added fat. (A 4-ounce patty reduces to 3 ounces (80 g) during cooking.)

Use the same seasonings with steak, calculating your portion size as directed three paragraphs below.

Variation 1. Italian Seasonings. Sprinkle liberally with garlic powder and onion powder with your choice of herbs such as oregano, basil, thyme, marjoram and parsley. Add a touch of fresh-ground black pepper. This recipe doesn't need salt, so don't add any until you serve the hamburger and taste it. After turning in the pan, spread hamburger with a teaspoon of ketchup or chilli sauce.

Variation 2. Chilli Seasonings. Sprinkle sparingly with chilli powder, paprika and a dash of cayenne pepper. Cumin and basil will make interesting additions to the flavour as well. Add salt after tasting at the table.

Lean beef and extra-lean hamburger average about 55 calories per cooked ounce. Serving size is 3 ounces (80 g) cooked (165 calories) on the 600/900-calorie rotations, 4½ ounces (125 g) cooked (248 calories) on the 1200-calorie rotations, and 6 ounces (175 g) cooked (330 calories) at the higher levels.

STEAK FLAMED IN BRANDY

Flavour your steak with your favourite seasonings and fry without fat. Just before serving, pour 2 dessertspoons of brandy over the steak and light fumes with a match. Let it burn out before serving.

Just about all of the calories in the brandy burn off, so figure about 55 calories an ounce for lean meat.

MARINATED STEAK

You can use either of the following two marinades with any cut of steak, but flank (or skirt) is one of the leanest cuts of meat and the marinade tenderizes it. In addition, the use of either marinade is excellent for outdoor grilling. If you use any other cut of steak, be sure to trim all the visible fat (most of the calories in any cut of steak come from fat, *not* protein).

2 pounds (1 kg) of flank or skirt
1 dessertspoon of salad oil
4 fluid ounces (110 ml) of dry white wine

1 small onion, minced
¼ teaspoon of thyme
1 bay leaf
2 cloves of garlic, minced
2 teaspoons of chopped chives

85

Steak must be marinated overnight to obtain the full tenderizing and flavouring effect. Use a covered bowl or two plastic bags (one might leak). (An extra tenderizing and even more flavourful effect can be obtained if you take the trouble to pierce the steak with the tines of a fork on both sides before putting it in the marinade, at intervals of about a ¼ inch/½ cm.)

Grill about 4 minutes on each side, basting with marinade as you turn. Use all of the marinade. Slice thinly on the diagonal to serve (it's both attractive and easy for the diner to deal with diagonal cuts), and cover with sauce from the pan. Add salt and pepper to taste at the table.

Here is an Oriental marinade that will have you salivating every time you think about it once you have sampled it:

1 dessertspoon of salad oil	¼ teaspoon of ground coriander
2 fluid ounces (50 ml) of soy sauce	1-inch (2-cm) cube of fresh ginger, peeled
2 fluid ounces (50 ml) dry red wine	and grated or minced (it must be fresh ginger –
4 cloves of garlic, minced	the powder just won't
4 shallots, minced	give you the flavour of
6 whole peppercorns	the fresh root)

Marinate overnight and cook as above.

Each 4-ounce (110-g) serving of cooked flank steak will contain about 220 calories.

Each 2 pounds (1 kg) of steak (raw weight) will yield about 6 servings. The exact number of servings depends upon the size you desire, and you must remember that there is about 25 per cent shrinkage from the raw to the cooked state.

HERBED PORK

4 lean pork chops, 1 to 1½ inches (2 to 3 cm) thick	2 tablespoons of soy sauce
	1 teaspoon of cornflour or flour

86

1 clove of garlic, minced
½ teaspoon each of
   rosemary, thyme,
   tarragon, oregano, sage
   and basil

Salt and fresh-ground
black pepper to taste

Trim all visible fat. Puncture the chops with the tines of a fork at intervals of about a ¼ inch (½ cm). Rub well with the cornflour or flour. Place the soy sauce, herbs, garlic and pepper in a shallow bowl and marinate the chops for at least 2 hours (preferably overnight). Be sure the chops are coated on both sides with the marinade and turn two or three times. This marinade is an excellent tenderizer. (Add a little more soy sauce if there is not enough to coat the chops, and leave a bit remaining in the bottom of your marinating bowl.)

Place chops in a shallow pan with 4 fluid ounces (225 ml) of water, cover, and simmer *very gently* for 45 minutes. Do not boil as this will toughen the meat. Remove chops. Pour off and save the liquid. If you have trimmed the meat well there will be very little fat on top of the liquid. Remove any that remains.

Return chops to the pan and brown on both sides. When done, place on warm plate. Return liquid to pan and heat, tasting occasionally to determine how much salt to add. You can add more water to taste, or perhaps 3 tablespoons of dry white wine (the alcohol will evaporate, leaving the flavour). It takes about 2 to 3 minutes to make this sauce.

Pour over the chops and serve (you might want to save a bit of the sauce for a baked potato if that is also on the menu).

Lamb chops can be made with a similar marinade. However, lamb chops should be dry fried, uncovered, without water, for about 7–8 minutes per side. Remove the chops and add either 4 fluid ounces (110 ml) of water or a 50/50 mixture of water and dry red wine to the drippings in the skillet and heat to make a sauce.

The lean meat, separated from all visible fat, will contain about 55 calories per ounce, but unless you do a perfect job of trimming, you should figure about 70 calories per ounce, or about 315 calories for a 4½-ounce (125-g) serving and 420 calories for a 6-ounce (175-g) serving.

POT ROAST OF BEEF

This particular roast is made with Italian seasonings.

2 pounds (1 kg) of lean beef (topside trimmed) or
2 pounds (1 kg) of flank steak or skirt
4 cloves of garlic, minced
2 medium onions, sliced
1 green pepper, sliced
4 stalks of celery, cut in 2-inch (5-cm) pieces
6 large carrots, cut in 2-inch (5-cm) pieces
12 new potatoes
1 bay leaf

1 dessertspoon of Italian seasonings*
1 28-ounce (790-g) tin of tomatoes
1 15-ounce (425-g) tin of tomato pulp
2 teaspoons of soy sauce
Dash of Worcestershire sauce
Salt and pepper to taste
Optional: 4 fluid ounces (110 ml) of hearty red wine .

Place meat in a large roasting pan and cover with minced garlic and slices of onions and green pepper. Place other vegetables and potatoes all around the meat.

Mix the soy sauce and Worcestershire sauce in either the tomatoes or the tomato sauce, and then add both to the roast (together with the wine, if you use it). Add all the other seasonings.*

Cook in a slow oven at 250°F (Gas Mark ½/130°C) for 4 to 5 hours, or until meat falls apart when prodded with the tines of a fork.

Makes 6 or 8 servings (3 or 4 ounces (80 or 110 g) of meat, cooked), which, with vegetables, will average 275 or 325 calories per serving, respectively.

* Use a commercial Italian seasoning, or mix your own from oregano, basil, marjoram, tarragon and thyme, about ½ teaspoon each, plus ¼ teaspoon of rosemary.

VEAL LOAF

1 pound of minced veal or best quality beef mince

1 15½-ounce (440-g) tin of dark kidney beans, drained

4 rounded tablespoons of dry breadcrumbs

1 egg

2 dessertspoons of soy sauce

⅛ teaspoon of cayenne pepper

16 fluid ounces (450 ml) of tomato sauce (see p. 222)

1 teaspoon of oregano

1 teaspoon of basil

Dash of Worcestershire sauce

Fresh-ground black pepper to taste

Purée beans in a food processor. Remove and add to minced meat. Blend in breadcrumbs, egg, soy sauce, Worcestershire sauce, black and cayenne peppers and about 2 tablespoons of the tomato sauce.

Mould into a loaf shape and place in deep baking dish. Cover with remaining sauce, and sprinkle with oregano and basil. If you like sprinkle with additional cayenne.

Bake 1 hour at 350°F (Gas Mark 4/180°C).

Makes 8 servings (4 ounces (110 g) of loaf, plus sauce) at about 220 calories per serving.

Poultry

ALMOND CHICKEN

3 pounds (1 kg 35 g) of chicken breasts, skinned and boned

4 tablespoons soy sauce 1-inch (2-cm) cube of fresh ginger, finely minced (or 1 teaspoon of dry ground ginger)

3 cloves of garlic, finely minced

3 ounces (80 g) of whole-wheat flour

3 ounces (80 g) of finely ground almonds

½ teaspoon of salt

½ teaspoon of pepper

2 dessertspoons of peanut or corn oil

In a large bowl, combine the soy sauce, ginger and garlic.

Cut the chicken into bite-size chunks and marinate in the soy mixture while you prepare the other ingredients.

In another bowl, combine flour, almonds and the rest of the seasonings. Add this to the chicken and toss until the chicken is coated with the flour mixture.

Heat the oil in a wok or large frying pan on high heat. When the oil is hot, add the chicken and turn the heat down to medium. Cook, covered, stirring often, for about 20 minutes.

Serve with rice and a green vegetable.

Makes 8 servings at 223 calories per serving, not including the rice and vegetables.

BAKED CHICKEN

There are countless ways to prepare poultry and I will present several other recipes in addition to the simplest roasting recipes later in this book. During the 600/900-calorie rotation of your diet it is probably best to keep the recipes simple, in order to be sure a few hundred extra calories don't sneak into your daily diet. Oven roasting is one of those simple but delicious ways to prepare chicken.

Line a baking pan with foil and lay out the joints of a small roasting chicken. Flavour with your favourite seasonings and bake at 300°F (Gas Mark 2/150°C) for approximately 1 hour. Skin before eating (much of the flavour of the seasonings will have penetrated to the flesh of the chicken during baking; however, add more at the table, if desired).

Try the following different combinations of seasonings for variety.

Variation 1. Sprinkle liberally with onion, minced garlic and Herb Salt (page 105). Or make your own selection of herbs, using one or more of the following: marjoram, oregano, rosemary, tarragon or thyme. Add fresh-ground black pepper.

Variation 2. Sprinkle with chilli powder, paprika and a dash of cayenne pepper. Add salt at the table after tasting.

Variation 3. Calories are significantly less if the chicken is skinned *before* baking. But skinning prior to cooking creates a problem since the meat is liable to dry out. You can prevent this by coating the skinned chicken with a basting sauce made from ½ cup of ketchup, 2 dessertspoons of soy sauce and 2 fluid ounces (50 ml) of sherry. Then sprinkle with other herbs of your choice. (Additional salt is not needed because of the soy sauce.) Cover the chicken lightly with a piece of aluminium foil for about half of the actual cooking time and it will stay moist.

White meat baked without the skin is about 45 calories an ounce, dark meat is about 50. On 600/900 rotations, the serving size is 3 ounces (80 g) cooked (135 and 150 calories for white and dark meat, respectively). On 1200-calorie rotations, the serving size is 4½ ounces (125 g) (208 and 225 calories for white and dark meat, respectively). On 1500- and 1800- calorie rotations, the serving size is 6 ounces (175 g) (270 and 300 calories for white and dark meat, respectively). Basting sauce will add between 15 and 30 calories per serving, depending on size.

LEMON-BAKED CHICKEN

About 3½ pounds (1½ kg) of chicken pieces, skinned
3 tablespoons of lemon juice
1 onion, cut into chunks
1 clove of garlic, finely diced

¼ teaspoon of thyme
¼ teaspoon of marjoram
¼ teaspoon of fresh-ground pepper
1 tablespoon of fresh parsley, chopped

Combine all ingredients in a 3-quart casserole dish and marinate for at least an hour, covered, in the refrigerator. Stir occasionally.

Bake, covered, in a preheated oven at 350°F (Gas Mark 4/180°C) for 1½ hours.

Serves 4 to 6. See Baked Chicken for the calorie count.

91

(This chicken is so good as a leftover you may wish to double the recipe.)

CHICKEN TOMASI

This dish is adapted from a traditional Hungarian recipe. We are not sure it originated in the town of Tomasi, but we like the name!

3 pounds (1 kg 35 g) of chicken pieces, skinned
2 teaspoons of butter
1 medium onion, chopped
1 clove of garlic, minced
5 teaspoons of paprika
¼ teaspoon of cayenne
4 fluid ounces (110 ml) of bouillon
8 fluid ounces (225 ml) of plain yogurt
3 tablespoons of low-fat milk
Salt and black pepper to taste

Melt 1 teaspoon of butter in a large saucepan and brown the chicken pieces. Remove the chicken from the pan and drain on paper towels.

Melt the remaining butter in the pan and sauté the onion and garlic, covering the saucepan, until the onions are clear.

Place the chicken back in the pan, sprinkle with paprika and cayenne and pour the bouillon in. Simmer, covered, until the chicken is tender.

Again remove the chicken from the pan, and remove the pan from the burner. Let the bouillon cool for several minutes. Cooling is essential to prevent the dairy products from curdling.

When the bouillon is lukewarm, stir in the yogurt and the milk until smooth. Replace the pan over low heat, add salt and pepper to taste, and put the chicken back in.

Reheat until hot – but do not let the sauce boil!

The chicken contains approximately 300 calories for a 6 ounce (175 g) serving. Add 10 calories for each tablespoon of sauce.

Serves 6 to 8.

Fish

POACHED FISH FILLETS

Poaching is about the simplest low-calorie way to pre-pare fish fillets as well as fish steaks, such as salmon or halibut.

2 pounds (900 g) of fish fillets or steaks (sole, cod, etc.)	1 bay leaf
	1 lemon, thinly sliced
	Herb Salt to taste (page
8 fluid ounces (225 ml) of dry white wine	105)
	Sliced lemon and sprigs
16 fluid ounces (450 ml) of water	of parsley for garnish
	Optional ingredients:
1 tablespoon of chopped fresh parsley	1 onion, thinly sliced
	1 carrot, thinly sliced

Combine wine, water, chopped parsley, bay leaf, thinly sliced lemon and Herb Salt, plus optional ingredients, and bring to the boil in a saucepan. Reduce heat and simmer for 30 minutes. Strain.

Divide fish into portions of approximately 4 to 8 ounces (110 to 225 g), depending on what your daily menu calls for (the weight will be reduced by 25 per cent during baking). Place in a casserole dish with bouillon. Cover and bake at 300°F (Gas Mark 2/150°C) for about 20 minutes, or until fish flakes when tested with a fork.

Remove fish to a warm plate with a couple of table-spoons of the fish bouillon and cover with foil to keep moist. Place the remainder of the bouillon in the saucepan and heat to reduce by half.

Pour over the fish before serving and garnish with additional lemon slices and parsley.

Shortcut Method: I have had excellent luck with this dish using a shortcut method that takes only about 5 minutes of preparation once you gather the ingredients.

Place your fish in the centre of a piece of aluminium foil large enough to fold over the fish. Place the foil and fish in a baking pan. Season with Herb Salt and any of the other ingredients from the above recipe that you like. Cut the

93

liquid ingredients in the above recipe to 4 fluid ounces (110 ml) of white wine and 4 fluid ounces (110 ml) of water. Pour directly over the fish and fold the foil tightly to make a perfect seal.

Place in a preheated oven at 300°F (Gas Mark 2/150°C) and bake for about 30 minutes, or until fish flakes when tested with a fork.

Let the fish cool a bit before serving. Taste the bouillon and reduce, if necessary, to obtain the strength of flavour you prefer. Then pour over the fish before serving.

Fish fillets will average about 50 calories an ounce, cooked. Serving size is 3 ounces (80 g) cooked on 600/900 rotations, 4½ ounces (125 g) cooked on 1200, and 6 ounces (175 g) cooked on higher intakes.

Serves 6 to 8 (depending on where you are in the Rotation Diet).

BAKED FISH FILLETS

1½ pounds (675 g) of white fish fillets (sole, haddock, etc.)
1 dessertspoon of oil
1 dessertspoon of lemon juice
2 dessertspoons of fresh parsley, chopped
1 lemon (6 wedges)
Salt and fresh-ground black pepper to taste

In the bottom of a shallow baking or grill pan, spread the oil, lemon juice and pepper. Swish the fish around in the pan, coating both sides. Sprinkle with parsley.

Grill 3–4 minutes on each side or until the edges are browned. Serve with lemon wedges, and add salt to taste at the table.

See Poached Fish Fillets for the calorie counts.

Serves 4 to 6 (depending upon where you are in the Rotation Diet).

BAKED OR GRILLED RAINBOW TROUT

4 small trout (about ¾ pound (340 g) each)
1 dessertspoon of oil

94

Herb Salt to taste (page 105)   Fresh-ground black pepper to taste

Preheat oven to 500°F (Gas Mark 9/240°C). Pour oil onto aluminium-lined baking pan, swish fish around well in the oil, season, and bake for about 12 minutes, or until fish flakes easily with a fork. You may grill if you prefer.

Serves 4. Edible portion, approximately 4 ounces (110 g) will contain about 125 calories.

ROYAL INDIAN SALMON

4 salmon steaks, 1 inch (2 cm) thick

4 tablespoons of chicken or vegetable bouillon

2 dessertspoons of lemon juice

½ teaspoon of fennel seeds, crushed

¼ teaspoon of cumin

¼ teaspoon of ground coriander

Dash of salt and fresh-ground black pepper

Place the steaks in a shallow dish. Pour the bouillon and the lemon juice over the steaks. Add the seasonings.

Marinate, covered, in the refrigerator for at least 2 hours, turning the steaks occasionally.

To cook, place the steaks on a foil-covered grill pan. Spoon 2 teaspoons of the marinade on top of each steak. Place under the grill for 6 to 8 minutes, or until slightly brown on the edges. Turn steaks over, spoon on the remaining marinade, and grill for an additional 6 to 8 minutes.

Note: This dish has a delicate, aristocratic flavour – not too spicy or hot in the way many people expect Indian cooking to be.

A 6 ounce (175 g) serving will contain approximately 330 calories.

Pasta

MY FAVOURITE PASTA

Meat Sauce

1 pound (450 g) of
extra-lean mince
1 large onion, chopped
1 stalk of celery, chopped
1 green pepper, chopped
1 28 ounce (800 g) tin of
tomatoes
1 6 ounce (175 g) tin of
tomato paste

1 dessertspoon of
Worcestershire sauce
1 scant teaspoon of chili
powder
½ teaspoon of oregano
½ teaspoon of basil
Salt and pepper to taste

Brown the first four ingredients (if you have bought extra-lean mince there will be no fat to pour off). Add the remaining ingredients and bring to the boil. Reduce heat immediately and simmer, uncovered, for about an hour or until sauce reaches desired consistency. You may add a small amount of water to taste, or 3 tablespoons of dry red wine, during cooking.

Makes 6 servings of about 125 calories each.

Served with 1 cup of cooked spaghetti (2 ounces/56 g dry weight) the total calories are about 325. Add 50 calories per dessertspoon of Parmesan cheese, if used.

Vegetables

The best ways to prepare most vegetables to keep the calorie content at a minimum are steamed, boiled in a very small amount of water, or cooked in a microwave, according to its directions. During the 600/900 rotation, we use no fats or other additions that will increase the calories unnecessarily – we concentrate on herbs. At higher intake levels you can dress your vegetables up with small amounts of fat and other caloric additions.

All vegetables can be eaten plain, or with just a sprinkle of salt (or, better, Herb Salt, page 105) and fresh-ground pepper, if you desire. The following recipes add a

96

little interest – you may not have considered how herbs and spices can turn the ordinary into the exotic. When you use herbs and spices for seasoning you will find it easy to reduce or eliminate both salt and fat in your cooking.

Remember that most vegetables are at their nutritious best when eaten raw. While I include tasty ways of cooking the vegetables in the Rotation Diet, you will do well to eat one vegetable raw each day. And cooked vegetables are best when served crisp.

ASPARAGUS

Caraway Asparagus
If you use fresh asparagus, cut off the tough part of the stalk and cook the spears in a small amount of water for about 12 minutes or until tender. You can also steam asparagus if you prefer, or use your microwave according to directions. The texture of the tips is best preserved by steaming the asparagus standing upright and covered in a deep saucepan. Peel back an inch (2 cm) or so of the outer stalks before placing them in the saucepan. Add about ½ teaspoon of caraway seeds for each 6 stalks of asparagus, plus fresh-ground black pepper to taste. (Follow directions on the package for frozen asparagus.)

Cold Dijon Asparagus
Mix 1 dessertspoon of Dijon mustard with 1 dessertspoon of plain yogurt and ¼ teaspoon of tarragon. Spread over chilled asparagus. Add salt and fresh-ground black pepper to taste.

Serving size is 6 stalks at 18 calories. Add 8 calories for the Dijon dressing.

GREEN BEANS ALMONDINE

10 ounces (275 g) of frozen french or runner beans	Dash of salt
	Dash of pepper
3 tablespoons of water	2 dessertspoons of slivered almonds

97

Cook beans in water until crispy tender, add remaining ingredients, and simmer for an additional 5 minutes.

Makes 4 servings of ½ cup at 38 calories per serving.

GREEN BEANS WITH CHIVES

1 pound (450 g) of fresh french or runner beans (2 10 ounce (275 g) packages frozen)
2 dessertspoons of chopped fresh parsley
1 dessertspoon of chopped chives (or spring onions)
1 teaspoon of Herb Salt (p. 105)

Steam or simmer (in 4 tablespoons of water) unseasoned beans until tender (or follow directions for your microwave). Sprinkle over other ingredients just before serving.

Variations. Beans can be made with 8 ounces (225 g) of mushrooms or 1 large sliced onion, without changing the calorie value of a ½ cup serving to any great extent.

Makes 8 servings of ½ cup at 18 calories per serving.

GINGERED BEETS

You can use tinned baby beets, or cook the beets yourself, leaving on about 1 inch (2 cm) of the stem and root ends. Small beets will take about ½ hour to cook in boiling water. I have not tried to cook them yet in my microwave.

Drain most of the liquid from the beets, and sprinkle each ½ cup serving with about ¼ teaspoon of ground ginger. You can add a couple of dessertspoons of cider vinegar if you want some extra zing. Top with a dessertspoon of chopped fresh parsley.

Serving size is ½ cup at 29 calories per serving.

BROCCOLI

Broccoli is one of my favourite vegetables. It not only tastes good, but it's a powerhouse when it comes to nutritional value – plenty of vitamins A and C, plus fibre. Broccoli is also a good source of calcium and iron. It should become one of your vegetable staples.

Broccoli is excellent when cooked in the microwave, steamed or simmered in 4 tablespoons of water or bouillon until it can be penetrated with the tines of a fork, but is still crisp. If you don't care much for broccoli without a sauce, just sprinkle each serving with a teaspoon of Parmesan cheese and you have the 600/900-calorie rotation version of Broccoli au Gratin.

Serving size is ½ cup at 30 calories per serving; add about 15 calories for the cheese.

BROCCOLI WITH BLACK OLIVES

1 large bunch of broccoli (about 1½ pounds/ 680 g)	2 ounces (56 g) of stoned black olives
1 dessertspoon of olive oil	3 tablespoons of Parmesan cheese
1 clove of garlic, minced	Salt and pepper to taste

Cook broccoli in a small amount of water for 10 minutes (or in a microwave according to directions). Drain. Sauté garlic in olive oil until lightly brown. Add broccoli and cook over low heat for 5 minutes (do not overcook). Add olives and heat 2 more minutes. Serve immediately and sprinkle with cheese. Add salt and pepper at the table.

Serves 4 at 90 calories per serving.

CARROTS

In my own diet, carrots run a close second to broccoli as my favourite vegetable. I like carrots sliced and cooked in the microwave with nothing but a bit of water (follow your own microwave recipe). Dill and/or chives make good seasonings.

Carrots à l'Orange

For this variation, add 1 dessertspoon of grated or finely slivered orange peel to each cup of matchstick or sliced

99

carrots before cooking. Add Herb Salt (page 105) to taste after serving.

And, of course, instead of the orange, you can use 1 dessertspoon of fresh (1 teaspoon of dried) dillweed or 2 dessertspoons of chives or chopped spring onions for variety.

Serving size is ½ cup at 23 calories per serving.

CARROTS WITH ONIONS

6 medium carrots, sliced
1 onion, chopped
4 tablespoons of water

Salt, pepper, and fresh parsley to taste

Place ingredients in saucepan, bring to a boil, and then simmer gently until cooked.

Makes 6 servings at 27 calories per serving.

BRAISED CARROTS AND CELERY

The word 'braise' refers to a method of cooking in fat, with very little moisture. Naturally, when it comes to weight management, the worst thing you can do in preparing meals is to use even a drop more fat than you need for flavouring. My 'braising' is done in the microwave, or in a small amount of water on top of the stove.

For each serving:

1 carrot, in ¼-inch (½-cm) slices

1 stalk of celery, in 2-inch (4-cm) slices

Place in pan with 4 tablespoons of water (the same amount of water regardless of the quantity of carrots and celery, up to a maximum of four carrots and stalks) and simmer until crisp, but definitely not soft.

Pour off water and mix with 1 dessertspoon of butter for all of the 4 servings (½ teaspoon per serving).

When using a microwave, follow the directions that come with your oven, and add a small amount of butter after cooking.

Chives are about the best accompaniment that I know

of for carrots and celery. Add about ¼ teaspoon of chives per serving, before cooking, if you like.

About 25 calories per serving.

SAVORY STEAMED CAULIFLOWERETS

Cut up a medium head of cauliflower into 2 inch (5 cm) flowerets and, for each cup of cauliflower, sprinkle with ½ teaspoon of oregano and ½ teaspoon of savory. Steam until tender.

Serving size is 1 cup at 30 calories per serving.

BAKED MARROW OR COURGETTE

Use a small marrow or an overgrown courgette. Cut in half lengthwise, spoon out seeds, and bake face down on aluminium foil at 350°F (Gas Mark 4/180°C) for about 45 minutes, or until tender. Season with salt and pepper to taste at the table. Try a sprinkle of cloves, ginger, or nutmeg for variety.

Serves 2 at 56 calories per half.

OLD THYMEY PEAS

Maybe you remember the old folk song Simon and Garfunkel made famous in the sixties: *Scarborough Fair.* Here's a recipe that uses all the lovely herbs mentioned in that song.

10½ ounces (300 g) of frozen peas, or 12 ounces (350 g) fresh
1 teaspoon of parsley

½ teaspoon of sage
½ teaspoon of rosemary
½ teaspoon of thyme

Cook peas in 4 tablespoons of water until barely tender. Add seasonings and cook 1 minute more before serving.

Variation. Peas go well with a squeeze of lemon and a pinch of basil (about ⅙ of a lemon and ½ teaspoon of basil per serving). Add salt and pepper to taste.

Serving size for either recipe is ½ cup at 57 calories per serving.

PEAS AND BABY ONIONS

1 package (10½ ounces/   ⅓ ounce (10 g) of butter
  315 g) of frozen peas, or   Herb Salt (page 105)
  12 ounces (350 g) fresh   Fresh-ground pepper to
1 large onion, sliced   taste

Sauté the onion in the butter until translucent. Add peas
and 4 tablespoons of water. Cook until tender.

This is a traditional dish with baked or poached fish. It
is especially complementary to salmon.

Makes 4 servings of ½ cup at 75 calories per serving.

BROWN OR WILD RICE

16 fluid ounce (450 ml)   Other seasonings to
  measure of brown or   taste – for example, 1
  wild rice   dessertspoon of
1 dessertspoon of oil or ⅓   chopped chives, spring
  ounce (10 g) butter   onions, or Herb Salt
32 fluid ounces (950 ml) of   (page 105) to taste,
  bouillon (meat or   depending on the
  vegetable)   bouillon

Melt butter in saucepan, add rice and stir until rice is
coated. Add bouillon, cover, and bring to boil. Reduce
heat and simmer gently for 45 minutes, or until all of the
liquid has been absorbed.

The rice will expand to double its original volume and
provide 8 ½-cup servings, which, prepared in this way,
will contain about 105 calories each.

SPINACH AND BROCCOLI CASSEROLE

1 pound 4 ounces (565 g)   4 fluid ounces (110 ml) of
  of frozen spinach   water
  (chopped)   1 14-ounce (400-g) tin of
10 ounces (285 g) of   mushroom soup
  frozen broccoli   4 rounded tablespoons of
  (chopped)   seasoned breadcrumbs

4 rounded tablespoons of grated Parmesan cheese	1 teaspoon each of garlic and onion powder
4 rounded tablespoons of grated Cheddar cheese	4 fluid ounces (110 ml) of low-fat milk
	Salt and pepper to taste

Cook broccoli and spinach in water until completely thawed (but not cooked). Stir in remaining ingredients, place in large casserole dish and cover with seasoned breadcrumbs. Bake at 350°F (Gas Mark 4/180°C) for 35–40 minutes.

Makes about 12 servings of ½ cup at approximately 85 calories per serving.

This is an excellent dish as a main course. Just double or triple the serving size, and calculate the calories approximately.

STIR-FRY SPINACH (OR OTHER GREENS)

1 pound (450 g) of fresh spinach (or other young green vegetables)	Herb Salt to taste (page 105)
1 dessertspoon of oil (olive oil preferred)	Fresh-ground black pepper to taste
1 medium onion, sliced thin	

Wash and drain greens. Heat oil in frying pan and sauté onions for 1 minute. Add greens and stir until leaves are wilted and greens are hot – about 1 minute more on medium heat.

Serve with a squeeze of lemon or a sprinkle of grated cheese.

Makes 4 servings at about 60 calories per serving.

BAKED TOMATO

2 large fresh tomatoes	1 dessertspoon of Parmesan cheese
1 clove of garlic, minced	
¼ teaspoon of tarragon	Fresh-ground black pepper to taste
¼ teaspoon of basil	

103

Slice tomatoes in half. Place in shallow baking pan, flat side up. Combine seasonings and cheese, and sprinkle over tomatoes. Bake at 350°F (Gas Mark 4/180°C) for about 30 minutes, or until tender.

Makes 4 servings at about 28 calories per serving.

STIR-FRY VEGETABLES

If you are already experienced in stir-frying, do your vegetables in the way you like them (as long as you keep the fat content down).

This is actually a method of using an ordinary frying pan that comes close to duplicating the results obtained with a wok.

1 thinly sliced green pepper
2 medium onions, thinly sliced
3 cloves of garlic, chopped
4 stalks of celery (2-inch /5-cm pieces)
4 large carrots (½-inch/1-cm pieces)
1 dessertspoon/⅓ ounce

(10 g) of butter or oil
small wedge of white cabbage, chopped
1 pound (450 g) of fresh green vegetables
2 dessertspoons of soy sauce
Fresh-ground black pepper
Pinch each of marjoram and thyme

Melt butter or heat oil in a large frying pan on low heat as you begin to slice your vegetables. I add to the pan as I slice them, the green pepper, carrots, onions, garlic and celery, in that order, stirring occasionally. Increase heat to medium for 2 to 3 minutes, then add cabbage, greens and marjoram and thyme. Cook on medium to medium-high heat, stirring almost continuously, until greens have wilted but other vegetables are still crisp. Add soy sauce and pepper to taste.

Serve with Brown or Wild Rice (page 102), which you will have started about 1 hour before the stir-fry, and 2 dessertspoons of grated cheese.

Serves four, each serving containing about 110 calories. Add about 90 calories for each half cup of plain cooked brown rice and 100 calories for the cheese. Add additional calories if rice is cooked with any added fat.

HERB SALT

½ teaspoon of basil
¼ teaspoon of dillweed
¼ teaspoon of salt
¼ teaspoon of thyme

¼ teaspoon of celery seed
¼ teaspoon dried parsley

Combine ingredients and grind with a mortar and pestle. Store in a small herb jar. Experiment with your own combination of herbs. You will soon find that Herb Salt is an excellent substitute for plain salt, and instead of about 2000 to 2200 milligrams of sodium per teaspoon, it has only 285 milligrams. Thus, a sprinkle of Herb Salt will give you perhaps 30 or 40 milligrams of sodium, rather than about seven times that much (200 to 300 milligrams) if you were to use plain salt.

PERMISSIBLE SUBSTITUTIONS AND OTHER ALTERATIONS TO THE ROTATION DIET

Substitutions

The daily menus for the Rotation Diet have been developed to provide maximum nutritional value at all caloric levels. That's why it's best to stick to them as closely as possible. In addition, my experience in reviewing thousands of eating diaries indicates that deviations are likely to lead to increased calories, and increased calories will tend to slow your weight loss. The reason for

the impact of deviations is usually quite simple to understand: most of us tend to prefer the foods that have more
calories (have more fat or are sweeter) in any given food
category!

Nevertheless, you can make substitutions if any particular food does not appeal or agree with you. Here are
the simple rules:

> When a serving of a vegetable is called for, you may
> substitute a serving of another vegetable.
> When a serving of fruit is called for, you may substitute a
> serving of another fruit.
> When a serving of a grain product or bread is called for,
> you may substitute a serving of any other grain product or
> bread.
> When a serving of meat, fish or poultry is called for, you
> may substitute a serving of another meat, fish or fowl.
> When a serving of a milk product is called for, you may
> substitute a serving of any other milk product.

If you substitute foods during the diet, make
sure you use the correct serving sizes whether
they are identical (as with vegetables, or as with
meat, fish or poultry) or equivalent (with milk
products, 1 ounce (28 g) of a hard cheese = 4
ounces (110 g) of cottage cheese = 8 fluid
ounces (225 ml) of milk; with grains, 1 ounce
(28 g) of dry cereal = 1 slice of bread = 5 whole-
wheat crispbread).

You should remember, however, that your nutritional
needs are best served by a wide variety of foods. In
addition, there is another potential value to a wide
variety of foods: variety in your choices of foods will
ensure that you do not take in particularly large amounts
of any given preservative or whatever pesticides are
used in growing a particular food product.

I could be very fussy about which substitutions are
most closely equivalent in calories, but I don't think it is
worth your effort to be concerned about 5 or 10 calories,

more or less. And as for other nutritional values, you will do best if you choose foods that are similar to each other as substitutions. For example, one variety of green vegetable for another, one citrus fruit for another, and so forth. But even here, you will not do much damage, provided you stick to the wide-variety principle, and do not continually eat just one or two foods from a given category.

Study the menus, and the recipes, and you will soon learn serving sizes if you don't already know them.

Skipping Meals, Combining Meals, Reversing the Order of Meals

Do you have to follow the menus exactly? Or can you eat breakfast for dinner and vice versa?

We have many people in the Vanderbilt Weight Management Program who juggle the foods around in the day to please themselves and it seems to work out very well. But, in order to be sure that you are obtaining adequate nutrition, *be sure that you end up eating what I suggest in each day's menu.* Make any substitutions from the appropriate categories. Sometimes changes of this kind do interfere with weight loss, especially if you end up eating everything at night (or at the end of whatever is your workday, before you go to sleep).

If you have unusual hours, try eating the meals in the order that they fit into your workday (breakfast first, etc.), and then make alterations to please yourself if this doesn't turn out to be satisfactory.

In other words, I really don't care when you eat.

During the 600-calorie rotations, just have two servings of a grain product, two servings of a milk product, two different vegetables, two different fruits and about 3 ounces (80 g) of lean meat, fish or poultry – and that's about as simple as I can make it!

During the 900-calorie rotations, add another grain product and another serving of lean meat, fish or poultry. There is also room for 1 teaspoon of fat or oil for seasoning or spread.

During the 1200-calorie rotation, make it a total of four

grains, two milk products, two different fruits and two different vegetables, and two servings of lean meat, fish or poultry. And you also have room for 1 dessertspoon of fat or oil for seasoning or spread.

Vegetarian Substitutions

Vegetarians can use the Rotation Diet by substituting a complementary protein dish composed of combinations of legumes, grains, seeds and nuts for meat, fish or poultry. A combination of a grain with a legume will provide the most complete protein with the fewest calories. A soy product such as tofu may also be substituted any time a food of animal origin is called for in the menus. Adding a small amount of cheese to plant foods will increase the quality of the available protein. A ½ cup of cooked beans with a ½ cup of cooked rice will approximate the caloric value of a 3-ounce (80 g) serving of lean meat (cooked).

DIET DRINKS
(AND THOSE WITH SUGAR)

I hope there is one thing that I can persuade you to do during the Rotation Diet, and that is to give up drinking diet drinks for the entire three weeks. I want you to see for yourself whether using diet drinks is keeping alive your taste for sweets, and ultimately leading you to over-eat sweets that contain calories.

I would be willing to bet that diet sweeteners are keeping alive your yen for sweets and leading you to over-eat. In fact, I'll give you odds because I have never yet met a person who is completely satisfied with the use of artificial sweeteners and who doesn't periodically overindulge on 'the real thing' in a way that is disastrous for weight control.

If I can persuade you to give up diet drinks, and if you are at all like participants in the Vanderbilt Weight Management Program, you will soon notice an increase in your taste sensitivity.

The use of diet drinks may be deadening your sensitivity to sweetness, leading you to require more than the normal amount of sweetness to satisfy your palate. If this has happened to you, and you decide to give up the use of artificial sweeteners, in a matter of just one or two weeks natural, unsweetened foods will begin to taste unbelievably sweet, and it will become much easier for you to stick with your diet or to increase your intake of more nutritious foods.

In my opinion, diet drinks (and artificially sweetened desserts) just turn on your appetite without satisfying it, possibly leading you to overeat at other times. When you need a drink, try water! If you crave something sweet, use your *safe fruit*. If you are thirsty and crave something sweet, do both – eat your fruit and have a drink of water.

The food processors who manufacture diet foods are capitalizing on the human preference for sweetness in food, and they may have you 'hooked'! Try stopping the use of diet preparations, and the difficulty you experience will prove my point.

Think about it for a few moments. Somebody 'out there' is making a fortune feeding you artificial diet sweeteners, products with no nutritional value, and you are gulping them up and staying fat!

If cutting out the use of all artificial sweeteners proves to be difficult, I hope that difficulty will make you really angry at the way that you are being manipulated for someone else's profit – angry enough at the fact that you've been 'hooked' to persevere in your efforts never to use an artificial sweetener again for the rest of your life.

Cutting out the use of all artificial sweeteners may turn out to be the crucial factor in your efforts to control your weight.

I am a pretty good example of how you can change in your preference for sweets. In contrast with the situation twenty-two years ago, today I use no artificial sweeteners and, for that matter, I add no sugar to any beverage. I use only small amounts of sugar in baking, usually half or less than what is called for in the usual recipe. (Don't worry

109

about the change in bulk when you do this – I have never found it necessary to make compensatory alterations in the other ingredients.) Compared with my taste for sweets when I was a fat man, my sensitivity to sweetness has increased to the point that most cereals, for example, even Grape-Nuts, taste too sweet to me even without added sugar. Dried fruits such as raisins and dates are at the limit of my tolerance for sweetness. And whereas half a pound of chocolate might have constituted a binge twenty-two years ago, two small bars of chocolate – perhaps 2 ounces (56 g) or a quarter of what I might have downed as a fat man – prove to be a perfectly satisfying binge today. Normally, it's possible to enjoy a single bar without turning on an insatiable yearning.

While I would much rather see you learn to use small amounts of sugar, honey or molasses whenever a sweetener is called for in baking or cooking, rather than an artificial sweetener, I am not rigid in this respect, provided the sweetener is blended with other foods and used in *small* amounts so as not to make the sweetness too intense.

How to Use Sugar

Don't use any drinks that contain 'straight sugar', that is, soft drinks. Sugar must be blended as a minor ingredient in the overall recipe for any food.

While white table sugar (sucrose) is found naturally in many foods, it has only been freely available *in its processed form* for about a hundred years.

Considering that about two million years have been involved in the evolution of the human capacity to deal with foods as they are found in our natural environment, it is safe to say that your body is not designed to deal with sugar 'straight', which, after all, is a relatively new product. In some people processed foods that are high in sucrose set off reactions that are not only terrible for controlling your weight, but lead to 'insulin overshoot'. Too much insulin will deplete your blood of circulating sugar (glycogen), leading to temporary symptoms of

110

hypoglycemia or low blood sugar. Although the disease *hypoglycemia* is rare, the temporary symptoms of low blood sugar in normal persons may lead to an increase in appetite. You should avoid using sugar straight, just as you should avoid using an artificial sweetener except as a minor ingredient in a recipe containing other ingredients.

Should you make an effort to give up completely using sugar or eating chocolates, cakes and pies?

I don't think so.

An effort to be completely abstinent may build up such a tremendous hidden hunger drive that the slightest deviation can end up in a monstrous binge. In Chapters 9, 10 and 11 I will show you how you can learn to be moderate in your eating habits, and how you can gain control over the tendency to binge on high-calorie foods. There is a happy medium in eating the foods you like best. You must build them into your diet intentionally. Planning to enjoy them, without the driven quality that often accompanies your eating of foods that you feel guilty about enjoying, may actually protect you against a binge.

Some successful people who have been through the Vanderbilt Program build one to two servings of a rich dessert or sweets into their daily maintenance diets. They are now active enough to prevent regaining any weight. I prefer to eat more nutritious foods. I have found my happy medium by including a rich dessert, or possibly some sweets, just once a week, or sometimes twice. In this way, I never feel that I am denying myself. However, by not eating such foods every day, I no longer have any yearning for them as a regular part of my diet.

I also make sure that the temptation to eat chocolate, biscuits and desserts is not present at all times by not keeping such foods in the house on a regular basis. Instead, we have bowls of fruit on display and eat whenever we feel inclined without worrying about the effects on our weight.

111

THE NUTRITIONAL VALUE OF THE ROTATION DIET

The Rotation Diet has been designed to approximate the United States Recommended Dietary Allowances of known major vitamins and minerals over the entire twenty-one-day period that you will use it. The same is true of the suggestions I will make for your maintenance diet.

At the level of 1200 calories and above (including my recommendations for your maintenance diet), the proportions of calories from carbohydrate, fat and protein are designed to meet the recommendations of the United States Senate Select Committee on Nutrition and Human Needs: 55 to 60 per cent from carbohydrate, 25 to 30 per cent from fat and 15 per cent from protein.

Crackpot claims to the contrary, there is no known diet that is more beneficial to your health than the recommendations of the Senate Select Committee on Nutrition and Human Needs.

When calories are reduced below 1200, such as on the 600/900-calorie rotations, the relative percentage from protein increases to around 40 per cent, fat decreases to about 20 per cent and carbohydrate decreases to 40 per cent. These changes are necessary on a temporary basis since it is important to include enough protein to make the diet palatable, maintain the body's store of protein and prevent the loss of your muscle tissue.

In spite of the nutritional value of the Rotation Diet, it may be important for you to use a multiple vitamin and mineral supplement while you are on the diet.

Substitutions during the diet may change your intake of certain nutrients. For example, if you do not include milk in your diet, and do not like sardines and tinned salmon but instead substitute cottage cheese or some other cheese as a calcium source, you will be relatively low on calcium. Although this is not likely to be dangerous on a temporary basis, it might be in the long run. If you do not take in enough calcium to provide for your

112

daily needs, your body leeches it from your bones, gradually weakening them. Then, when you reach a more advanced age, you may be more susceptible to osteoporosis than you would have been with an adequate intake. Thus, I think it would be wise to include a calcium supplement in the form of calcium gluconate, calcium lactate or calcium carbonate.

There are two other reasons you may need temporary vitamin supplements. First, if you don't care for red meat, you may end up low in some of the B vitamins and iron, since red meat tends to be a major source of these nutrients in most Western diets and substitutions of other meat products or vegetables may not be as rich. Lack of these nutrients leaves you feeling weak and lethargic.

Second, while on a reduced-calorie diet, the body's need for vitamins and minerals may change. Although there is no evidence for this effect that I know of, dieting does stress the body and your need for stress-related vitamins – the B-complex vitamins and vitamin C – may increase. Furthermore, recent research indicates that vigorous exercise may change one's needs for certain B vitamins and iron, and this may occur for you as you change from a sedentary to an active person. A multiple vitamin and mineral tablet will help take care of all of these possibilities.

What brand of vitamin and mineral supplement is best? I recommend that you visit your chemist and choose a brand of a multiple vitamin and mineral tablet that contains, in general, amounts that approximate the Recommended Dietary Allowances (RDAs) of the major vitamins and minerals. I would not get anything with higher dosages because too much of certain nutrients may also be bad for you, and your diet, with the permissible substitutions, will still be a healthful one.

Discuss supplementing your diet with your doctor or nutritionist, and get your pharmacist's help in choosing the appropriate tablet. And don't be concerned if a few of the nutrients are not exactly at the 100 per cent level of the RDAs in the information provided on the label. *Just be sure that you avoid megadoses* and ask the pharmacist to guide you in the choice of supplement if you are uncertain.

SHOPPING LIST FOR WOMEN'S MENUS OF THE ROTATION DIET

Here is a shopping list to make it easy for you to buy exactly what you will need for the Rotation Diet. I am not entering quantities for you; enter your own in the space provided in case you want to buy enough for the family, or for another person who is going on the Rotation Diet with you. Look at the Week 1 menus, decide upon any substitutions, and add them to this list.

In addition, it is a good idea to check the recipes that are suggested for each day in case you happen to be out of any of the items you will need for cooking.

Week 1 and Week 3

FRUIT
Grapefruit _____
Apples _____
Bananas _____
Berries (in season) _____
Cantaloupe _____
Other (for *safe fruit*) _____

GRAINS
Whole-wheat bread _____
Whole-wheat crispbread
(low salt) _____
Breakfast cereal _____
_____
_____

DAIRY PRODUCTS
Milk (skim or low-fat) _____
_____
Cottage cheese (low-fat) _____
Hard cheese _____

MISCELLANEOUS
Mayonnaise (optional) _____
_____
No-cal or low-cal dressing _____
_____

No-cal beverages (tea, coffee, herb
teas, etc.) _____
_____
Eggs _____
Peanut butter _____

VEGETABLES

Free Vegetables: check choice of
Celery _____
Chicory _____
Chinese cabbage _____
Courgette _____
Cucumbers _____
Endive _____
Lettuce _____
Parsley _____
Radishes _____
Watercress _____

Other vegetables:
Cauliflower _____
Beetroot _____
Broccoli _____
Carrots _____
Green beans _____

114

THE ROTATION DIET FOR WOMEN AND MEN

Asparagus _____   Mince for hamburgers _____
Peas _____

                                      HERBS AND SPICES
                                      _____
MEAT, FISH, POULTRY   _____
Chicken _____
Fish fillets _____
Tuna (tinned in brine) _____   OTHER (for food preparation)
Salmon (tinned) _____   _____
Sardines (optional) _____   _____

                            Week 2

FRUIT   No-cal or low-cal dressing _____
Grapefruit _____   _____
Apples _____   No-cal beverages (tea, coffee, herb
Bananas _____   teas, etc.) _____
Berries (in season) _____   _____
Cantaloupe _____   Eggs _____
Pears (optional) _____   Peanut butter _____
Fresh pineapple (optional) _____   Almonds, slivered _____
_____
Raisins _____   VEGETABLES
Other (for *safe fruit*,   *Free vegetables:* check choice of
    fruit salad) _____   Celery _____
_____   Chicory _____
                                      Chinese cabbage _____
GRAINS   Courgette _____
Whole-wheat bread _____   Cucumbers _____
Whole-wheat crispbread   Endive _____
    (low salt) _____   Lettuce _____
Breakfast cereal (including porridge oats) Parsley _____
_____   Radishes _____
Brown (or wild) rice _____   Watercress _____
Pasta _____
                                      Other vegetables:
DAIRY PRODUCTS   Spinach _____
Milk (skim or low-fat) _____   Celery (if not ticked above) _____
_____   Potatoes _____
Cottage cheese _____   Baby onions _____
Hard cheese _____   Mushrooms _____
Parmesan _____   Marrow _____
Yogurt (for Chicken Tomasi) _____   Broccoli _____
                                      Carrots _____
MISCELLANEOUS   Green beans _____
Mayonnaise (optional) _____   Tomatoes _____
_____   Peas _____
Black olives _____   Green peppers _____
Chives _____   (Other for stir-fry) _____ _____

                            115

Dark kidney beans (for Mexican
 Bean Spread) _____

MEAT, FISH, POULTRY

Chicken _____

Fish fillets _____

Tuna (tinned in brine) _____

Salmon (tinned, optional) _____

Sardines (optional) _____

Mince (for pasta sauce) _____

Beefsteak _____

Beef for pot roast (topside, flank) _____

Salmon steaks _____

Pork chops _____

HERBS AND SPICES

_____

_____

_____

SHOPPING LISTS FOR MEN'S MENUS

For all three weeks of the Rotation Diet men should use
the shopping list of Week 2 for women as their basic list,
and check the daily menus to determine what, if any,
substitutions they are going to make. There are only a
few meals that will require any changes or additions to
the basic shopping list of Week 2 for women. These
include Veal Loaf on Day 12 and a suggestion for Baked
Trout on Day 14.

116

7

The Rotation Diet
Activity Plan

As they say, let's call a spade a spade.

I know that, if anything is likely to put people off about a weight-management programme, it's the suggestion that they need to get physically active. That's why many weight-loss plans tend to play down the need for physical activity.

But I know both the absolute necessity for physical activity in weight management as well as how you feel about it at this time.

Talk about what it feels like! When I was a fat child and a fat man, I felt obscene. I didn't walk, I waddled. I was embarrassed to try anything physical because I was convinced that I would be awkward and lousy at it. If I so much as walked on a low wall along the street when I was a kid, my mum used to scream, 'Watch out, Dick! You'll fall off.' I avoided gymnasiums. I certainly did not want to let anyone look at all my fat in its naked form. And until I was thirty-five years old, there was no way that anyone could convince me that it could possibly *feel good* to be physically active.

I assure you that you can do away with all these negative feelings. Follow my advice and I can also assure you that *nothing* will ever make you *feel* thin in the way that being active does. If you are at all like me, losing weight by itself does not make you feel like a thin person. No matter what the mirror says, there is still a sense of being fat. All of this changes when you become an *active* thin person.

To begin with, you may feel an increase in your motivation to become more active if you face the facts: if you are sedentary, it will be almost impossible for you to manage your weight without finding some way to increase your activity level to the point that nature intended.

Until the invention of the car, and the availability of electricity in our homes and places of work, the average person had to walk seven or eight miles each day. And those people who didn't have to walk quite that much still ended up expending just as much energy because their work required standing, moving around and a lot more muscle! For the first few million years of our existence as a distinct species of animal, until about a hundred years ago, human beings had to burn up about 500 calories more energy each day in our work, in maintaining our homes (chopping wood, shovelling coal) and in obtaining food, since there was no electric refrigeration. Our bodies were designed for a high level of physical activity, and our appetites are matched to that level of activity. Because of the nature of life in previous times, we could eat about 500 calories more each day a hundred years ago, and we were not as likely to get fat as we are today because we had to burn up all those extra calories working to stay alive.

Although the need for energy expenditure has decreased significantly in our technologically advanced society, our appetite for food has not. In fact, there is a tendency for inactive persons to eat more than moderately active persons. This may occur, perhaps, out of boredom or as a result of tensions that would normally be lowered through physical activity.

Physical activity is a great regulator of appetite. When

sedentary people become active, they actually tend to eat less than before. Then, as activity levels increase, food intake seems to increase only to the extent that it matches output.

In addition, as long as you remain an active person, Mother Nature puts a special fat-burning mechanism to work to help you stay thin. If you happen to over-eat, but are immediately active without missing a day, your body will rev up even higher than it normally does in physical activity, as though trying to help you burn off the extra calories you ate the day before. Nature appears to be working to help you stay thin in order to be better at whatever physical thing you ask yourself to do. But consistent physical activity is required. The mechanism will not work as well if your activity becomes sporadic.

SOME ACTIVITIES ARE BETTER THAN OTHERS FOR WEIGHT CONTROL

When it comes to controlling your weight, you get the biggest payoff when you engage in any physical activity that requires you to move your whole body through space.

Just taking a brisk walk burns about twice the calories of doing calisthenics. While swinging your arms and lifting your legs feel like hard work, when you move your whole body through space you move your entire body weight. Moving your whole body feels easier than those arm swings because your body was built for walking. Walking uses your largest muscles (in the buttocks and thighs), and these muscles are placed in the middle of your body. This placement makes for very efficient movement. In contrast, arm swings use smaller muscles and the weight that is being moved extends outward from the moving muscles. That makes for inefficient movement, which is experienced as being harder and is more tiring, in spite of the fact that it burns far fewer calories.

So, the first principle of the Rotation Diet activity pro-

119

gramme is: move your whole body through space to get the most calorie-burning benefit for every minute that you engage in physical activity.

This principle makes it easy to see what activities are best for weight management: walking, swimming and gentle jogging (when you get down to desirable weight). These are followed by bicycling (because it also uses the major large muscles in the thighs and buttocks), bouncing on a mini-trampoline and exercises that may move your whole body up and down, but generally in one place rather than through space. Thus, most aerobic dance routines do not give you quite the weight-management benefits of a brisk walk.

Racket sports can be an excellent route to weight control, provided you learn to play at an advanced level and spend more of your time moving around than standing still and socializing. As you know, tennis was my daily sport for many years, until I discovered the joys of jogging. Squash is easier to learn than tennis, and you will tend to burn more calories at squash than at tennis in any given period of exercise time.

Rowing – usually on the machines found in many gyms and exercise studios – has recently become a popular weight-management and conditioning activity. It works in spite of your not having to move your whole body through space because it uses so many of the muscle groups throughout your entire body. Rowing can be a valuable activity for people who cannot do weight-bearing exercise, such as walking, because of injury to their legs or leg joints. However, if you have back problems, discuss the benefits and risks of rowing with your doctor, and be sure to start slowly against little resistance until you see how it feels.

YOUR OVERALL ACTIVITY GOAL

Your activity goal is to burn the same number of calories each day that it presently takes to keep the extra fat you now have on your body alive and well!

Let me put it another way: once you have lost your excess weight, your goal is to burn enough calories each day in physical activity to equal the number of calories it used to take to support the extra fat you previously had on your body when you were heavier and inactive.

Because I know the facts from both personal and professional experience, there is little that annoys me more than the claim made by many commercial weight-control experts who have packaged foods and powders to sell that diet is more important in weight control than exercise. You probably have heard the statement that 'It takes thirty-five miles of walking to lose a pound of fat.' Weight-control experts who remind you of this fact then go on to extol the virtues of their particular diet.

I have no argument about the virtues of diet versus exercise when it comes to *losing weight*. Simply put, diet wins. That's why I have worked to develop the Rotation Diet. But this completely misses the point about the value of physical activity.

The real question is, 'What amount of physical activity will it take to keep you at your desired weight, once you have lost all the weight you want to lose?'

Here are the important facts:

It takes about forty-five minutes a day of brisk whole-body activity to equal the number of calories it used to take to support approximately 3 to 3½ stone (18 to 23 kg) of extra fat on a sedentary, fat body!

It takes about an hour a day of brisk whole-body physical activity to equal the number of calories it used to take to maintain approximately 4 to 5 stone (27 to 34 kg) of fat on a sedentary, fat body!

(I cannot be more exact than these approximations because of individual differences in metabolic rates.)

Yes, it may take thirty-five miles of walking to lose a pound, but just forty-five minutes of extra walking each day (or a similar amount of time in some other brisk whole-body movement) will keep between 3 to 3½ stone of fat from ever accumulating, or from ever reaccumulating, on your body!

Lose whatever weight you wish to lose with the

121

Rotation Diet. The Rotation Diet will get your weight off just about as fast as any quick-weight-loss diet, without the risks of those diets. As you lose your excess weight, increase your activity level to burn up all the calories that your body formerly used *just to keep its fat alive*. Follow the weekly activity goals that I am about to give you and at the end of just three weeks you will be burning up enough calories to keep 18 to 23 kg of fat off your body. Then you may return to your former food intake when you begin your maintenance diet, but you can be confident that you are now active enough *TO PREVENT ALL THE FAT YOU HAVE LOST FROM EVER RETURNING.*

YOUR WEEKLY ACTIVITY GOALS

Whatever your level of physical condition, no objective can be more important, and no principle is more fundamental, than this: NEVER HURT YOURSELF.

Competitive athletes may have reasons to exert themselves to the point of injury. The payoff for being a champion may be worth it to them in dollars, even if they end up hobbling around for the rest of their lives. But you and I don't have to go, nor do we need to go, to this extreme in order to control our weight and achieve overall good physical condition. If you hurt yourself, your activity programme goes for a burton. Believe me, once you have become an active person and experienced the joys of being active, if you have to stop you are going to feel terrible! And your feelings will go from terrible to even worse than terrible when you see your weight going up all over again.

As for weekly goals, it is very simple. A beginner in physical activity should aim for:

1. Fifteen minutes a day the first week
2. Gradually increase until you are at thirty minutes a day by the end of the second week
3. Then increase until you reach forty-five minutes a day by the end of the third week

122

Even though you have not lost 3 to 3½ stone (18 to 23 kg) in three weeks, at the end of this time you will have the security of knowing that, should you need to lose that amount you are *already* doing enough in the way of physical activity each day to keep it all off for good. Just use the Rotation Diet one or two times more during the next few months, and you will make it all the way to your desired weight, and you will stay there for good.

The above guidelines for time (forty-five minutes a day) will work when you choose *any* continuous whole-body movement as your activity (walking, bicycling, swimming, jogging). If you choose a racket sport such as tennis, you need to think more in terms of an hour to an hour and a half, and it needs to be singles tennis, not doubles. Until you become an intermediate to advanced tennis player, you will burn more calories taking a brisk walk than you would in an equal amount of time playing tennis.

Can you take a day off? Yes, if you are tired or feeling under the weather. You should certainly not be active when you have a fever. But extra walking (if nothing else) in a sedentary person's life should become a daily habit.

I will return to more specifics about physical activity later in this chapter.

WHICH ACTIVITY WILL BE BEST FOR YOU?

The next principle of the Rotation Diet activity pro-gramme is to experiment until you find at least one activity that you really like. It should be something that makes you feel good physically, and that has, in fact, a 'moral' impact: you find yourself motivated to continue because you feel a better person for having done it.

You may find that it is better to have two different activities that you like, rather than one. Not only will this be more interesting, but you are less likely to overdo and injure any particular group of muscles when you alternate activities on a daily basis.

Nothing can be more important, however, than finding some physical activity that becomes a personal expression of your hidden talents and skills. If you take your activity as an 'exercise prescription', it will end up feeling like a dose of medicine. Experiment with different activities until you find at least one that makes you fancy getting good at it. As you get better at whatever you have chosen, your increasing strength, skill and endurance will begin to contribute to your self-concept in a way that equals the other things you do in life that make you feel a worthwhile person.

I hope you will take what I am saying very seriously because *our long-term follow-up of people who have been in the Vanderbilt Weight Management Program shows that physical activity is likely to do more for your feelings of well-being and your physical self-concept than does weight loss.* Since this statement is particularly true for me, I'd like to tell you about the role that physical activity has played in my own successful fight against fat, and the continuing role that it plays in maintaining my health and good spirits. I know that it holds similar promise for you, if you will only give it a chance.

WHAT ACTIVITY HAS MEANT TO ME

I learned a great deal about what it takes to make physical activity an important part of daily life from personal experience. The very first thing I learned was its value in weight maintenance. I discovered that, after losing a stone (7 kg) or so during my three weeks of dieting, I could return to my former food intake without gaining weight *provided* I played an hour and a half of singles tennis each day. I have measured my food intake over periods of several weeks, and it averages 2960 calories per day. I can say with a great deal of confidence that *nothing* works like physical activity for weight maintenance.

124

Without realizing it, however, I stumbled on to another very important key to the success of an activity pro-gramme – the contribution it made to my self-concept.

All the while I was growing up as a fat child with about as poor a physical self-concept as anyone could have, I had an uncle who was an expert tennis player. He was my childhood idol. His name was Jules Daniels, and I watched him play with some of the best tennis players in the country. But Jules wouldn't even show me how to hold a racket. I'm sure he felt that anyone as fat as I was could never be a tennis player. And while I might have dreamed about becoming a tennis player, I never thought that it was possible either.

My good old doctor friend, Ed Tarpley, changed all that when he said that I had to become active if I ever wanted to get my weight off, keep it off and help prevent further heart problems. I remembered Uncle Jules and asked Ed if he would approve of tennis. He did, and he gave me the advice to start slowly and moderately.

I borrowed a tennis racket and, with the wife of one of my colleagues, went out in my street clothes to a tennis court near my office. I wanted to see if I had any talent for the game and if I could imagine myself ever getting good at it. I found, somewhat to my surprise, that I had much more co-ordination than I expected. Within a few days I was out on the court again, and within two weeks I was playing at least a half an hour every day. I began to have those dreams again of 'being a tennis player' like my Uncle Jules.

I began to take tennis lessons and I was soon playing singles tennis every day for an hour and a half. Not only did it keep my weight down, but I began to look forward to those three weeks on my diet because each time I lost 15 pounds I could scamper around the court a great deal faster!

I played most of the time with players who were about equal to me in skill. That is the way to have the most fun and keep both participants interested. But I kept working at my game and improving. Finally, at the end of my first year, I got up the courage to ask one of Nash-

125

ville's best players to knock up with me. This man, Dr Milt Bush, became one of my closest friends. In addition to being a well-known pharmacologist and a professor in the Pharmacology Department at Vanderbilt, Milt was, at that time, the part-time coach of the Vanderbilt tennis team. He was a nationally ranked player and his triumphs included both the United States Grass Courts Championship and the Canadian Open Clay Courts Championship when he was sixty-five years old.

One of the things that made Milt such an inspiration was that he won those national championships in spite of having only one arm! If anyone knew what it means to conquer adversity, and to become a champion in spite of it, Milt did. I would meet him after team practice, and we would knock up together. Occasionally he might drop a stroke or two. My game began to improve by leaps and bounds.

Soon I began to think of myself as 'a tennis player'. I wasn't playing for the sake of my health any more, or for the weight-management benefits. These benefits became incidental to the effect tennis was having on the way I thought of myself as a person. There I was, 'fat little Dicky', leaping around the court and winning tennis tournaments! The trophies became so numerous that I had to start storing them in a cupboard. People who have never been fat can never appreciate the thrill formerly fat people experience when they discover their hidden physical talents and skills.

So this is what I mean about searching for a physical activity that can contribute to your self-concept. Perhaps you, too, have had a childhood dream about being athletic, but have felt too embarrassed to talk about it or pursue it. Perhaps you, too, have had a secret idol who was a physically active person. I certainly hope that you, too, have dreamed of becoming a tennis player, or if not a tennis player, a dancer, a swimmer or any other kind of active person. If you have had such dreams, or kindle them now, and if you then begin to engage in that activity, you will not have to worry about being fat EVER AGAIN. Being active will carry a value for you that is just

126

as important to your sense of being worthwhile as the work you do for a living and the roles you play in your personal relationships as a father, mother or servant to others in your community.

There is every likelihood that becoming active will lead you to find some new and special friends, just as I found Milt Bush.

For twenty years until his death a year ago at the age of seventy-seven, Milt and I looked forward to our weekly tennis match, and the couple of beers that followed, every Friday afternoon. It became a tradition, something so important and valuable in our lives that we felt deprived if anything interfered. Milt died in the way many tennis players would most prefer, of a heart attack in the middle of a tennis match. I know that he preferred to leave his life in this way, because he had often told me of his desire never to linger here in poor health or to be limited in his physical and mental abilities. Today there is one trophy that is not put away – it's the one Milt and I shared when we won the Music City Invitational Doubles Tournament here in Nashville several years ago. It stays on the mantelpiece in my study and helps preserve the memory of a friendship I never would have known, and an experience I never would have had, had I not made the attempt to become 'a tennis player'.

MAXIMIZING THE VALUE OF PHYSICAL ACTIVITY

When is the best time to be active?

How vigorous must I be?

Is it better to exercise for forty-five minutes all at once, or can I break it up?

How can I tell when any exercise – for example, swimming or bicycling – is equal to the weight-management benefits of forty-five minutes of brisk walking?

The Best Time to Exercise

The best time to exercise is when it feels the best to you, and is most convenient! Any other consideration is relatively minor. And as for the relative weight-management benefits of different activities, in general, brisk activity, of whatever kind that involves moving your whole body through space, burns about 100 calories every fifteen minutes. Time of day can affect this value to the tune of about 5, or at the most, 10 per cent.

However, since 5 or 10 per cent of your daily expenditure in activity can equal enough calories to gain, or to *prevent* the gain of, a considerable amount of weight over time, you might want to consider the following guidelines.

You can get extra calorie-burning benefits if you exercise after eating. Your body has to work to digest your food. Normally, it takes about 10 per cent of the caloric value of the food you eat to digest it. If you eat 1000 calories, the digestive process will take about 100 calories' worth of energy. However, you can increase by almost double the work it takes to digest food if you take a walk, *at a moderate pace*, after eating. Thus, if you need to walk back to work after a 1000-calorie lunch, and your walk is at least a mile in length, you will burn up about 200 calories in the digestive process. However, if you eat lunch near where you work, and there is no need to walk afterward, so that you just plop back in your chair after eating, you will use up only half that amount.

If you are one of those people who has a great deal of difficulty losing weight, even on a very restricted diet, nothing will equal the value of adding some physical activity around mealtimes. Here is an example: if, before you ate, you had to walk fifteen minutes to reach the location where you were going to have lunch, and then, after eating, you had to walk fifteen minutes to return to work, the total *extra* energy that you would be expending would equal about 300 calories (200 involved in the walking itself, and another 100 over and above the usual cost of digestion). That is enough energy to keep about 3

128

to 3½ stone (18 to 23 kg) of fat *off* your body. Let me put it another way: if a person who normally did this amount of activity every day around mealtime were to stop, and did not change the level of food intake, he or she would gradually gain between 3 and 3½ stone during the next twelve to eighteen months!

As for time of day for physical activity – morning versus evening – the most convenient time is the best time, and the best time is whenever it feels best and suits you. Every other consideration is, once again, relatively minor.

At best, time of day can affect your caloric expenditure through exercise by an amount that's similar to the effect of walking after meals – about 5 to 10 per cent. If you wish to obtain the benefit of burning an extra 5 to 10 calories for every brisk mile that you walk, exercising at the end of the day appears to be the way to do it. It works in the following way.

Late in the afternoon, your metabolic rate is likely to be at its highest point. This is a result of our inborn daily cycles of activity. If we wake and sleep according to the day-night cycle, our metabolic rate is lowest at about 5 a.m. and highest between 4 and 8 p.m. If we exercise when our metabolic rate is at a high point, the ceiling on energy expenditure seems to open up and we use more calories than usual. Thus, if you exercise before dinner, you may burn more calories than you might at five o'clock in the morning. I am happy to say that the effect seems to be greater for overweight persons than for normal-weight persons. Although time of day may amount to a small quantity on a daily basis, say 15 to 30 calories each day, on a year-round basis it can amount to several pounds.

If you happen to be a morning person, and by that I mean a person who wakes up and is, within moments, bursting with energy, I have a word of encouragement for morning exercise. In comparison with the evening person, your metabolic rate is already higher, and you can expect at least some extra calorie burning during physical activity even in the morning.

Exercise Intensity

What do I mean by 'brisk'?
 Simply this:

 First, be as vigorous as you can without hurting yourself,
 Second, be as vigorous as you can while still finishing 30 to
 45 minutes of exercise feeling refreshed, not exhausted.

These are the principles that I use, and since I jog anything from 30 to 35 miles a week and have never had a
running injury, I certainly feel confident in recommending them to all walkers and runners. In addition,
since I almost always finish an hour's jog feeling more
refreshed than when I started, I know that one doesn't
have to work to exhaustion for weight control! So, just
find your best cruising speed – one that you can maintain
for whatever period you choose to be active.

 (However, if you do decide to exercise intensely, that
is, to the point where you are breathing very hard or
actually get 'out of breath' for a few minutes at a time, be
sure to 'cool down' slowly. You should follow very
intense activity with five minutes of moderate or gentle
movement before stopping altogether. This cool-down
will prevent the pooling of blood in your legs, reduce the
burden on your heart and help prevent cramping in your
other working muscles.)

How Long Must You Exercise?

It is probably best to have one session each day of at least
a half an hour in length. The reason I suggest that you try
at least thirty minutes at a stretch is as follows.

 If you move briskly and continuously for at least thirty
minutes you may experience an elevation in your metabolic rate that can last several hours after you finish
exercising. This 'residual metabolic elevation' after a
brisk walk can burn off between 50 and 100 calories
more during the two to four hours after exercise than you
would ordinarily burn following a period of inactivity.
We have measured this effect in our laboratories, and in

130

my own case, after an hour's jog, I tend to burn up over 10 per cent more calories during the next six hours than I normally would burn if I had not been active.

There is another reason for exercising at least thirty minutes at a stretch – perhaps even forty-five or more – which is psychological in nature. It seems to take that long for your entire body to get into the rhythm of the movement. Walking, jogging, swimming, or bicycling in a safe place or indoors on a stationary bicycle begins to have meditational or hypnagogic effects after thirty or so minutes. When you enter into steady rhythmic movement, many physiological functions become co-ordinated in a steady state: breathing, heart rate, the movement of your arms and legs – in fact, the movement of almost all the major muscles of your entire body that are involved in maintaining your posture as you go through the various stages of each step. The refreshing, relaxing, 'other-consciousness' effect is so great that yoga masters have, in fact, stated that meditation in motion (as in walking or jogging) is superior to medi-tation at rest. The so-called 'runner's high', when it is experienced, seems to require at least forty-five minutes of continuous movement. Having tested many forms of meditation and many relaxation techniques, I can say that for me nothing can equal the refreshing, relaxing effects of an hour's gentle jog in the woods near my home.

But, once again, you have to decide what works best for you. As I indicated earlier, many persons who seem to be especially resistant to losing weight find that walking around mealtimes for fifteen-minute periods, three or four times each day, with two of these fifteen-minute walks right after meals, facilitates weight loss more than any other approach to activity.

If you have especially difficult problems in losing weight, you might try walking at mealtimes until you lose your weight. Then, get out there and work up to forty-five minutes of continuous activity of the kind I have just described. The ultimate psychological benefits of pro-longed activity in one single period may then begin to outweigh all other considerations for you, as they do for me. And there is no question that single long periods of exercise work perfectly for long-term weight management.

Exercise and Appetite

Exercise has some additional beneficial weight-management effects on appetite. Although these benefits are valuable any time of the day, they seem especially useful for those many persons who tend to eat like pigs at night.

If you exercise at the end of the day, it may depress your night-time eating urges. Exercise causes your liver to secrete glycogen and your fat cells to release fat. This increases the levels of sugar and fat in your bloodstream. Your brain senses this increase, which mimics the levels of fat and sugar in your bloodstream after eating, and it causes you to feel a decrease in appetite.

Exercise increases the level of epinephrine secretion from your adrenal glands. Epinephrine is a fat-mobilizing hormone: when you get active, epinephrine is released from your adrenal glands in order to stimulate your fat cells to release fat for energy. However, epinephrine is similar to amphetamine in its effects on appetite – it decreases your desire to eat. (One way you can recognize this effect is to notice the decrease in salivation that occurs during and after exercise.) Thus, when you exercise at the end of the day, you may experience a decrease in your appetite for the rest of the evening.

Finally, exercise at the end of the day may suppress night-time appetite in another way. Exercise elevates your body temperature. In fact, the internal body temperature of a person who has been engaging in vigorous physical activity can approach 104°F (40°C). That's equivalent to running a considerable temperature. Although you will feel great rather than ill after being active, this elevation in body temperature can have somewhat the same appetite-suppressing effects as the fever that accompanies illness.

132

THE ROTATION DIET ACTIVITY PLAN

I can vouch for the appetite-suppressing effects of evening exercise – and these effects are not always appreciated by my wife! She knows that it will be an hour or so before I feel like eating after a jog in the evening, and it sometimes annoys her to have to wait too long if we have planned to have dinner together. Keep this in mind if you begin to prefer evening exercise!

Although the appetite-suppressing effects of activity are great and worth working for, the emotional and psychological effects are even greater. I have already discussed some of these effects above. But there is even more for you to anticipate and experience. If you are now an inactive person, it may be hard for you to believe that, short of illness, *the more tired and aggravated you are before you get physically active, the better you will feel afterward*. Nothing will invigorate you and prepare you for a day of profitable work more than some brisk activity in the morning, and nothing will relax you and relieve you of the aggravations of a hard day at work more than some brisk activity before dinner. Indeed, it's at the end of the day, when you may feel drained of energy, that a brisk walk, jog, tennis match or dance class is most elevating and refreshing, physically and mentally. Once you have experienced these effects, there is a good chance you will become addicted to your daily activity, and then it's really 'bye-bye, fat'.

CAN YOU INCREASE YOUR METABOLIC RATE THROUGH EXERCISE?

Yes, you can. But you should be clear about what increasing your metabolic rate really means, both in principle and to you personally.

Simply put, your resting metabolic rate refers to the number of calories it takes to support a pound of your body weight for a given period of time, say, twenty-four hours (should you remain at rest for that period of time).

Technically, metabolic rate is often calculated as calories burned per square metre of your body surface, but thinking in terms of a pound of body weight is easier to understand and more useful in weight management.

At the start of our programme, we find that there is tremendous variability in the resting metabolic rates of our participants. A few people, generally women, need fewer than 6 calories a day to maintain a pound of body weight in the resting state, whereas others, generally men, may need 9 or even 10 calories to maintain a pound of body weight in the resting state. Thus, a 14 stone (90 kg) person who needed, say, 7 calories per pound of body weight each day would have a resting need for 1400 calories, whereas another 200 pound person with a need for 10 calories per pound of body weight would need 2000 calories at rest over a twenty-four-hour period.

Men tend to have higher metabolic rates than women because, even when fat, they have as part of their total body weight a larger percentage of muscle tissue. Muscle tissue is considerably more active than fat tissue, even at rest – which means that muscle tissue burns more calories just maintaining itself – circulating nutrients and regenerating itself – than does fat tissue. Even at rest, muscle tissue may burn two or even three times more energy than does fat.

One way to change your resting metabolic rate is to change the composition of your body. That is, increase the amount of muscle tissue relative to the amount of fat. This will happen naturally by making sure that when you lose weight you lose only fat, or that, while losing weight, you slightly increase the amount of muscle on your body through appropriate exercise. In this way, when you calculate your metabolic rate, it will go up in terms of the calories you need each day per pound of weight.

I am happy to report that people who get active in the manner I advise add, on the average, between 2 and 3 pounds of muscle for each 20 pounds lost. When you consider that up to half the weight you lose on diets without becoming active can be muscle tissue, this is an important advantage of the Rotation Diet and the activity

134

programme. If 10 of the 20 pounds lost on a diet is muscle tissue, you will be lowering, not increasing, your metabolic rate.

This becomes important when you consider the *total* number of calories it is going to take each day to maintain your weight at rest when you finish dieting. Here are the facts: *your total needs at rest are very likely to drop, in spite of an increase in the need per pound of weight!*

Think about it for a moment and you will see why: a given person who weights 14 stone (90 kg) at the start of a weight-loss campaign and loses 3½ stone (22½ kg), ending up with a body weight of about 11 stone (68 kg) has a body to keep alive and move around each day that is 25 per cent smaller. If that person needed 7 calories per pound of body weight before dieting, then the total daily need at rest would come to 1400 calories. If that person increased the need to 8 calories per pound of body weight at rest, which is, in fact, a considerable increase in metabolic rate, not likely to be obtained by many people, the *total daily calorie need at rest would still end up at only 1200 calories.*

So you see, you can get an increase in metabolic *rate*, but, with a large amount of weight loss, an increase in rate is not likely to compensate completely for the loss in the *total* daily need for calories.

But think of the disaster that would occur for weight management if you not only lost weight but also *lowered* your metabolic rate. If that 14 stone person whom I have been using as an example had even a slight decrease in metabolic rate (which would occur with the loss of muscle mass through dieting without becoming active) – say, down to 6½ calories per pound of body weight – at 11 stone the total daily need would have fallen to 975 calories! Even if the needs had not changed, but remained the same at 7 calories per pound, the total need for calories would be reduced to 1050 at rest.

Now, of course, I think you see another reason why you must be active virtually every day for at least forty-five minutes to achieve permanent weight management. *It is during the forty-five minutes of brisk activity itself and*

*during the residual metabolic elevation that can burn
some additional calories when you finish being active
that you burn up all the calories it used to take to keep
alive all that extra fat you now have lost.*

And this is why I rant and rave – and why I will rant and
rave once again, right here and now – against the
dietmongers who want to sell you quick and easy
weight-loss schemes without laying it all on the line and
demanding, whenever physically possible, that you
become an active person.

I cannot emphasize this too strongly: if you do not get
active and stay active, you've got a snowball's chance in
hell of maintaining any weight loss.

You will face semi-starvation for the rest of your life if
you remain sedentary and want to control your weight.
Just like everyone else in our affluent, over-nourished
society, you are, and will be for life, surrounded by delicious, irresistible, high-calorie foods. Is it any wonder that
95 per cent of dieters put their weight back on again?

I certainly hope you have an itchy feeling in your feet
right now. So, go out for a walk, and then come back and
read the next section on how to calculate the calories you
burn in various physical activities.

HOW TO CALCULATE THE CALORIES
BURNED IN PHYSICAL ACTIVITY

Compared with sitting at a desk, or lounging around
watching TV, you will burn approximately three times
more calories walking at a moderate pace (3 miles per
hour).

When you work up to a brisk pace (4 miles per hour)
you will burn almost five times more calories than you
burn while sitting.

And if you lose enough weight to begin a little bit of
gentle jogging, say, at a pace of a mile in ten minutes (6
miles per hour), you will burn between nine and ten
times the calories you burn sitting still.

Table 7.1 presents estimates of calories burned by the

Table 7.1 Energy Expenditure in Physical Activities*

ACTIVITY	5	10	15	30	45	60
			MINUTES OF ACTIVITY			
Walking						
moderately, 3 miles per hour	22	44	66	132	198	264
briskly, 4 miles per hour	33	66	99	198	297	396
Rebounding†						
brisk walking tempo,						
little foot lift	22	44	66	132	198	264
jogging tempo,						
foot lift of 4–6 inches	33	66	99	198	297	396
running, high knee						
lifts, or kicks	68	136	204	408	612	816
Badminton	34	68	102	204	306	408
Cycling						
leisure, 5.5 miles per hour	22	44	66	132	198	264
leisure, 9.4 miles per hour	35	70	105	210	315	420
Chopping wood						
average tempo	30	60	90	180	270	360
Dancing						
moderate tempo	18	36	54	108	162	216
continuous, intense aerobic	59	118	177	354	531	708
Gymnastics	23	46	69	138	217	276
Horse riding						
trot, English style	39	78	117	234	351	468
Martial arts, judo, karate						
continuous drill	68	136	204	408	612	816
Rowing						
moderate pace	26	52	78	156	234	312
Running (flat surface)						
a mile in 11½ minutes	47	94	141	282	423	564
a mile in 9 minutes	68	136	204	408	612	816
a mile in 8 minutes	73	146	219	436	655	874
a mile in 7 minutes	81	162	243	486	729	972
a mile in 6 minutes	88	176	264	528	792	1056
a mile in 5½ minutes	101	202	303	606	909	1212
Skiing						
moderate, downhill	42	84	126	252	378	504
cross country	50	100	150	300	450	600
Squash	74	148	222	444	666	888
Stair climbing						
down, rate of 1 step per second	17	34	51	102	153	204
up, rate of 1 step per second	72	144	216	432	648	864
Swimming						
continuous freestyle, slow	45	90	135	270	405	540
continuous freestyle, fast	55	110	165	330	495	660
Table tennis	24	48	72	144	216	288
Tennis						
singles	38	76	114	228	342	456

* Estimates taken from Martin Katahn, *The 200 Calorie Solution*, Norton, 1982. All values are approximate for a person weighing 11 stone (70 kg).

† Rebounding exercise must move at a faster pace than walking on a level surface because of the assistance given to your movement by the springing action of the minitrampoline.

average 11 stone (70 kg) person in a number of different activities over different time periods. All estimates of this kind are rough, because of the great variability in our metabolic rates to begin with. The calories you end up burning in any activity are some multiple of this basal rate. A person who burns about 60 calories per hour at rest will burn approximately 300 calories per hour during a brisk walk. Another person, with a higher rate to begin with, say, 80 calories per hour, will end up burning around 400 per hour during a brisk walk.

Here is a rough rule of thumb that will do about as well as anything short of testing in a metabolic laboratory to predict how many calories you burn in various activities.

If you do any whole-body activity that feels to you the equivalent of walking at a moderate pace (3 miles per hour), you are likely to be burning something between 225 and 325 calories an hour.

If you do any whole-body activity that feels to you the equivalent to walking at a brisk pace (4 miles per hour), you are likely to be burning something between 350 and 450 calories per hour.

If you do any whole-body movement that feels the equivalent of gentle jogging (6 miles per hour), you will be burning something between 650 and 750 calories per hour.

Women will burn fewer calories than men, and lighter people fewer calories than heavier. A woman who weighs less than 8½ stone (54 kg) is quite likely to fall below the range I've suggested, whereas men over 14 stone (90 kg) may exceed it.

I usually tell participants in my groups that there are two easy ways to think of the value of physical activity without getting obsessed by calories.

First, you will burn around 100 calories for every fifteen minutes of brisk activity. When you get into things that involve considerable running around, you will approach 150 calories burned every fifteen minutes.

Second, and the most important thing of all, is that in just forty-five minutes to one hour a day of physical activity you can burn 20 to 25 per cent of your total daily intake of calories. This is a great way to have your cake and eat it, too, since it means you won't be adding an ounce of fat to your body and can eat like a normal human being without dieting.

THE VALUE OF PHYSICAL ACTIVITY IF YOU SUFFER FROM VARICOSE VEINS

I mentioned earlier in this book that I suffered from varicose veins even as a child and had my first attack of thrombophlebitis (blood clots and accompanying inflammation) at the age of twelve. Bouts with clots and inflammations continued to plague me throughout my life until about seven years ago. Losing weight and becoming a tennis player helped, but didn't completely prevent their occurrence.

But the attacks ceased entirely after I became a jogger.

The dramatic reduction in the problems I was having with my legs the moment I became a runner puzzled me, so I began to read about the effects of running on the circulation and the blood itself, and to ask questions of all my physician friends. This is what I discovered.

Continuous vigorous physical activity changes the clotting characteristics of the blood, reducing what is called fibrinolytic activity, which is one of the factors that increases the tendency of the blood to clot. By jogging on an almost daily basis, I was remedying what has been a family tendency for generations. Tennis playing evidently was either not vigorous enough or did not involve enough sustained activity (as does jogging) to accomplish this result.

The effect of sustained physical activity on the characteristics of your blood is quite interesting. During intense activity, the ability of the blood to coagulate increases. This is a built-in tendency that serves to protect you, just in case you are injured. Evidently, when you stop and return to the resting state, there is a rebound in the other direction, so that at rest coagulation is less likely.

Of course you should not start to jog if you are over-weight and suffer from varicose veins. But I suggest you discuss the following total programme for self-care with your doctor. From what I have learned in my study of the problem, I believe that about 50 per cent of people who suffer from varicose veins, phlebitis and thrombophlebitis will benefit tremendously from following it. Your varicose veins will not go away, but they are not nearly as likely to hurt or become inflamed, nor is your blood so likely to clot, if you put this programme into effect.

A PREVENTION PROGRAMME FOR OVERWEIGHT PEOPLE WHO SUFFER FROM VARICOSE VEINS

Except where noted, there is scientific evidence to support the help you can receive by following each of these preventive steps. The first and the last steps are probably the most important beneficial changes that you can make in caring for yourself.

1. Get down to ideal weight.

2. Do not eat large meals (it can interfere with circulation to your legs).

3. Do not wear obstructive, tight-fitting clothing for the same reason.

4. Do not eat high-fat meals, which clog your blood with a high fat content. (I do not have strong evidence that high-fat meals will slow the blood flow and increase clotting in your veins, although there is very strong evidence that a high-fat diet, especially a diet high in the saturated fat that comes from meat products, is correlated with deposits of fatty substances on the walls of the coronary arteries and with coronary heart disease. This is purely intuitive advice on my part.)

5. Do not stand in one place for more than a few minutes at a time – keep moving. Flexing your calf muscles aids circulation. Flexing also helps when you have to sit in one place for a long period.

6. Elevate your legs at every opportunity to assist the flow of blood back to your heart.

7. Raise the leg end of the mattress you sleep on so it is about two inches higher than your waist (you can fold a blanket and slip it under the mattress).

8. If you should suffer from gnawing pains in your legs at night, turn around in bed, put your legs up over the headboard, and stay that way for about fifteen minutes to let blood drain from your legs. You can also do a back-stand: rest on your back on the floor or bed, lift your legs and hips to the vertical position, supporting yourself with your hands on your hips, and hold this position for several minutes. Your weight will rest on the backs of your upper arms from the elbows to the shoulders. However, if you have high blood pressure, check with your doctor about the advisability of these positions before you attempt to do either of them.

9. At the first sign of any problem, elevate your legs and gently massage them, with the motion going toward your heart. If you do not have an anti-inflammatory drug at hand, take one aspirin tablet and get in touch with your doctor.

10. If you receive any sort of bruise to your legs that might cause an inflammation or a clot, put an ice pack on it immediately.

11. Be careful in the use of elastic stockings or bandages. Sometimes these can obstruct circulation and hurt, rather than help, the condition. If you need to use support hose, experiment until you find the very best possible style for your condition. You need to talk this over with your doctor, and be sure to tell him what effects the support you are presently using are having. If there is pain, the support hose is probably not helping, and may be doing additional damage. No matter who prescribed or fitted it, when support hose begins to hurt, get it off immediately and get in touch again with your doctor. You may need another prescription.

12. *Above all, as you lose your weight, begin to gradually increase your walking.* I believe that vigorous walking, *worked up to in both speed and time very grad-*

141

ually to the forty-five minutes per day that I am recommending, will accomplish the same thing for you that jogging has done for me. However, as long as you are overweight, you must be very moderate and very careful, or you can aggravate, rather than help, the condition.

To gain the most benefit from continuous vigorous physical activity, and to be able to pursue it with more benefits than risk for varicose veins, you must be at the very best weight that you can possibly achieve.

All my suggestions are designed to prevent or to minimize trouble with varicose veins. My suggestions are not a *treatment* for phlebitis, thrombophlebitis and varicose veins. These are medical conditions that require medical treatment. While I have not needed them in years, I still carry with me, in my tennis bag and in my suitcase on trips, the blood thinner, the clot-dissolving enzyme and the anti-inflammatory drug that my doctor has prescribed in case of trouble. You need medical supervision, too, but discuss the preventive measures I have just prescribed with your doctor. I believe that they can help you, as they have helped me, prevent inflammations and clots and that they will lessen a very aggravating problem.

8

Taking a Break from Dieting: The Transition to Maintenance

Why do you have to stop now and take a break from dieting? If you have more weight to lose, why can't you just continue using the Rotation Diet over and over again until you lose all the weight you need to lose?

And, if you have reached your goal weight, why do you have to make a 'transition' to maintenance? If you haven't lowered your metabolic rate and reduced your need for food, why can't you begin your celebration immediately and eat anything and everything you want to eat right away, without gaining weight?

The answer to the questions in the first paragraph is quite simple and brief: there are four reasons why you have to take a break from dieting, and they are all equally important.

First, a break in dieting guarantees that there will be no slowdown in metabolic rate.

Second, the break increases your motivation to be as perfect as possible during each three-week period that you use the Rotation Diet. Longer periods of dieting encourage small deviations, followed by larger deviations, finished off by complete collapse.

Third, if you have problems controlling your appetite, you are not as likely to begin to overeat after only three weeks of dieting (especially because of that little respite during the second week) as you are if you had forced yourself to endure several more weeks or months of deprivation. Long periods of dieting build up powerful hidden impulses to binge.

Fourth, you need the practice in maintaining small weight losses on your way to complete success. It is much easier to manage maintenance after three separate 10- or 15-pound losses than it is to manage your weight after losing 2 to 3 stone (13½ to 20 kg) all at once. With each 10- or 15-pound loss you discover what you need to do in your diet and activity programme, and you begin to incorporate the metabolic benefits that go with increased physical activity and improvements in your diet. You have already learned some of the things you need to do to raise your metabolic rate and to increase your total daily metabolic needs in previous chapters. I will discuss some additional metabolic benefits that you can obtain from improving the quality of your diet later in this chapter.

Now to answer the questions in the second paragraph. Why do you have to make a 'transition' to maintenance? Why can't you eat anything you want right now, immediately after finishing the Rotation Diet?

The reason is water retention.

Because we tend to blame 'water retention' for a number of things when our weight fluctuates, I think you should be clear about the way your body varies in its water balance, apparently whimsically (but really lawfully) increasing and decreasing its total water content while still tending to hover around some central point. There are a number of factors involved in causing these fluctuations, and they can all come into play and affect your weight at any time, including this period when you must take a break from dieting.

First of all, haven't you noticed how your body weight tends to jump around within a range of about 3 to 5 pounds over a one- to three-day period? For example, take a time when you are not on a reducing diet. You go

144

out to a party on a Sunday evening, have a couple of glasses of wine, some snack food, perhaps a rich main course, and then dessert. You wake up 3 pounds heavier the next morning. In order to gain a true 3 pounds of *fat* weight, you would have had to eat about 10,500 calories *more* than your normal intake. (Each pound of body fat contains about 3500 calories.) You know darn well you haven't binged to that extent. You may have had 1500 extra calories, but certainly not 10,500. How can you gain 3 pounds on 1500 calories?

Now take the opposite situation. It's the middle of the week, you haven't been on a reducing diet, you haven't been near any desserts or alcohol, and you have been too busy to cook anything except plain food. Perhaps, in addition, you ran out of salty snack foods. Over a three-day period you may have eaten 500 calories a day less than you did over the last weekend. Now, on Thursday morning, you find yourself 3 pounds lighter than you were on Monday. What accounts for this?

As I indicated, it's a question of water balance.

The human body is, on average, about 72 per cent water. This means that a person weighing about 10 stone (63½ kg) has a body that contains about 7 stone (45 kg) of water. Muscle tissue, for example, is 75 to 80 per cent water, blood is almost 100 per cent water, and the sugar energy stores in your liver (glycogen) are dissolved in a ratio of one part sugar to three or four parts water. In addition, there is a considerable amount of fluid all around our body cells. Thus, given 7 stone or more of water in our bodies, it is easy to imagine that there are many different factors that might cause the body to vary by 3 to 5 per cent (3 to 5 pounds) in its water content, overnight.

SOME FACTORS AFFECTING WATER BALANCE

Sodium

Most of us know, of course, about the effects of the

sodium in table salt and in monosodium glutamate (MSG). Sodium is one of the nutrients that can cause a major amount of water retention when we take in more than our kidneys can dispose of quickly. There is enough sodium in just one spoonful of pickle to cause a 1-pound weight gain in susceptible people. And, since most persons who have a weight problem also tend to retain more than the average amount of water, I tell participants in our programme that it's 'a pound a pickle'. Similarly, if you have what is essentially a low-calorie Chinese meal, you can show a 2- or 3-pound weight gain the next morning without having overeaten by one single calorie. The gain is due primarily to the sodium in the MSG and, possibly, too much soy sauce.

Changes in Calorie Intake

Although you may be aware of the effects of too much sodium on your body weight, you may not understand how an increase in the caloric content of a day's food intake *of only 500 calories* more than was eaten the previous day can also lead to a 1-pound weight gain. The body responds to a change in caloric intake just as it would to a dose of sodium, and, up to a total of about 2000 calories more than your usual intake, you can gain weight at a rate of about 1 pound for each 500 extra calories.

Most people give themselves double trouble when they go off the deep end and begin to overeat. They combine an increase in sodium consumption (high in most dip and snack foods) with an increase in calories. Overeat by 500 calories each day for three days (or stuff in 1500 extra calories in one day) and, in addition, fail to watch your sodium intake, and you can easily gain 5 pounds (2 kg). This sort of weight gain is especially likely to happen to sedentary people because they do not do anything in the way of physical activity that can get rid of some water via perspiration and respiratory activity.

You can see the most dramatic illustration of rebound water retention (technically called 'the rehydration

146

effect') after a diet in people who have stopped all food intake and been on a complete fast in order to lose weight. A few years ago I visited one of our country's famous fasting programmes and watched obese men who had just finished three weeks of fasting in a medically supervised programme gain 7 pounds in five days on a refeeding diet *of only 600 calories per day!* Since the average loss was under 20 pounds this meant they were regaining weight faster than they had lost it.

Stress, Over-exertion, and Alcohol

Two other factors that can cause several pounds of water retention, without overeating, are severe stress, which I hope you will never face at any time of your life, and unaccustomed physical activity of a high intensity or prolonged duration.

With respect to stress, weight gains of 6 or 7 pounds have been noted in people experiencing the onset of divorce proceedings, the death of a person dear to them or a war. And after unusually hard exercise, you may overshoot the mark in your fluid intake. In addition, any inflammation of your muscles and joints following unusually intense or prolonged exercise will be associated with fluid retention.

Temporary water retention is a very common occurrence among active people who suddenly increase their level of activity. It has happened to me. The very first time that I ran an eight-mile course, which was three miles farther than I had ever run before, I expected to be lighter the next day. In spite of not having overeaten, I gained 2 pounds instead. It took me a while to associate the gain with the amount of fluid I had drunk, and the slight soreness in my leg muscles and joints. Of course, temporary water-weight gains as a result of overexercising are not seen in people who maintain a steady exercise programme. Normally, exercise is an important element in eliminating excess water retention.

Finally, the use of alcohol leads to water retention in many people. Even beer drinkers! You may spend the whole night running to the bathroom as you drink your beer, but you are likely to end up retaining more water than you started with.

Although the Rotation Diet has given you a quick weight loss without predisposing you to a rebound gain in your *fat* weight, you are still just as susceptible as you ever were to a temporary but terribly discouraging gain due to water retention, *unless* you follow my guidelines for making a transition to maintenance. And, by the way, these guidelines are generally effective in preventing water retention due to any cause, including periodic water retention during the menstrual cycle, and they will help keep you from bloating whether or not you are on a diet. In any event, I know just how discouraging an overnight gain of several pounds can be, so let's be sure it doesn't happen to you!

GUIDELINES FOR MAKING A SUCCESSFUL TRANSITION TO MAINTENANCE

The first thing I want to say is, DON'T WORRY. You will be able to eat again like a normal human being and not gain weight! You will be able to return to the style of cooking you prefer (unless it was loaded with fat!) You will be able to eat out and, while eating out, be able to eat as others eat. But you must follow each of my guidelines. You cannot go off the deep end and immediately binge to celebrate all the weight you have lost. And you can *never* return to a sedentary life-style (assuming you have increased your activity level) without endangering your weight. You have just got to keep burning up, on a daily basis, all the calories it used to take to keep the fat you have just lost alive on your body, or it will start creeping back!

Increase Food Intake Slowly

Of all the guidelines, this is probably the most important.

If you increase food intake too quickly, you will probably increase both calories *and* sodium. Assuming that you have just completed the twenty-one days of the Rotation Diet, do not increase your food intake to more than 1200 calories for each of the next three days if you are a woman, and 1800 calories a day if you are a man.

To make the transition to maintenance as easy as possible, we suggest that women in the Vanderbilt Weight Management Program use the 1200-calorie menus of Week 2 of the Rotation Diet (page 60), and men the 1800-calorie menus (page 66).

If you want to be absolutely sure you will not gain weight, use the Week 2 menus for a whole week. When our participants use the Week 2 menus for a full week, they usually lose about two more pounds. You may do this, too, if you like, since it gives some insurance against water retention when you add more calories next week. The two additional pounds that you lose in the fourth week after beginning the Rotation Diet will be ALL fat loss.

After women have been on the 1200-calorie menus for at least three days (or a week, if you prefer), they should increase to 1500 calories. Stick with 1500 calories for three days, using the 1500-calorie menus that I have laid out for men (pages 64–6, and pages 204–6 in the Alternative Menus), if you wish to make it easy for yourself.

With daily brisk activity of at least forty-five minutes, women should be able to reach a daily intake of around 1800 calories some time during the fifth week after beginning the Rotation Diet. Use my 1800-calorie menus as guides (pages 66–9 and pages 206–10 in the Alternative Menus). You can, if you like, consider this week your 'break from dieting' and start all over again next week. But I always took at least a month off between rotations and you may be happier and more successful if you do the same. It gives you practice in maintenance and keeps motivation at peak levels.

After spending three to seven days on 1800 calories, men also go up by 300-calorie increments, first to 2100 calories for three days, then to 2400 calories.

Thus, no matter what your sex, you see that you must think in terms of 300-calorie increments until you determine where your weight will stabilize with your new level of physical activity. Since we are all different, it must necessarily be a testing process.

For those of you who don't wish to follow my menus, and for men going up to 2100 and 2400 calories, to be on the safe side I would suggest adding only extra servings of fruits, vegetables and lean meat, poultry or fish to meet the 300-calorie increases. You can build your own menus using my recipes, since these recipes will give you the calorie contents for each serving. For other foods, see the calorie guide on pages 238–44 for quick calorie estimates. In general, note the following.

Half-cup servings of all vegetables except *free vegetables* will contain around 25 calories.

The average-size piece of fruit will run around 60 calories, with small fruits (such as a plum) containing around 40 calories and large fruits (a large apple) containing about 80 calories.

You can consider *lean* meats, fish and poultry to contain about 55 calories per ounce, and you will not be far from correct. But watch out for the fat! Fatty meats can run over 100 calories per ounce.

What about the 'goodies': puddings, sweets, alcohol?

If you choose to include dessert, snack foods or alcohol, rather than the fruits, vegetables and lean meat, fish or poultry that are preferable when you first increase calories, you should add only one serving of such foods on any given day, until you determine just how such increases affect your weight. Since no one can predict exactly what will happen until it's tried, it's up to you to find out for yourself. If your weight goes up on just one serving, you can be absolutely certain that it is due to water retention. It is impossible to gain a pound of fat on one serving of any dessert or one glass of wine! (You may gain more than a pound of water if you get into salty snacks, however. But again, it is not a gain in fat weight.)

If you use all the other guidelines that I give you in this chapter, you should not gain a single pound during your transition to maintenance. If you gain any weight at all, you will stabilize at a point very close to your lowest weight. Then, if you eliminate, *for just one day*, all of the sweet foods, alcohol and salty snacks that put you at the high point in your water balance, that increase in water weight will drop off just as quickly as it was gained. Working in this way you can find out how susceptible you are to water retention from desserts, alcoholic beverages and salt, and you can be certain that as you add or eliminate them from your diet you are simply playing with a pound or two of water weight.

Are there some foods that affect your metabolic rate, so that eating them can elevate that rate and help you stay thin?

Yes, there is a way that the food you eat affects your total metabolic needs and it is *very important* for you to understand how it works so you can put the principles to work in order to help you maintain your losses in the future. But that is a long-term rather than a short-term matter, and it needs some detailed explanation, so I will wait until the end of this chapter to discuss it. Right now I want to give you the other guidelines for making the transition to maintenance without gaining any weight – even water weight.

Avoid Excess Salt

A bowl of onion soup, a couple of dessertspoons of blue cheese dressing, some pickle to go with a cheese or salami sandwich, and you will be a few pounds heavier tomorrow morning.

Don't cook with salt – add it to taste at the table. And learn to use herbs and spices as I suggest in my many recipes.

Here is a list of foods high in sodium. Be moderate in their use when they have other nutritional value. For example, be moderate in your consumption of most cheeses. They are an important source of calcium, but they also tend to be high in sodium (see page 74 for a comparison of the sodium content of some popular

151

cheeses). Avoid foods that contain not much more than just sodium and fat (for example, bacon, sausages and many cooked meats) and prepare the foods that appear in this list, which are normally nutritious foods, without the salt that has been used in the noted method of preparation (for example, corned beef, smoked fish – beef and fish are normally nutritious foods, but here they are prepared with excess salt).

anchovies and anchovy paste
bacon
baking powder
beef: corned
bouillon cubes (except low sodium; check label)
celery salt (celery *seed* is fine)
cereals (check labels and choose the ones with the least salt per serving)
cheese (blue, Cheddar, processed, Camembert; use in moderation)
corn, popped with salt added (okay plain)
crab, canned
crispbreads dotted with salt (check label or be guided by taste)
fish: cod and haddock, smoked and salted

frozen meats (check labels)
ham
ketchup in large quantities
olives
peanuts, salted
pickles and bottled sauces
potato crisps and other similarly salted snack foods
processed luncheon meats
sauerkraut
sausages, frankfurters
soups, tinned
soy sauce (1 teaspoon of soy sauce has about 285 milligrams of sodium; 1 teaspoon of salt has 2000 milligrams of sodium)
tinned vegetables (check labels)
Worcestershire sauce

Eat Naturally Diuretic Foods

Some foods have a natural diuretic function. They stimulate your kidneys to rid your body of water, rather than close them down as do the salty foods listed under the heading above. Naturally diuretic foods tend to be relatively high in potassium content, compared with their sodium content.

Here is a list of foods that will help you get rid of excess water. The most effective ones seem to be fresh pineapple, asparagus, citrus fruits and green vegetables. Combine these foods with lean meat and cottage cheese, and you can lose several pounds of water overnight.

apricot
asparagus
banana

beef (lean)
broccoli
cantaloupe

152

chicken
cottage cheese
figs
grapefruit and grapefruit juice
lamb (trimmed)
milk, skim and low-fat
nuts, unsalted
pineapple, fresh

potato
prunes and prune juice
oranges and orange juice
raisins
tomato
tuna, drain off brine
turkey
watermelon

ONE-DAY WATER-LOSS DIET

Just in case you ever experience water retention, here is a day's menu that will get rid of several pounds of excess water. Women who experience periodic water retention find it particularly helpful, especially when it is combined with the daily exercise that I recommend. It will also do wonders for your mood since water retention is often associated with an increase in negative emotions such as depression.

Up to 1 pound (450 g) of extra-lean beef, fish or chicken, prepared without skin
Up to 1 pound (450 g) of low-fat cottage cheese
Asparagus, broccoli, fresh pineapple or melon and citrus fruits

You can use this diet for two days if necessary, and you can eat up to a full pound of lean meat, fish or poultry and 1 pound (450 g) of low-fat cottage cheese each day. You can also eat all the named fruits and vegetables, plainly cooked, in almost unlimited quantities. To be on the safe side, however, the first time you use the diet, try a serving each of two different vegetables, and a serving each of two different fruits. This will show you how well the diet can work for you when followed in its most perfect form.

If you have been retaining an extreme amount of water, you can lose 5 or more pounds (2 kg) on the One-Day Water-Loss Diet. Although I do not normally retain fluid, I have tried this diet after a big weekend and lost 3¾ pounds. The combination of a high protein content together with naturally diuretic fruits and vegetables does it. But do not use a diet such as this for more than two days. Over longer periods of time, you should eat a wide variety of foods to assure yourself of adequate nutrition.

153

Be Physically Active

DON'T MISS A DAY! If you are in good health, by the time you make this transition to maintenance you will be walking briskly for forty-five minutes a day, or engaging in some other physical activity. Between the activity itself and the residual elevation in your metabolic rate that stays with you for a few hours after your activity, you will be burning off between 300 and 400 more calories each day than you did before you began the Rotation Diet. As you begin to increase your calories to stabilize your weight, your new activity level will be burning off enough calories to keep the fat you lost during the three weeks of the Rotation Diet from ever returning to your body.

Almost as important as the fat-burning power of physical activity is its aid in preventing water retention. Normally, on any given day, we lose almost as much water through perspiration and respiration as we do through the kidneys. (Our breath is saturated with moisture when we exhale.) When we are active, we can lose one to several pounds of water through perspiration and, as we increase our breathing rate, we can double the loss of moisture through respiration. *You can retain several pounds of water on any day that you skip your activity session.* So it is absolutely essential that you maintain your activity level during the transition to weight maintenance.

Drink Eight Glasses of Water Daily

I repeat these directions because drinking eight 8-fluid-ounce (225-ml) glasses of water daily is as important to weight maintenance as it is to weight loss. *Don't make the mistake of thinking that cutting back on water can prevent water retention.* Just the opposite! Adequate fluid intake stimulates the kidneys and helps to reduce water retention, and your body has to burn some calories in the process. In addition, adequate water intake will keep you regular and prevent the gain of a pound or two

154

of refuse weight. Always use water in place of the dietetic beverages you might have used in the past. This will help prevent the reawakening of your sweet tooth!

Remember Your Safe Fruit

Perhaps the one most important dietary change that has stayed with me in my twenty-two years of weight maintenance has been the substitution of fruit snacks and desserts for junk foods and other dense-calorie foods (foods high in fat and sugar). I have mentioned previously how I nibble on fruit all day long – it's many different kinds now, not just grapefruit, and it's really not quite all day long, just two or three snacks. Right now, in a large bowl, in plain sight in the kitchen, is a very attractive selection of grapes (two kinds), oranges, the crisp apples that have just come into season, bananas and grapefruit. I can eat to my heart's content, never be hungry, and never worry about being fat again.

I think you, too, will find weight maintenance simple if you substitute 'safe fruit' (that is, all fresh fruit) for your previous snack foods. Similarly, if you make a practice of eating all kinds of fruits, including dried fruits of all kinds, for desserts, instead of pies, cakes and biscuits, you will have your weight problem licked. Try it. Make a fruit substitution for processed snack foods and for most of your desserts (not all, of course – you will find that that isn't necessary in maintenance). I guarantee that you will feel a great deal better as well as make a success of maintenance when you substitute fruit for most of the 'junk food' that might now be in your diet. Fruit substitutions are great for your digestive processes and will go a long way to help you deal with your sweet tooth, if you have one. (For a deeper understanding of the 'junk-food' problem, and a definition of 'junk food,' see the additional discussion on pages 180–3.)

There you have it. I know that you have worked hard to lose the weight you have lost. Having been on the yo-yo myself during the first thirty-five years of my life, before I found out how to maintain my own weight loss, I know how frustrating it can be to let your weight start creeping up again. Follow my guidelines in making your transition to maintenance and you, too, will achieve permanent weight control. Here they are, once again, in summary form:

---

1. Increase Food Intake Slowly
2. Avoid Salt and Salty Foods
3. Eat Naturally Diuretic Fruits and Vegetables
4. Be Physically Active on a Daily Basis
5. Drink Eight 8-fluid-ounce (225-ml) Glasses of Water a Day
6. Make All Fruit Your 'Safe Fruit' and Substitute them for the Junk Food in Your Diet

---

Now we are ready to discuss the *permanent* metabolic benefits that you can obtain by making one very significant change in the quality of your diet.

HOW TO INCREASE YOUR METABOLIC NEEDS BY DIET

Although a calorie is a calorie in the laboratory, all calories are not the same to the human body.

For a long time even the best, most informed nutritionists claimed that it didn't matter where your calories came from. They said that all calories meant the same thing in terms of energy to the human body. Recent research disproves this statement.

Fat, for example, is easily converted to a form that your body can use for energy, and it's very easy to convert dietary fat to *body* fat for storage. Thus it is especially easy to gain weight if you happen to eat more fat than your daily energy requirements.

Carbohydrates and protein need a great deal more digestive work to convert their energy than does fat, and this results in a 'wasting' of some of the energy. That is,

156

while the calorie count for a carbohydrate or protein food may be accurate in your calorie book, your body doesn't end up using all the listed calories for energy in vital processes. Some of the calories are burned up and thrown off as heat.

Similarly, if you should overeat on either carbohydrates or protein, the body has to work much harder to change these nutrients into fat than it does to change dietary fat into body fat.

In fact, it takes between four and five times more energy to convert carbohydrate and protein to fat than to convert dietary fat to body fat.

Perhaps this will become intuitively evident if you just imagine a quantity equal to two teaspoons of fat or oil sitting in a dish next to a fairly large apple. Both food items will be about equal in calories as measured in the laboratory apparatus that determines how many calories they each contain (about 70 to 80 calories). But your body will have to work a lot harder to change the calories in that apple into body fat than it has to work to change the calories in that fat or oil into body fat.

It takes about 5 per cent of the energy content of dietary fat to convert it to body fat. It takes 20 to 25 per cent of the energy in carbohydrate and protein to turn these nutrients into body fat.

Obviously, if you substitute carbohydrate or protein calories for fat calories, you can end up eating many calories more and still not gain any weight. Even though your total calorie count is up, you have increased your metabolic needs by making the body work harder in the process of digestion. So, you don't gain any weight.

Other Values of a Diet Low in Fat and High in Dietary Fibre

There are two other factors that prevent weight gain when you increase complex carbohydrates in your diet (whole-grains, fruits, and vegetables) and decrease fats.

First, these foods, and only these foods, contain dietary fibre. Fibre is included in the calorie counts in your calo-

157

rie books, but the body doesn't digest these calories! Our stomachs and intestines don't have the appropriate enzymes to break down that fibre (other animals do). So, depending on the particular carbohydrate foods you eat, perhaps 10 per cent or even more of the total listed calories passes right through your system as roughage.

Second, as an extra metabolic benefit, the fibre contained in the complex carbohydrates will tangle up about 10 per cent of the dietary fat you eat, and that, too, will pass right through your system without being digested.

So, can you, in fact, 'increase your metabolism through eating'? If you substitute complex carbohydrates for fats in your diet, the answer is yes. If you cut your fat consumption in half and, instead, start eating fresh fruits and vegetables and whole-grain products, you will end up needing a couple of hundred extra calories each day, over and above what you are presently eating, just to maintain your present body weight. This amounts to a considerable increase in your total daily metabolic needs.

YOU HAVE NOW DISCOVERED THE MAGICAL CURE FOR OBESITY

I have taken a great many pages to explain the details of the Rotation Diet and to show you how you can make a transition to maintenance that will keep off all the weight you have lost in the last three weeks. If you have more weight to lose, after a week's or a month's break from dieting (it's up to you), go back on the diet.

When you reach your desired weight, you also know a magical cure for obesity that will prevent every single pound of lost fat from ever reaccumulating on your body. The magical cure for obesity – everything I have said in this book, in fact, that leads to permanent weight management – can be boiled down to five little words:

EAT LESS FAT AND WALK

In the next three chapters I will tell you some things you can do from both a practical and a psychological standpoint to put this magical cure to work on a permanent basis. I wish there were some way around it, but the magical cure is not a one-time remedy – it only works when you use it on a daily basis.

9

The Weight-Mastery Quiz: Testing Your Weight-Management Confidence

At the first meeting with new participants in the Vanderbilt Weight Management Program I do something that may seem a little strange to you: I give each person a delicious bar of milk chocolate for their very own! This is not meant to be some kind of sadistic joke. It is, in fact, the first step toward complete mastery over their appetite for foods that, in the past, have stimulated them to overeat.

I am going to show you how to achieve the same mastery for yourself, which you can do on your own by following the same procedures that we use in our programme. Before I do this, here is a quiz that will identify your most serious weight-management problems and the areas of weight management in which you have the least confidence in your ability to succeed.

WEIGHT-MASTERY QUIZ[*]

Directions: Here are descriptions of three typical situ-

[*] This quiz is based on a questionnaire developed by Dr David Schlundt, Department of Psychology, Vanderbilt University, Nashville, TN 37240, and

160

ations in each of six areas that present major weight-management problems for overweight persons. Imagine yourself in each situation (or think of one from your own experience that is similar to it, which you are likely to encounter on a frequent basis). Then, rate the confidence you have in your ability to carry out the behaviour that would lead to greater control over your weight problem. Use a scale that ranges from 0 to 100 per cent confidence. If you have complete lack of confidence in yourself – that is, you feel that you would never be able to act appropriately – give yourself a 0. If you think that you might respond correctly about 50 per cent of the time, give yourself a 50. And, if you feel that you have complete confidence, give yourself a rating of 100 per cent. For convenience in scoring, do not use intervals smaller than 5 per cent (50, 55, 60, etc.) in making your ratings.

CONFIDENCE

RATING

Problem Area Number 1: Resisting Temptation

1. It's 6:00 pm and you are in the middle of preparing a delicious dinner. How confident are you that you will wait until the meal is served before eating anything?   _____

2. You are spending an evening home alone and you are tempted to snack on a high-calorie food. How confident are you that you will resist the urge to snack?   _____

3. You are watching TV and some high-calorie snack foods (biscuits, crisps, soft drinks, beer, etc.) are brought into the room. How confident are you that you will watch TV without eating a high-calorie snack?   _____

---

adapted with his collaboration for research in the Vanderbilt Weight Management Program. You may obtain the complete research version by writing directly to Dr Schlundt and asking for the diet questionnaire. Please enclose international reply coupons for £1.10p to cover the postage and handling expenses.

Problem Area Number 2: Social Eating

4. You are having dinner with your family and someone picks up the platter that contains a favourite dish, says, 'Let me give you a little more,' and begins to fill your plate. How confident are you that you will be able to say 'No, thanks' and stick to your food plan? _____

5. You are at a party for a friend and someone offers you a slice of cake, or other high-calorie food that is not on your food plan. How confident are you that you will turn it down? _____

6. You enjoy a good celebration and are out to dinner at a fine restaurant with friends. How confident are you that you will celebrate without overeating? _____

Problem Area Number 3: Food Choice

7. You have finished dinner and the choice of fruit or cake (or some other high-calorie dessert) is available. How confident are you that you will choose fruit instead of cake? _____

8. You prefer to prepare high-calorie meals (flavouring with butter or other fat, frying foods, using sauces that are high in calories). How confident are you that you will prepare low-calorie dishes instead? _____

9. You are out to eat in a fine restaurant that offers you a choice of both low-calorie and high-calorie dishes at every course. How confident are you that you will make *only* low-calorie choices? _____

Problem Area Number 4: Exercise

10. You have begun an exercise programme but find that family, friends or business obligations begin to make demands and interfere. How confident are you that you will stick with your daily exercise programme? _____

162

11. You are asked by another person to go for a walk (or engage in some other physical activity), but you are feeling tired and kind of low. How confident are you that you will overcome these feelings and say yes to the walk (or other activity)?   _____

12. You plan to exercise after work today (or at the end of the day, before dinner) but you feel tired and hungry when the time arrives. How confident are you that you will exercise anyway?   _____

Problem Area Number 5: Overeating

13. You are at a party surrounded by tasty, high-calorie foods. You have already eaten more than you should, but are tempted to continue. How confident are you that you will stop eating right now?   _____

14. Instead of putting food away after a meal, you find yourself eating the leftovers. How confident are you that you will put the food away without eating any?   _____

15. You over-eat at supper when you are tired and hungry on returning home. How confident are you that you will not over-eat?   _____

Problem Area Number 6: Negative Emotions

16. You crave things to eat when you are lonely, blue or bored. How confident are you that you will find another way to cope with these feelings and not over-eat?   _____

17. You have just had an argument with a family member and you are upset and angry. You are standing in front of the refrigerator and you feel like eating everything in sight. How confident are you that you will find some other way to make yourself feel better?   _____

18. You are anxious and tense after a very trying day. You have the urge to get a chocolate bar (slice of pie, cake, etc.) How confident are you that you will find a more constructive way to calm down and cope with your feelings? _____

Scoring

Score yourself in the following way. How many of the three items within each of the six problem categories receive confidence ratings of 50 per cent or less, 55 to 70 per cent, 75 to 85 per cent or 90 per cent or greater? Write down the number in the chart below.

	NUMBER OF ITEMS RECEIVING:			
CATEGORY:	50% or less	55 to 70%	75 to 85%	90% or greater
Resisting Temptation	_____	_____	_____	_____
Social Eating	_____	_____	_____	_____
Food Choice	_____	_____	_____	_____
Exercise	_____	_____	_____	_____
Overeating	_____	_____	_____	_____
Negative Emotions	_____	_____	_____	_____

Interpreting Category Scores

If your ratings of any two of the three questions in a category fall within the two lowest levels of confidence, either the 50 per cent or less level or the 55 to 70 per cent level, this is a problem area that is likely to pose an extreme threat to your weight-management efforts.

Any category in which two of the three ratings fall *below* the highest level of confidence (90 per cent or greater) is likely to pose a less serious, but still significant, problem area.

Any category that receives two or more ratings in the 90 per cent or greater level of confidence is not, as a problem area considered in its entirety, likely to pose a major threat to weight management. However, a low confidence rating in any specific situation must be dealt with if that situation occurs with great frequency.

Interpreting Individual Items

Low ratings on individual questions can be very significant, even though your confidence in the two related situations within the same category of weight-management problems is higher. This is particularly true, as I have just indicated, if you must face that situation frequently. Anything less than a 90 per cent confidence rating in a situation that you must face almost daily, or even once a week, can be disastrous. It means that, no matter how competently you deal with other situations that threaten your control over your weight, you are repeatedly facing one that you don't know how to deal with. Your frequent failure in this situation keeps pushing you back a step for every step of progress made during the rest of the week. You end up playing with the same 5 pounds (2 kg) – losing and gaining, losing and gaining – and you can never reach your goal that way.

To increase your effectiveness in dealing with weight-management problems, we will work with individual situations. So, do the following.

Go back over your ratings for individual situations in the Weight-Mastery Quiz and pencil in two stars by any question that received a confidence rating of 50 per cent or less.

Then put one star by questions that received confidence ratings of 55 to 85 per cent.

You will use the techniques that I discuss in the next chapter to work on the double-starred situations first, if you have any, and the single-starred situations next.

Our goal is to boost your confidence in all areas of weight management to the 90 per cent confidence level or higher. Once you reach the 90 per cent confidence level in all the situations that present weight-management problems, you can feel much more certain that you will be able to manage your weight in the future. And I'm happy to say that it doesn't take *absolute* perfection (which you might have inferred from one of my previous statements above). For example, you will not need to succeed at all times in resisting temptation, but

165

you will need to feel secure that, in the main, you can succeed when you need to. You just need to get from a confidence level of 50 or 60 per cent up to 90 per cent. Then you will be able to engage in the sort of 'controlled bingeing' that poses no threat to your weight.

This is where the chocolate bar that I give new participants in the Vanderbilt Weight Management Program can play its part in the development of a sense of weight-management mastery. The bar is symbolic of all the foods that are difficult to resist right now and that tempt you to make a poor food choice or to overeat.

In the next two chapters I'll show you how you, too, can use a sample of the junk food that most often tempts you to overeat to increase your own sense of weight-management mastery.

10

Four Steps to Mastery: Building Weight-Management Confidence

In order to make the best use of the procedures I am going to describe in this chapter, you really do need to have a chocolate bar or some other form of junk food at hand. However, whether or not you have already gone out to purchase that junk food is not as important at this moment as your understanding of why such foods pose a problem for weight management, and how you can learn to deal with them. If, after you read this chapter, you feel that what I have described might be helpful, then you can purchase your chocolate bar and get to work developing a new and higher level of weight-management confidence.

I want to discuss chocolate as my example because so many persons have trouble dealing with chocolate bars or other chocolate-flavoured dessert foods. And it's no wonder that they do. A chocolate bar is not a 'normal food' – it's a 'supernormal food'. It's a scientific blending of the flavours that humans like best. Fat is its primary ingredient (60 per cent of the calories in chocolate come from fat), followed by sugar, perhaps a pinch of salt to bring out the flavour and, of course, the chocolate, which,

167

unless blended with fat and sugar, tastes absolutely terrible. It's the creative blending of chocolate with fat and sugar that enables chocolate to work its magic.

Chocolate-flavoured foods, as well as other sweet and fatty dessert foods, are designed to turn on appetite even when your hunger has been satisfied. When such foods appear, you begin to salivate, and your pancreas begins to secrete extra insulin in preparation for dealing with the sugar in the food. Both of these reactions actually make you feel hungry, even though you have already eaten. Indeed, every cell in your body seems to turn on all over again and scream, 'Eat, eat!'

Sweets and most other foods that fall into what is called the 'junk-food' category are very hard to resist because of their 'supernormal' status. If you have a choice of one of these foods (chocolate, cake, pie, biscuits) or a more natural food, such as fruit, the supernormal food is almost certain to win. Thus it becomes very hard for an over-weight person to exercise an appropriate choice of foods for weight control when 'supernormal' foods are present to compete with normal foods at any given meal or snack time.

After I hand out the bar of chocolate to our group of weight-management participants, I ask them whether they can, even in their imagination, see themselves doing exactly what it will take to live with that chocolate (or whatever food most tempts them to over-eat) and not eat it when it is constantly present in their environment. You might take a moment and do the same thing: can you, in your imagination, see yourself in situations with all of the foods that tempt you most doing exactly what you are going to need to do for the rest of your life to control your weight?

If you can't even *imagine* yourself doing what you need to deal with these situations effectively, how can you ever expect to do it in reality?

Because it is a natural physiological reaction to 'turn on' in the presence of 'supernormal' foods, the very best strategy for permanent weight management is to control their presence, that is, rarely allow yourself to be in their presence so that you do not have to battle constantly with temptation.

But such control over yourself or your environment is not always possible. I know many of you will have families that bring junk food in unexpectedly, and you may feel that the members of your family who do not have a problem with their weight should not have to be inconvenienced by your desire to eliminate junk food from the home. Besides, wouldn't it feel great to know that you can control your 'binging' without gaining weight? Although we normally do not keep quantities of high-calorie foods around the house recently we have been celebrating Christmas with house guests and dinner parties. We have one of my wife's incomparable chocolate cheesecakes in the refrigerator, one of my daughter's delicious pumpkin pies on the kitchen table and a quart of my own homemade rum-raisin ice cream in the freezer. (The ice cream is pretty good, too.) Twenty-two years ago I might have overeaten and gained weight with all these delicious desserts around the house, but not today. I am enjoying these creations – every single one of them – but in moderation. You, too, can learn to enjoy the foods you like best, in quantities that pose no danger for weight control, by practising the four steps to weight-management mastery.

FOUR STEPS TO WEIGHT-MANAGEMENT MASTERY

You will find it helpful to have one of your own problem areas in mind as I discuss the four steps to weight-management mastery. So go back over the results of the Weight-Mastery Quiz. Pick out one of the areas in which you have the least confidence in your weight-management ability. This will be the first area of personal concern that you will work on. Keep this problem area in mind to compare with my illustrations as I discuss the techniques.

We use a four-step process to increase your confidence to the maximum. Normally, you will complete all four steps to assure mastery, and because the procedure for gaining confidence and achieving mastery in weight management is very similar to the techniques used by highly accomplished actors, concert musicians and champion athletes, I am going to use some analogies from these fields to illustrate what I mean.

First, you will need to ask yourself what it is that you need to know and do in order to achieve weight-management mastery in the problem area you have identified. If you don't know what you need to know and do, you can't even take the first step. Sometimes we think we know what we should do to solve a particular weight-management problem, but when we try it, we meet unforeseen consequences. In the past, you may have given up on your efforts to change or control a potential weight-gain situation, but not this time. When you are confronted by unforeseen consequences it simply means that these consequences are your real problems and that you may need some additional skills or knowledge to deal with them.

Second, you need to be able to see yourself clearly, in your imagination, carrying out successful weight-management behaviour, just as Olympic champions see themselves performing to perfection in the heat of competition. Champions don't become champions if they imagine themselves failing before they even take to the field!

Third, you may find it helpful to set up rehearsal situations in order to practise what you are learning, just as athletes practise and perfect their skills in protected, 'practice' situations before they enter their tournaments. (This step is not always possible, and can sometimes be eliminated, but it should be used whenever possible.)

Fourth, you must expose yourself to the situation that poses the problem and test yourself in reality, just as the athlete does by entering competitions. Perhaps you start with those situations that are easiest to handle and work up to the big time, as musicians and actors do by taking their shows on the road and doing 'warm-ups' before hitting Broadway or London's West End.

The relative importance of each of these steps varies with the situation. In addition, as you practise my suggestions, you should expect to develop your own unique approach to using this four-step strategy. My hints will show you how to get started. In the end, you will be your own best weight-management problem solver.

The methods for dealing with all kinds of food problems, such as resisting temptation and making appropriate food choices, are similar, so I will explain the methods for all food-related problems using one illustration. Then I will show you how to apply the four steps to the exercise situation.

A short workbook section is the basis of the next chapter. In this chapter I will show you how to practise our four steps to weight-management mastery in the presence of your choice of junk food. It will help you to reach at least the 90 per cent confidence level in dealing with that food. And it will show you how to use the procedure in each of the personally relevant situations on which you have scored below 90 per cent confidence in the Weight-Mastery Quiz.

First, some illustrations.

PROBLEM AREAS SUCH AS RESISTING TEMPTATION, SOCIAL EATING AND POOR FOOD CHOICE

Step 1: Necessary Knowledge and Skills

It is most likely that you have some idea of what it will take to deal with these problem situations, especially if you have read one of the innumerable behavioural approaches to weight control that are already available, or if you have taken part in a weight-management programme such as Weight Watchers. If you haven't found it possible to implement what you have learned, and, unfortunately, our research shows that over 85 per cent of people who have been in behavioural weight-management programmes do not continue to use even one of the control strategies that they learned, these four steps to mastery will help you.

Let's assume that you are in one of the situations described in the Weight-Mastery Quiz. To make it difficult, we will choose a situation that does not permit you to avoid being in the presence of tasty foods.

You are preparing a tasty, full-course dinner.

The question is: what can you do to prevent yourself from nibbling while you are preparing the food?

Consider some of the possible strategies. If you have allowed yourself to become over-hungry by skipping meals earlier in the day, do you want to nibble on a free vegetable? If you are not really hungry but just find that your appetite turns on in the presence of good food, will you chew gum or keep a toothpick in your mouth? Wear a surgical mask? I know some people who wear surgical masks every time they cook a tempting dinner!

Could you just brave it out by imagining how each bite will end up on your hips and keep a size 16 or 18 instead of a perfect 10 or 12?

I am sure you can think of some additional possibilities for preventing eating at this time. It's up to you to decide what substitute behaviour or mental attitude might, with practice, become strong enough to defeat the urge to eat high-calorie foods unnecessarily.

Then you go to Step 2 and do something you have probably neglected to do in the past.

Step 2: Using Fantasy and Your Imagination

Now comes the key – something you have probably never considered doing, nor have you realized its importance. It is being able to see yourself clearly, in your imagination, carrying out your intentions to perfection. I want to elaborate on the importance of this step.

I know that there are many areas in your life in which you are a success. When it comes to performing in these areas, you never think twice — you have no doubt at all about your ability to do what it takes to be successful. If you took a moment to think through what you do in these other areas (even if it is just making a bed or, at perhaps a more complex level, getting your professional jobs done) you would see yourself in your mind's eye carrying out appropriate acts. But I know that you will have difficulty seeing yourself being this successful with weight-management behaviour, at first.

Having given many concerts in my first career as a violinist, and having become a pretty fair tennis player at a later age, I know what mental work it takes to build self-confidence and then to expose yourself in the arena for the true test of your ability. Actors, musicians and champion athletes all visualize themselves on the set, the stage or the field, going through the motions that lead to success. We learn to do this as children, and this mental activity is an essential part of practice, just as essential as the physical part. If the actor, musician or athlete has never learned how to fill his mind with success fantasies, it is quite likely that he will have an anticipation of failure that can become a self-fulfilling prophecy. You may be in this latter situation when it comes to weight management — you expect failure and you get it!

Unfortunately, we tend to forget the role of success fantasies as we grow older. Perhaps we become accustomed to our limitations and, for lack of knowledge or skill, fail at things, such as controlling our weight, that we could really learn to master. Perhaps we feel sheepish about fantasizing, as though it is not a grown-up thing to do.

It's time to start putting your childhood gift for fantasy and imagination back to work again!

So pick an approach to mastering those eating urges when you are preparing a meal, and take some time to imagine yourself being completely successful in your performance. It is important to visualize yourself clearly in the situation, actually experiencing the difficulty that you have faced in the past. Then, visualize yourself going through the specific actions that will lead to mastery, and boldly carry them out in your mind's eye.

173

Let me emphasize that *attention to specific behaviour* is very important in this fantasy process. For example, champion tennis players put their major effort into visualizing perfect strokes and their plan of attack. They spend much less time dreaming of the trophy! This is where most persons who attempt to use fantasy as an aid to change make their crucial mistake. They dream about the end product, whereas they should be concentrating on the *means* to that end. As a concert violinist it was one thing to dream about being a success on the stage, but I soon learned that the most profitable time had to be spent mentally rehearsing the bowing and fingering of every selection I was to perform, and hearing the music I was working on in my mind's ear as I watched the score flow by my closed eyes. Working mentally with a great deal of attention to detail, I was able to increase my technical security and I never had a memory slip.

You, too, will build confidence in the technique as you practise, and as you continue with the next steps in the mastery process. And by the way, the time when you are out walking alone, or engaging in any other solitary physical activity, is one of the best times for productive fantasy. That's when you can engage in the mental practice that is necessary to learning to control your weight. Soon you may find that you are applying mental practice or rehearsal to many other things in your life. Today, being alone in some physical activity has become my best time for mental practice, and it makes going for a jog in the woods my best time for preparing classes and speeches and outlining articles and books. Try it – being alone during a walk or a jog may become your most productive and creative time as well.

Step 3: Setting Up a Rehearsal Situation

Before you put yourself to a major test, it is always good to practise in one that minimizes the difficulties so that you can build your skills.

In the food-preparation situation, practise making a small meal, or preparing only one simple dish. In addition, begin with practice at a time when the temptations to eat inappropriately are slight. Making breakfast, lunch or a snack is a good time. After going through what is required in your imagination, set up your kitchen in a way that will minimize the temptation to nibble (don't have a large array of particularly tempting foods around), make your meal, carry it to the table and sit down to eat in accordance with your plan. Review what you did (and did *not* do), and get it firmly established in your mind so that, if asked, you could repeat every detail accurately.

One of the best ways to build up your strength to resist eating in this situation (and in others that I will describe in a moment) is to invite a friend over to observe you as you demonstrate your procedures for gaining control. Explain what you are about to do and imagine that your friend is your coach. Then, practise in front of your coach.

And don't forget to give yourself some credit for success. Have you ever seen the raised fist of the champion tennis player after a great shot? You need to do a little of the same as you accumulate your weight-management victories.

Step 4: Exposing Yourself to the Real Test

After a few successes in your rehearsal situations, you are ready for the real thing. Before you try it, see yourself as a success in your imagination, going through the entire process from beginning to end. And, as in rehearsal, it may prove helpful to invite someone in to watch, explaining beforehand what you are about to do. Public commitment helps increase the incentive to succeed. For example, continuing with the food-preparation situation, announce that tonight is the night for putting your approach to preventing nibbling to work. Then, invite members of the family to drop in and observe you acting like a weight-management champion. And invite *them* to be your food tasters!

Additional Examples for Other Eating Situations

As I indicated, you must become your own best problem

175

solver, but I may be able to assist with some other hints.

In the category of *resisting temptation*, when you feel the urge to eat in the evening, or at weekends when you have nothing else pressing to do for a few moments, or when those snack foods are likely to pop up in front of you as you watch TV, it is good to have some alternative activity available to replace eating or a substitute food that you have practised turning to in your imagination and rehearsal. We practise saying 'No, thanks' in our groups when we work on *social eating* situations. First we use our imagination, then we rehearse and role-play with real, tempting high-calorie foods that I bring to the group meetings for this special purpose. Then we send our participants home to set up practice situations.

With *food choice*, you might imagine that cake and fruit are both available as desserts, either at home or in a restaurant. Then, fantasize yourself executing the behaviour you desire for weight control. Get closer to reality by actually buying yourself that symbolic chocolate bar, set it out on a table together with a piece of any kind of fresh fruit that you like, pick up the fruit and put the bar away (it is better out of sight!) and eat your fruit.

The food-choice situation is one that is helped by mentally rehearsing the rewards of a correct choice. These rewards are often postponed to the future and they are not as naturally strong as the taste of cake, biscuits or chocolate. Although a correct choice of fruit rather than junk food would either get you closer to your weight goal, keep you at the desirable weight, or simply help you stay healthier, a 'supernormal' food is a very strong physiological stimulus to eating. If it is present right in front of you, it can overwhelm all other considerations – that is, unless you put thoughts of future consequences right at the forefront of your consciousness and then move with dispatch to a correct choice.

Finally, with *over-eating*, most of us have the urge to throw in the towel the moment we make the first deviation from our eating vows. It is very important that you begin to see yourself in a different light. Yes, it is possible to *begin* to over-eat and *still stop yourself*. Work through the familiar fantasy steps that you have used in the other eating problem areas: imagine yourself beginning to over-eat, and then exerting control. It is most important that you see yourself returning immediately to your eating and activity programme, so that one skirmish lost does not lead to losing the entire war.

One of the best rehearsal strategies for learning to deal with over-eating is to buy a food item that frequently tempts you to over-eat, in a single portion, and set up a situation in which you can eat it slowly and with pleasure. It helps to do things like this before an audience as you talk through what you are experiencing and doing – so invite a friend to be with you as you practise. Be sure to allow up to twenty minutes for observing yourself and your reactions after you finish eating, so that you can see how your appetite begins to turn off and how the urge to continue disappears. Then store the image of the experience in your memory so you can draw on it as needed.

MAINTAINING YOUR EXERCISE PROGRAMME

What do you need to do when every bone in your body seems to say it would be so much more pleasant to sit down after a hard day, with a snack at your side, rather than go for a walk?

What can you do to deal with a feeling of fatigue when the feeling, in fact, doesn't result from physical exertion? When, instead, it is more mental than physical?

How will you deal with the demands of daily living when each and every one of them begins to seem more important than taking that walk or going to your dance or exercise class?

Step 1: Choosing the Strategies that Can Lead to Success

As I have said in a previous chapter, nothing proves to be a greater remedy for fatigue and sluggish feelings than the very physical activity you have the urge to resist.

Once you have become an active person, you will still have a resistance to exercise at odd times, but you will be able to envision the refreshing and relaxing feelings that follow activity. Getting this anticipatory feeling up front in your imagination can become all the incentive you need to start.

In addition, learning to say no to outside demands and putting your health priorities at their deserved levels, for just forty-five minutes or so a day, are, in my opinion, an inalienable right! I think you, too, should cultivate this attitude and then consider what it will take to negotiate with others to obtain the time and support.

Step 2: Using Fantasy and Your Imagination

You start by imagining that one of the situations has occurred, for example, a fatigue situation, and that you have developed a plan. You then imagine how you will feel when you are really, really tired and resistant, but know that the feelings stem from frustrations you encountered at work or result simply from the stress of being forced to work sitting down all day. (The sitting position, when it is necessary for most of your workday, causes a significant amount of physical stress, especially to the lower back and shoulders, and leads to a great deal of fatigue.) Then, clearly see yourself overcoming these resistant feelings and setting out for a walk. Just imagine how it will feel to get out of the house and take a breath of fresh air. Or imagine how it will feel when no one knows where you are and cannot bother you for forty-five minutes. Imagine the feeling you will have when you finish – both physical and mental. And, once again, in your imagination, give yourself the congratulations you deserve for having been able to accomplish a most important weight-management activity.

Step 3: Rehearsal

The practice behaviour I am about to suggest may seem paradoxical, but it works very well in developing an amazing amount of control over your feelings. It has, in fact, been used as a therapeutic procedure with top-flight athletes who were having trouble performing at peak level.

The next time you are about to go for a walk, or engage in any other physical activity, hesitate for just a moment before you begin. Now, even though you are feeling full of energy, imagine instead that you are feeling very tired and not at all in the mood for activity. Go ahead and do it – turn on your very *worst* feelings. Then, after just a few moments, turn on your energy and begin your exercise with vigour. You will find that you have a great deal of ability to switch your feelings on and off. Switch back and forth, and see how it feels. Then, the next time you feel tired and sluggish, turn on your vigour switch, get moving, and in moments you will feel truly invigorated.

Similarly, if you have problems negotiating for personal time, imagine and rehearse what it will take to bargain for what you need with your family or with your boss. I know some very busy (and very successful) people who felt that they had to work incessantly. They had luncheon meetings and after-work business cocktail meetings every day, and they carried their briefcases loaded with work home every night. If you are in the same circumstances, your first step is to imagine that change is possible, followed by a little rehearsal, which might include talking over a strategy for changing the situation with a friend or business associate.

Step 4: Testing Yourself in the Real Situation

After you have gone through the steps above, you are ready for the real test. You now have a good strategy for dealing with fatigue. Use it and you will achieve virtual perfection in handling all fatigue problems (but remember not to force yourself into activity when you are ill, especially when running a temperature).

When it comes to negotiating for personal time, most of the people I have worked with have found that they were their own worst enemies. You don't have to work every waking hour, and you can get the cooperation of your family if you approach family responsibilities as a family sharing proposition. Begin with the attitude that you will cooperate with others so that they can get what they need to lead happy and fulfilling lives, and that they, in turn, owe you help in getting forty-five minutes for yourself and your health.

Best of all, you are more than likely to discover that an activity break, even a brief one, at some point during your actual working hours will lead to greater productivity and job satisfaction. It works so well that some corporations are beginning to make activity breaks a required part of the working day. Why not work fewer hours, get more done, and enjoy your work more, all at the same time? If you cannot manage longer periods of time, at least experiment with some fifteen-minute work breaks. You may have to force yourself to take these breaks at first. But after a while you may be quite surprised at the results, in both productivity and good feelings.

A NOTE ON JUNK FOOD

Before you begin to use the workbook and the four steps to weight-management mastery, I think you will be able to raise your motivation to deal with junk foods to a maximum if you understand what a junk food really is.

A 'junk food' is a food that supplies a larger percentage of your total daily need for calories (the amount it takes to maintain your weight) than it does of the Recommended Dietary Allowance of any single essential vitamin or mineral.

Read some food labels and you will see exactly what I mean. For example, take the label from a chocolate bar. It is, say, a 1¾ ounce (50 g) bar, which you can pick up anywhere. The label may say that it contains 230 calories. If you are a woman who needs about 1800 calories a day to maintain your weight at the present time, 230 calories is almost 13 per cent (actually 12.7 per cent) of

180

the calories you need to maintain your weight. However, the most that this chocolate bar contains of any one essential vitamin or mineral is just 8 per cent of the Recommended Daily Amounts of calcium (because of the milk content). In other words, junk foods contain relatively more weight-maintaining calories than they do health-sustaining essential nutrients such as vitamins and minerals.

If you will think about it for just a minute, I think you will see that, if your diet is composed to a large extent of junk foods, you will reach (or go beyond) your required number of weight-maintenance calories *but you will still be undernourished in terms of essential vitamins and minerals.* Although I cannot prove this point, I think another reason that many people may be stimulated to over-eat when their diets contain many junk foods is that their bodies are pushing them to take in enough food to meet its nutritional needs in vitamins and minerals.

A serving of a truly nourishing food contains a larger percentage of at least three or four of the essential vitamins and minerals – those nutrients you need to maintain health and fitness – than it does of your total daily need for calories.

Now consider how you can ruin a perfectly nourishing food. Take a potato, for example. A 3½ ounce (90 g) baked potato contains about 90 calories (compared with the 230 calories in just 1¾ ounces of milk chocolate). Ninety calories is only 5 per cent of the total calories that it takes to maintain your weight (at 1800 calories per day). But that 3½ ounce baked potato *is a powerhouse when it comes to nourishment.* For each 5 per cent of your total daily calories, it contains (based on the Recommended Daily Amount) approximately:

7% of your daily protein needs
8% of your phosphorus needs
10% of your thiamine needs
13% of your niacin needs
33% of your vitamin C needs
plus about 25% of the suggested minimum for potas-

181

sium and a broad array of traces of other vitamins and minerals. (That potassium content makes it excellent for helping to prevent water retention, since the potato contains almost no sodium and a high potassium-to-sodium ratio helps the kidneys eliminate excess water from the system.)

Now, look what happens when you peel and fry this otherwise nutritious potato and convert it into chips: a similar 3½ ounce (90 g) serving will add up to approximately *275 calories!* You have added over 180 calories' worth of fat! And you will have almost succeeded in converting that poor potato into a junk food. In a 90-calorie serving (that's less than 1.2 ounces (35 g) or just about three or four little strips, rather than a whole baked potato), you will obtain only:

    3.5% of your daily protein needs
    4.6% of your phosphorus needs
    4% of your thiamine needs
    7.7% of your niacin needs
    11% of your vitamin C needs
    and only about 11% of the suggested minimum for potassium.

In just about every way, except for fat calories, you cut the nutritional value of a potato by about two-thirds when you eat chips. EVERY TIME YOU EAT FRIED FOODS, THIS IS WHAT YOU ARE DOING: YOU ARE TRIPLING THE CALORIES PER SERVING OR, FOR EQUAL CALORIE SERVINGS, CUTTING THE OTHER NUTRITIONAL VALUE OF YOUR FOOD BY ABOUT TWO-THIRDS!

Begin to read some of the labels on those foods that tempt you to over-eat. Check all dessert and snack foods, including salty, rather than sweet, snacks. You will see that in just about every case they contain a larger percentage of your total daily calorie needs than they contain of even *one* vitamin or mineral. By eating a large amount of junk food, you may be keeping yourself fat *and malnourished* at the same time!

Because we vary in our daily need for calories at maintenance levels, I suggest you use the following rule of thumb for determining whether a food falls into the 'junk' category: Examine the label and simply calculate whether it contains 5 per cent of the RDA of at least one vitamin or mineral for every 100 calories. Thus, if a serving of some snack, according to the label of the package, is 100 calories, it ought to have 5 per cent of at least one essential vitamin or mineral listed; if a serving is 200 calories, it ought to have 10 per cent of at least one vitamin or mineral.

Really nutritious foods that you can use as snacks, such as the grapefruit that I used as my safe fruit, have a much higher percentage of essential vitamins and minerals than they do of weight-maintenance calories. For example, 100 calories' worth of grapefruit (I prefer pink varieties) contains 7% of the RDA for iron, 22% of vitamin A, 12% of thiamine, 5% of riboflavin, 5% of niacin, 192% of vitamin C and about 14% of potassium. And since grapefruit contains virtually no sodium, that high potassium content makes it an excellent food for persons who tend to retain water.

If you have difficulty making good food choices, I hope these words will increase your motivation to reduce permanently the junk food in your diet and begin to make more nutritious substitutions for snacks and desserts. I also hope that I have motivated you to make some of the other changes I suggest, such as increasing your activity level if you are a sedentary person. If so, I think using the workbook for the four steps to weight-management mastery, which I present in the next chapter, will help you maintain the initiative you have taken in beginning the Rotation Diet.

11

A Weight-Mastery Workbook

I know you are going to be reluctant to do this, especially after my discussion of junk food at the end of the previous chapter, but you must go to the shops and buy a chocolate bar or a packet of biscuits, or whatever other junk food that has, in the past, been part of your weight-management problem. Pick your most-difficult-to-deal-with junk food!

But before you purchase your junk food, rate yourself on the following question, just as you did on the Weight-Mastery Quiz in Chapter 9:

> You have enough of your favourite junk food in the house to last you (and your family) a month. How confident are you that you will be able to live with that junk food for a full month and not eat any? Let me phrase the question another way: *What is the probability that you will be able to keep that food in the house for a full month and not eat any?*
>
> Your rating:_____

How did you rate yourself? Zero per cent? Fifty per cent?

From now on, after you complete the first exercise I am about to describe, this will all be different.

After you have used the four steps to weight-management mastery with the junk food that you will purchase as your tool and your symbol, your relationship with junk food will be completely different. You are going to end up at least 90 per cent confident of your ability to manage your appetite for such foods.

An increase in confidence to deal with junk food can have a tremendous impact for the better on your ability to control your weight, because, if you are anything like participants in the Vanderbilt Weight Management Program, the increase in rated confidence is closely translated into action. Suppose you have just rated yourself at the 50 per cent confidence level. An increase to 90 per cent confidence means that you will be successful in resisting junk food (if you choose to) four out of the five times that you might previously have eaten some (or more than 'some').

Let me remind you once again that we are not after abstinence. We are aiming for an increase in control to the point where you can decide, with great confidence, on when and where it will be time for a 'controlled binge'.

For this first exercise to be of maximum value to you, you must not use any junk foods that are already in the house. You must use some food that is especially purchased for this exercise, so that you can clearly see the role that your state of mind can play in controlling eating temptations. This will become clear to you as you go through the exercise in a way that cannot be communicated through reading about it. So, make a special trip and buy your special, 'symbolic' junk food. Trust me – take my word that it is best if you do it this way and do it!

HOW TO USE YOUR SPECIAL JUNK FOOD AS A TOOL AND A SYMBOL OF YOUR ABILITY TO DEAL WITH TEMPTATION

Step 1: What Would You Need to Do to Succeed in Not Eating This Food during the Next Month?

Perhaps the first thing that occurs to you is to not buy it in the first place! Avoiding temptation is a number one strategy and one worth using as a matter of course, considering the natural physiological reactions to the sight of 'supernormal' foods. But not buying the food or giving it away (which many of our participants in the Vanderbilt Weight Management Program suggest as a means of avoiding temptation) would defeat the purpose of the exercise. Your objective is to increase your ability to have junk foods in your immediate environment and not eat them in amounts that would lead to a weight gain.

In the space below, list the things that you might possibly do that would prevent you from eating this food during the next month. Here are a few suggestions that we discuss in our weight-management groups:

Hide it – get it out of sight.

Wrap it in 'plain brown paper' and stick it in the freezer.

Put it out in plain sight and practise sitting next to it without eating it.

Review carefully the effects that over-indulgence in junk food will have on your weight.

Think about the effects not eating it and substituting a more nutritious food will have on your weight and your health.

Think about how you feel after you eat junk food and how much more positive you will feel about yourself if you don't, or if you eat only a planned amount.

Think about using it in a 'controlled binge' after you finish twenty-one days on the Rotation Diet.

186

What do you think will work for you? (It helps to write down your thoughts about potential strategies.)

_____

_____

_____

_____

Step 2: Use Your Imagination in Mental Rehearsal

This is a key step that many people, otherwise well versed in all the behavioural eating-control strategies, fail to use. Before you attempt to implement any strategy that might help you control your inclination to eat this junk food during the next month, go through the entire process involved in implementing your approach very carefully in your imagination. See the process through in great detail from beginning to end. Experience the difficulties in your fantasy, if you anticipate any, but, by all means, see yourself as being ultimately successful, and celebrate that success in your imagination.

Be sure to visualize yourself as being in the presence of this food, at least for some certain limited time, before you imagine yourself getting it out of sight, and see yourself successfully resisting any urge to eat it. Feel the urge, if you anticipate any, but visualize yourself doing whatever it will take not to eat any.

Then, as part of another scene, try visualizing yourself eating your junk food at a time when you have planned to include some such foods in your diet, for example, after three weeks on the Rotation Diet. If you are at all like me, I suspect that you will want to enjoy some dessert foods at appropriate times, without losing control. So, it is valuable to work such situations into your mental rehearsal.

Step 3: Physical Rehearsal and Practice

After you have had a session or two of mental practice in which you have planned how you will deal with your junk food, do it in reality. Do exactly what you have been rehearsing in your fantasy. This is another instance in

187

which it can help to have an audience, or to announce your intention publicly, and then do it! Even if it all sounds crazy to your friends, you will increase your ability to deal with junk food if you talk about what you are doing with other people, and if you illustrate what you are doing in reality.

And remember that one of the most important things you can do, when junk food is not in your food plan, is to be able to say, unequivocally, 'No, thanks' when someone offers you some junk food. Using the junk food you have purchased as a prop, ask a friend to offer it to you and practise saying 'No, thanks' until it becomes automatic – at least as easy to say as, 'Well, I really shouldn't – ' as you used to say, when you previously reached for the junk food and were about to 'blow it'.

Step 4: Testing Yourself in the Real World

BEFORE GOING ON TO THIS STEP, REPEAT THE QUESTION TO YOURSELF THAT I INTRODUCED AT THE BEGINNING OF THIS CHAPTER IN THIS SLIGHTLY MODIFIED FORM: How confident are you that you can be in the physical presence of your symbolic junk food, or any other tempting junk food, and not eat it? You are ready for the real-world test when you can answer that question with a 90 per cent level of confidence.

Keep repeating Steps 1 to 3 until you reach at least a 90 per cent confidence level.

Then, put yourself in the line of fire intentionally. Plan to go out with family or friends to any party or restaurant where junk food is a standard part of the menu, or put yourself in the presence of junk food in any convenient way, such as going to a tea shop or an ice cream parlour. Have your rehearsed strategies clearly in your mind. See if you can plan a situation with minimal temptation at first. However, if you have worked through the other three steps, you will probably be able to deal with just about any junk food temptation.

When you have worked through this exercise with

your symbolic junk food, I think you will see why I wanted you to purchase it specially. From now on, every time you purchase any sort of food that previously incited you to overeat, you will purchase it in the frame of mind you have cultivated with your symbolic food. I think you will find that you have developed something that, in the past, you might have called *willpower*. But you will also find that controlling your appetite for such foods will not feel like the struggle you might have associated with that word. You now have a new, and well-practised, repertoire of responses for resisting junk-food temptations and making better food choices.

USING THE FOUR STEPS TO WEIGHT-MANAGEMENT MASTERY IN YOUR OWN MOST RELEVANT SITUATIONS

So much for the junk food practice. Now let's get on with one of your own double-starred situations (or single-starred situations if you do not have any marked with double stars).

Go back to the Weight-Mastery Quiz and choose one of the scenes about which you are least confident. In the space below, rewrite the scene so that it is an accurate representation of what you actually face. Describe the scene in whatever detail is necessary for completeness – who is there, what the room looks like, how it feels, etc. The more detailed and complete, the better.

_____
_____
_____
_____
_____

Before going any further, consider once again how confident you are that you can carry through appropriate weight-management behaviour in this situation and write it down in the space below.

Confidence rating in your ability to carry out an appropriate weight-management behaviour in the above situation is _____

Now you are ready to lead yourself in the four-step plan to weight-management mastery.

Step 1: Write Down All the Things that Occur to You that Might Help You Deal Successfully with This Situation

If you have trouble developing a plan of action, reread the last two chapters for some hints.

_____
_____
_____
_____
_____

Step 2: Practise Your Solutions in Your Imagination

See yourself performing in exactly the way it will take to be a complete success. Remember, it's the *means* to success that you must mentally rehearse – each and every step – and this is different from 'dreaming' about being successful. Take time to work on it, every day if necessary. We tell participants in the Vanderbilt groups to spend at least five minutes a day for a week, if necessary. And, interestingly enough, just five minutes a day seems to be enough.

Step 3: Set Up a Practice Situation

Insofar as is possible, set up some physical rehearsals or practice sessions. This step is not always possible, but use my musician, actor and sports analogies of Chapter 10 to help you design whatever warm-ups you can think of.

Step 4: Test Yourself in the Real World

Before going on to Step 4, ask yourself the confidence question once again to determine whether you have reached the 90 per cent level. That's the time to proceed with the real-world test. Keep everything you have been working on in the forefront of your consciousness as you intentionally subject yourself to the troublesome situation.

DEALING WITH THE UNFORESEEN CONSEQUENCES OF CHANGE

The moment you try to change anything about yourself or your dealings with other people, something unforeseen happens. You may fail to be able to carry out your practised intentions because you have not correctly identified the problem!

Think about this for a moment: the things that happen to you as you go about making changes which prevent you from carrying out your intentions, are what constitute your real problems. I will give two examples.

A simple one first, to illustrate the point: you eat too fast and you are told that it is helpful to slow down by putting your knife and fork down between bites, or for two minutes in the middle of a meal. You put them down and then what happens? You don't know what to do with your hands; you don't know what to say to the people around who are staring at you; you get very fidgety waiting for two minutes to pass. What's the real problem? It's learning to deal with what happens after you put the knife and fork down!

A more difficult one: you are a woman and agree with me that you have a right to forty-five minutes' exercise a day for your personal well-being and you rehearse what you will say to your mate to negotiate for this time. He agrees in principle, but he pouts or acts surly every time it is his turn to take over the family responsibilities to help you accomplish your objectives. This upsets you and leads to an argument. Your problem is not knowing how to deal with a sulky husband.

When unforeseen consequences arise as a result of your efforts to make changes, DON'T ACCEPT DEFEAT. Just redefine the problem and put it back into my four-step weight-mastery procedure. Think about possible solutions to these unforeseen consequences, go through the three preliminary steps before attempting to deal with the situation in reality, and TRY AGAIN – AND AGAIN, if necessary.

And keep telling yourself one indisputable fact: the difference between successful people and unsuccessful people is that successful people never give up!

12

Alternative Menus for the Rotation Diet

I asked our nutrition consultant to the Vanderbilt Weight Management Program, Ms Rachel Willis, RD, to design some alternative menus for the Rotation Diet to show you the interest and variety that you can add to a healthful weight-reduction and weight-maintenance diet. Except for breakfasts, which are often the same, I asked her to be as different as possible from the standard menus in the design of the meals and in her style of cooking, and, of course, to maximize the nutritional value of the food selections at every calorie level of the Rotation Diet plan. She has come up with some great recipes, illustrating styles of food preparation from all over the world, while using tricks for saving calories and enhancing flavours in everything from soups and salads to main courses and some great desserts.

You can choose a complete day from the Alternative Menus to substitute for any equivalent day in the standard menus on your second time around (Week 3) of the Rotation Diet. Just make sure you are at the appropriate calorie level. Several days at each level of the Rotation Diet, from 600 to 1800 calories, are included among the Alternative Menus.

If you do not feel like sticking with any full day in its entirety, you can mix and match your own meals. The calories are listed for all recipes in this chapter, as well as for the standard recipes in Chapter 6. Choose a standard breakfast at each level, if you like, and repeat it for several days if that will make your food choice easier. (If you choose a fortified cereal for breakfast, such as Bran Flakes or Raisin Bran, you will help ensure that the nutritional value of your diet closely approximates the RDAs even at 600 calories per day.)

For lunch and dinner, however, be sure to include a wide variety of different foods both during your twenty-one days on the Rotation Diet and in maintenance.

If you design your own menus at any time during the Rotation Diet, remember the formula:

Women — *For Weeks 1 and 3:*
    600 calories for three days
    900 calories for four days
    For Week 2:
    1200 calories for one week
Men — *For Weeks 1 and 3:*
    1200 calories for three days
    1500 calories for four days
    For Week 2:
    1800 calories for one week

MAINTENANCE

Women

The 1500- and 1800-calorie menus in this chapter are perfect for women as you build up to your maintenance intake after the Rotation Diet. Try them to ensure that you do not regain any weight. You can alternate these menus, or substitute them, for the 1500- and 1800-calorie-per-day menus that I suggest for men in Chapter 6. If you wish to follow your own inclinations on your way to maintenance, be sure to increase by only 300

194

calories per day, and stick with 1500 for several days before going up to 1800.

Men

On entering maintenance, men should also remember to increase from 1800 calories per day, up to their maintenance levels, in amounts of about 300 calories per day. Be sure to stay with 2100 calories per day for several days, checking your weight, before moving up to 2400. It is best to increase your calories with fruits, vegetables, whole grains and lean meats, but you can try a serving of a dessert or alcoholic beverage if you like. Check my quick calorie guide in Appendix A to make sure you do not increase by too much too rapidly.

Everyone

Remember that *free vegetables* and your *safe fruit* are available at all times, and that a substitution of fruit of any kind for junk-food snacks will go a long way toward preventing weight gain after you have used the Rotation Diet to reach your goal.

MEAL PREPARATION WITH THE ALTERNATIVE MENUS

Any of the dishes marked by an asterisk in the Alternative Menus that follow will have a recipe in this chapter, right after the daily menu plans. Some of the dishes from the standard menus have been included, so even if you do not see an asterisk after a dish in the Alternative Menus, be sure to check the index or go directly to Chapter 6 to find some cooking suggestions. If you follow your own inclinations, remember to prepare food in a plain fashion, without added fat or sugar, except as permitted in each rotation. All weights in the following menus are cooked weights. The calorie counts in the recipes allow for shrinkage due to cooking.

195

600-Calorie Rotation

MENU 1

Breakfast
½ grapefruit
½ cup of porridge
½ teaspoon of cinnamon
4 fluid ounces (110 ml) of skim milk
Coffee or tea

Lunch
8 fluid ounces (225 ml) of bouillon
Open-faced sandwich: 1 slice of whole-grain bread, 1
ounce (28 g) of lean meat, and Dijon mustard
Unlimited free vegetables
No-Cal Salad Dressing
½ cup of peach slices
4 fluid ounces (110 ml) of skim milk
No-cal beverage

Dinner
2 ounces (58 g) of veal cutlet, or fillet steak, grilled or
baked in foil
Fresh spinach salad
No-Cal Salad Dressing
½ cup of cooked brown rice
No-cal beverage

MENU 2

Breakfast
8 fluid ounces (225 ml) of plain yogurt
1 cup of berries, sliced
1 slice of whole-grain toast
Coffee or tea

Lunch
Chef salad: 1 ounce (28 g) of turkey, carrots, peppers,
celery and unlimited free vegetables
No-Cal Salad Dressing
5 whole-wheat crispbread
No-cal beverage

Dinner
1 cup of cooked red beans
½ cup of cooked brown rice
2 dessertspoons of grated cheese
½ cup of cauliflower
½ grapefruit
No-cal beverage

MENU 3

Breakfast
Cheese toast: 1 ounce (28 g) of cheese and 1 slice of
whole-grain bread
1 orange
Coffee or tea

Lunch
Tomato stuffed with 2 ounces (50 g) of shrimps or tuna
tossed salad of free vegetables
No-Cal Salad dressing
5 whole-wheat crispbread
1 apple
No-cal beverage

Dinner
Egg Drop Soup*
Turkey and beansprout sandwich: open-faced with 1
slice of whole-grain bread, 1 ounce (28 g) of turkey, and
Dijon mustard
¼ cantaloupe
No-cal beverage

900-Calorie Rotation

MENU 1

Breakfast
1 low-fat Whole-Wheat Breakfast Cake*
2 dessertspoons of maple syrup
8 fluid ounces (225 ml) of skim milk
choice of fruit
coffee or tea

Lunch
2 ounces (50 g) of Baked or Roast Chicken
1 cup of Spinach Salad
No-Cal or Lo-Cal Salad Dressing
½ cup of fresh fruit
No-cal beverage

Dinner
1 Grilled Herring
½ cup of cooked carrots
1 cup of Herb and Garlic Brussels Sprouts*
1 baked potato
⅙ ounce (5 g) of butter or 2 scant teaspoons of sour
cream
No-cal beverage

MENU 2

Breakfast
8 fluid ounces (225 ml) of skim milk
½ cup of hot cereal
½ teaspoon of cinnamon
2 dessertspoons of raisins
Coffee or tea

Lunch
8 fluid ounces (225 ml) of soup (your choice)
Open-faced sandwich: 1 slice of whole-grain bread with
2 ounces (56 g) of lean meat, sliced tomato, and Dijon
mustard, lettuce salad with carrot, celery, and cucumber
No-Cal or Lo-Cal salad dressing
½ grapefruit
No-cal beverage

Dinner
2 ounces (56 g) of Chicken Sesame*
¾ cup of cooked brown rice
¾ cup of marrow or courgette
1 cup of fresh fruit
No-cal beverage

MENU 3

Breakfast
1 ounce (28 g) of dry cereal
4 fluid ounces (110 ml) of skim milk
1 orange
Coffee or tea

Lunch
4 ounces (110 g) of Medley Casserole*
½ cup of Peas and Pods*
4 fluid ounces (110 ml) of skim milk
½ grapefruit
No-cal beverage

Dinner
3 ounces (80 g) of Paprika Pork Goulash*
½ cup of noodles
1 cup of broccoli
1 pear or peach
No-cal beverage

MENU 4

Breakfast
½ cup of cooked cereal
2 dessertspoons of raisins
8 fluid ounces (225 ml) of skim milk
Coffee or tea

Lunch
8 fluid ounces (225 ml) of bouillon
1 roll of Rolled Ham and Vegetables*
tossed salad
No-Cal or Lo-Cal Salad Dressing
5 whole-wheat crispbread
1 apple
No-cal beverage

Dinner
4 ounces (110 g) of Chicken Divan*
1 baked potato

199

⅙ ounce (5 g) of butter or 2 scant teaspoons of sour cream
½ cup of cauliflower
1 cup of berries and melon balls
No-cal beverage

1200-Calorie Rotation

Remember that when you reach the 1200-calorie level, or above, you may add ⅓ ounce (10 g) of butter or other fat or 1 dessertspoon of oil within the calorie guidelines. You may also add 3 *safe fruits* within the calorie guidelines.

MENU 1

Breakfast
8 fluid ounces (225 ml) of skim milk
½ banana
2½ ounces (70 g) of dry cereal
Coffee or tea

Lunch
salad: lettuce, tomato, radish, green pepper
Lo-Cal Salad Dressing
6 whole-wheat crispbread
8 fluid ounces (225 ml) of plain yogurt
1 cup of berries
No-cal beverage

Dinner
4 ounces (110 g) of Baked Fish in Spring Herbs*
1 serving of Oven-fried Potatoes*
1 cup of cooked cabbage
1 apple
No-cal beverage

MENU 2

Breakfast
8 fluid ounces (225 ml) of skim milk
½ cup of porridge with cinnamon
2 dessertspoons of raisins
1 slice of whole-grain toast
Coffee or tea

Lunch
8 fluid ounces (225 ml) of Broccoli-Cauliflower Soup*
5 whole-wheat crispbread
1 ounce (28 g) of Cheddar cheese
tossed salad
Lo-Cal Salad Dressing
½ grapefruit
No-cal beverage

Dinner
3 ounces (80 g) of Veal in Mushroom Sauce*
6 stalks of steamed asparagus
5 ounces (145 g) of new potatoes, boiled
1 cup of fresh fruit
1 slice of whole-grain bread
No-cal beverage

MENU 3

Breakfast
8 fluid ounces (225 ml) of plain yogurt
1 cup of berries and melon balls
1 slice of whole-wheattoast
Coffee or tea

Lunch
1 serving of Chicken Oahu*
Salad of free vegetables with Lo-Cal Salad Dressing
4 Toasted Oat Thins*
1 apple
No-cal beverage

Dinner
4 ounces (110 g) of Halibut Steak with Vegetables*
1 cup of Carrots Aloha*
¾ cup of Peas and Baby Onions
1 cup of sliced peaches
No-cal beverage

MENU 4

Breakfast
8 fluid ounces (225 ml) of skim milk
1 low-fat Whole-Wheat Breakfast Cake*
2 dessertspoons of maple syrup
½ banana
Coffee or tea

Lunch
8 fluid ounces (225 ml) of Egg Drop Soup*
Chicken and Swiss Salad*
½ melon
No-cal beverage

Dinner
4 ounces (110 g) of Spicy Orange Pork*
1 serving of Herb and Garlic Brussels Sprouts*
½ cup of brown rice
tossed green salad
Lo-Cal Salad Dressing
4 fluid ounces (110 ml) of unsweetened stewed apple
No-cal beverage

MENU 5

Breakfast
8 fluid ounces (225 ml) of skim milk
1 wedge of German Fruit Puff*

Lunch
1 serving of Cheddar Chili Pie*
Unlimited free vegetables
Lo-Cal Salad Dressing
6 whole-wheat crispbread
1 pear
No-cal beverage

Dinner
4 ounces (110 g) of Chicken Teriyaki*
1 serving of Chinese Fried Rice*
1 cup of steamed courgettes

1 serving of Honeydew De-Light*
No-cal beverage

MENU 6

Breakfast
8 fluid ounces (225 ml) of skim milk
1 slice of whole-wheat toast
1 teaspoon of jam or marmalade
1 orange
Coffee or tea

Lunch
8 fluid ounces (225 ml) of soup (your choice)
2 slices of whole-grain bread
2 ounces (50 g) of chicken
Unlimited free vegetables
Lo-Cal Salad Dressing
½ melon
No-cal beverage

Dinner
4 ounces (110 g) of lean grilled steak
1 cup of cooked brown rice
1 cup of french or runner beans
1 cup of peach slices
No-cal beverage

MENU 7

Breakfast
½ grapefruit
1 egg, boiled or poached
2 slices whole-wheat bread
1 teaspoon honey
Coffee or tea

Lunch
8 fluid ounces (225 ml) of bouillon
Turkey and beansprout sandwich: openfaced with 1
slice of whole-grain bread, 1 ounce (28 g) of turkey and
Dijon mustard

1 serving of Spinach Caesar Salad*
1 banana
No-cal beverage

Dinner
4 ounces (110 g) of Chicken Cordon Bleu*
1 serving of Spicy Green Beans*
1 small baked potato
1 slice of Tropical Coconut Crust Pie*
No-cal beverage

1500-Calorie Rotation

MENU 1

Breakfast
8 fluid ounces (225 ml) of skim or low-fat milk
1 cup of hot cereal
2 dessertspoons of raisins
4 fluid ounces (110 ml) of grapefruit juice
coffee or tea

Lunch
10 ounces (300 g) of Veal Stew*
5 whole-wheat crispbread
1 apple
No-cal beverage

Dinner
4 ounces (110 g) of Chicken Oahu*
1 cup of steamed broccoli
½ cup of Island Rice*
2 Chewy Raisin Cookies*
No-cal beverage

MENU 2

Breakfast
1½ ounces (40 g) of dry cereal
1 banana
8 fluid ounces (225 ml) of skim or low-fat milk
Coffee or tea

204

Lunch
6 ounces (175 g) of cottage cheese
6 whole-wheat crispbread
1 cup of steamed cauliflower
½ small melon
No-cal beverage

Dinner
12 ounces (350 g) of Shrimp Jambalaya*
1 cup of Green Beans and Mushrooms
1 cup of cooked carrots
5 whole-wheat crispbread
1 slice of Tropical Coconut Crust Pie*
No-cal beverage

MENU 3

Breakfast
8 fluid ounces (225 ml) of plain yogurt
1 cup of berries
1 slice of whole-wheat toast
Coffee or tea

Lunch
8 fluid ounces (225 ml) of soup (your choice)
2 slices of whole-grain bread
2 ounces (56 g) of brine-packed tuna
Unlimited free vegetables
Lo-Cal Salad Dressing
1 banana
No-cal beverage

Dinner
1¼-wedge of Lean and Perfect Pizza*
tossed salad
Lo-Cal Salad Dressing
1 cup of fruit
No-cal beverage

205

MENU 4

Breakfast
8 fluid ounces (225 ml) of skim or low-fat milk
1 wedge of German Fruit Puff*
Coffee or tea

Lunch
4 ounces (110 g) of Quick Pork Fry*
tossed green salad
Lo-Cal Salad Dressing
1 apple
No-cal beverage

Dinner
4 ounces (110 g) of Halibut Steak with Vegetables*
1 serving of Stovetop Spinach Casserole*
1 small baked potato
1 slice of whole-grain bread
1 piece of fruit
No-cal beverage

1800-Calorie Rotation

MENU 1

Breakfast
½ grapefruit
8 fluid ounces (225 ml) of skim or low-fat milk
1 poached egg
2 slices of whole-wheat toast
1 teaspoon of jam or marmalade
coffee or tea

Lunch
6 ounces (175 g) of Paprika Chicken*
1 serving of Potato Salad*
6 stalks of cooked asparagus
tossed salad
Lo-Cal Salad Dressing
1 pear
No-cal beverage

Dinner
8 fluid ounces (225 ml) of Egg Drop Soup*
1 serving of Oriental Stir-Fry*
1 serving of Chinese Fried Rice*
1 slice of fresh pineapple
3 Chewy Raisin Cookies*
8 fluid ounces (225 ml) of skim or low-fat milk

MENU 2

Breakfast
8 fluid ounces (225 ml) of skim or low-fat milk
1 cup of hot cereal
2 tablespoons of raisins
1 slice of whole-wheat toast
1 dessertspoon of peanut butter
Coffee or tea

Lunch
4 ounces (110 g) of Pepper Beef Burger*
1 wholemeal roll
1 cup of steamed cauliflower
Spinach Caesar Salad*
1 orange
Coffee or tea

Dinner
1 Grilled Herring*
1 small baked potato
tossed salad
Lo-Cal Salad Dressing
1 slice of whole-grain bread
1 serving Honeydew De-Light*
No-cal beverage

MENU 3

Breakfast
8 fluid ounces (225 ml) of skim or low-fat milk
3 ounces (80 g) of dry cereal
1 banana
1 slice of whole-wheat toast

1 teaspoon of jam or marmalade
Coffee or tea

Lunch
8 fluid ounces (225 ml) of soup (your choice)
4 ounces (110 g) of roast turkey
2 slices of whole-grain bread
Lettuce, beansprouts and Dijon mustard
Unlimited free vegetables
Lo-Cal Salad Dressing
1 pear
No-cal beverage

Dinner
5 ounces (145 g) of Oriental Chicken Stir-Fry*
1 cup of steamed carrots
1 slice of whole-grain bread or 1 wholemeal roll
2 Apple-Nut Bran Squares*
8 fluid ounces (225 ml) of skim or low-fat milk
No-cal beverage

MENU 4

Breakfast
1 wedge of German Fruit Puff*
8 fluid ounces (225 ml) of skim or low-fat milk
Coffee or tea

Lunch
5 ounces (145 g) of Savoury Turkey Roll*
1 cup of broccoli
1 slice of whole-wheat bread
½ cup of cooked brown rice
1 apple
No-cal beverage

Dinner
4 ounces (110 g) of Veal in Mushroom Sauce*
5 ounces (145 g) of mixed new potatoes and peas
1 cup of cooked cabbage
1 serving of Green Beans Almondine

½ cup of sliced apricots
8 fluid ounces (225 ml) of skim or low-fat milk
No-cal beverage

MENU 5

Breakfast
8 fluid ounces (225 ml) of skim or low-fat milk
1 cup of berries
2 slices whole-wheat bread
2 dessertspoons of cream cheese
1 apple
Coffee or tea

Lunch
8 fluid ounces (225 ml) of Broccoli-Cauliflower Soup*
1 cup of carrots
4 ounces (110 g) of baked fish
1 slice of whole-grain bread
1 orange
No-cal beverage

Dinner
4 ounces (110 g) of Slim Southern-Style Fried Chicken*
1 cup of brown rice
6 stalks of cooked asparagus
tossed salad
Lo-Cal Salad Dressing
2 tinned pear halves
No-cal beverage

MENU 6

Breakfast
½ grapefruit
2 Whole-Wheat Breakfast Cakes*
2 dessertspoons of maple syrup
8 fluid ounces (225 ml) of skim or low-fat milk
Coffee or tea

Lunch
8 fluid ounces (225 ml) of soup (your choice)

209

2 turkey and beansprout sandwiches, open-faced: each
with 1 slice of whole-grain bread, 1 ounce (28 g) of turkey
and Dijon mustard
1 cup of Brussels sprouts
1 slice of fresh pineapple
1 serving of Honeydew De-Light*
No-cal beverage

Dinner
4 ounces (110 g) of Sesame Scallops*
1 baked potato
Spinach Caesar Salad*
Choice of assorted vegetable relishes: carrots, celery,
radishes, cucumber, etc.
1 slice of Pineapple Bread*
No-cal beverage

RECIPES

Soups

BROCCOLI-CAULIFLOWER SOUP

12 ounces (350 g) of fresh
chopped broccoli
12 ounces (350 g) of fresh
chopped cauliflower
1 small onion, chopped
12 fluid ounces (330 ml) of
bouillon
¼ teaspoon of ground
mace

1¼ pints (700 ml) of skim
milk
1 dessertspoon of
cornflour
½ teaspoon of salt
⅛ teaspoon of pepper
⅓ cup of grated cheese

Cook broccoli, cauliflower and onion in the bouillon until
tender. Pour half the vegetables, along with half the
bouillon, into a blender or food processor and blend until
smooth. Remove and blend the remaining vegetable
mixture, along with the mace. Return all the blended
mixture to rinsed pan.

Blend 4 fluid ounces (110 ml) of cold milk with the cornflour and add to pureed vegetables. Add remaining milk, salt and pepper, and cook until thick and hot, stirring. Blend in cheese and stir until melted.

Makes 8 servings at 71 calories per serving.

EGG DROP SOUP

10 fluid ounces (275 ml) of bouillon

10 fluid ounces (275 ml) of water

2 dessertspoons of chopped spring onion

1 egg, slightly beaten

Combine bouillon and water in saucepan and bring to boil. Add onion and reduce heat. Gently stir in beaten egg, and simmer for three minutes or until egg is set. Serve immediately.

Makes 4 servings of about 4 fluid ounces (110 g) at 35 calories per serving.

Salads

CHICKEN AND CHEESE SALAD

4 fluid ounces (110 ml) of plain yogurt

2 dessertspoons of mayonnaise

1 tablespoon of fresh chopped parsley

1 teaspoon of horseradish sauce

1 teaspoon of prepared mustard

¼ teaspoon of rosemary

¼ teaspoon of garlic powder or 2 cloves garlic, minced

1 head of lettuce

12 sliced green pepper rings

6 slices of hard cheese, 1 ounce (28 g) each

6 slices of sweet red onion

6 slices of cooked chicken or turkey, 1 ounce (28 g) each

24 sliced cucumber rounds, ¼ inch (½ cm) thick

12 tomato slices

Blend together yogurt, mayonnaise, parsley, horseradish, mustard, rosemary and garlic. Cover and chill while preparing the rest of the salad.

211

Remove core of lettuce head. Cut lettuce crosswise to get 6 slices, ½ inch (1 cm) thick. Place lettuce slices on serving plates. Top each lettuce slice with 2 green pepper rings, 1 slice of cheese, 1 slice of onion, 1 slice of chicken or turkey, 4 slices of cucumber and 2 slices of tomato. Top each serving with 2 dessertspoons of yogurt mixture.

Makes 6 servings at 224 calories per serving.

POTATO SALAD

3 medium-sized cooked potatoes, diced
8 spring onions, chopped
2 stalks of celery, chopped
1 dessertspoon of mayonnaise
1 teaspoon of prepared mustard
1 teaspoon of dillweed
½ teaspoon of garlic powder or 3 cloves garlic, minced

Combine all ingredients in a large bowl, and chill at least one hour.

Makes 4 servings at 102 calories per serving.

SEASONED TOMATO SALAD

8 fluid ounces (225 ml) measure of fresh chopped tomato
½ teaspoon of basil
½ teaspoon of oregano
1½ teaspoons of lemon juice
Several sprigs of fresh parsley, chopped

Combine all ingredients, cover and let marinate in the refrigerator for an hour or more.

Makes 1 serving of 52 calories.

SPINACH CAESAR SALAD

1 clove of garlic
10 ounces (300 g) of fresh spinach
3 tablespoons of chopped onion
2 tablespoons of mayonnaise

2 fluid ounces (50 ml) of
Italian salad dressing
(3–4 tablespoons)
1 dessertspoon of lemon
or lime juice
¼ teaspoon of salt

⅛ teaspoon of black
pepper
3 slices of whole-wheat
bread, toasted, cubed
3 dessertspoons of grated
Parmesan cheese

Cut garlic clove in half and rub salad bowl with the cut ends. Discard garlic. Trim and shred spinach and add to salad bowl. Add onion. Combine mayonnaise, salad dressing, lemon or lime juice, salt and pepper, and pour over spinach. Toss warm toasted bread cubes with cheese and pour onto salad.

Makes 8 servings at 67 calories per serving.

Main Courses

BAKED FISH IN SPRING HERBS

1 pound (450 g) of white
fish fillets (sole works
best)
1 dessertspoon of
vegetable oil or

⅓ ounce (10 g) of butter
1 lemon
1 scant teaspoon each of
dried parsley, chives
and rosemary

Melt butter and pour into shallow baking dish. Arrange fish in dish. Cut lemon in half and squeeze over the fish about 1 dessertspoon of juice from one-half of the lemon. Sprinkle with herbs. Slice the remaining lemon into thin slices and arrange on top of the fish.

Bake at 500°F (Gas Mark 9/240°C) for 12 to 15 minutes, or until fish flakes easily with fork.

Makes 4 servings of 4 ounces (110 g) each, at about 115 calories per serving.

GRILLED HERRING

8 small herring
5 fluid ounces (150 ml)
tomato juice
2 tablespoons of vinegar

1 teaspoon of paprika
⅛ teaspoon of salt
⅛ teaspoon of black
pepper

Slash each herring twice on each side and arrange in shallow baking dish. Combine remaining ingredients and pour over fish. Marinate, covered, in refrigerator for 1 hour, turning once. Remove fish and place on grill pan. Brush with marinade and grill 4 to 5 minutes, about 4 inches (10 cm) from heat. Turn and baste again with marinade. Grill another 4 to 5 minutes, or until fish flakes easily with a fork and pulls away from bone.

Makes 8 servings at about 200 calories per serving.

CHEDDAR CHILLI PIE

1 pound (450 g) of lean beef mince

1 large onion, or 4 spring onions, chopped

2 cloves of garlic, chopped fine

1 tin (28 ounces/800 g) of tomatoes

1 tin (15 ounces/425 g) of kidney beans, with juice

6 ounces (175 g) of cornmeal

3 ounces (80 g) of grated Cheddar cheese

2 dessertspoons of chilli powder (or less, depending on taste)

1 teaspoon of ground cumin

¼ teaspoon of cayenne pepper

½ teaspoon of crushed red pepper (if available)

½ teaspoon of black pepper

Dash Tabasco sauce

10 fluid ounces (330 ml) of skim milk

2 eggs, lightly beaten

Salt and pepper to taste

Sauté beef, onion and garlic until brown. Drain off fat. Add tomatoes, beans and bean juice, ¾ cup of cornmeal, ½ cup of cheese and spices. Cook over low heat, stirring occasionally, for about 15 minutes. Pour into casserole dish.

In the same saucepan, combine the milk, the rest of the cornmeal and salt and pepper to taste. Stir over low heat until the mixture thickens a little. Add the remaining cheese and the eggs, stirring until smooth. Pour this over the beef mixture. Bake uncovered at 375 degrees for 30 minutes or until crust is lightly browned.

Makes 8 servings at 308 calories per serving.

CHICKEN CORDON BLEU

4 chicken breasts, skinned and boned
Nonstick vegetable cooking spray
4 thin slices of ham, ½ ounce (15 g) each
4 thin slices of cheese, ½ ounce (15 g) each
3 ounces (80 g) of whole-wheat flour
½ teaspoon of garlic powder
½ teaspoon of onion powder
¼ teaspoon each of salt and black pepper
1 egg
2 teaspoons of water
3 ounces (80 g) of dry breadcrumbs, sifted

Pound chicken breasts with mallet and cut each breast in half. Spray a frying pan with cooking spray and lightly brown chicken on both sides. Remove from pan.

Place a slice of ham on each of four pieces of chicken; place a slice of cheese on top of each piece of ham. Top each with one of the remaining chicken halves and pat dry.

Combine flour and seasonings in a shallow bowl. In another bowl, lightly beat egg and water together with 10 or 11 strokes. Place the breadcrumbs, finely sifted, in a third bowl. Dip the chicken into the flour, carefully coating all sides and then removing excess flour. Slide chicken through egg mixture and let excess drip off. Then dip in breadcrumbs. Place on an oven-proof plate, and let stand for 15 minutes. Preheat oven to 350°F (Gas Mark 4/180°C) and bake for 15 minutes.

Serves 4 at 316 calories per serving.

CHICKEN DIVAN

1 pound 4 ounces (565 g) of fresh broccoli
12 fluid ounces (330 ml) of cold water
3 dessertspoons of cornflour
5 fluid ounces (150 ml) of skim milk
2 dessertspoons of dry sherry
1½ cubes of instant chicken bouillon

⅛ teaspoon of nutmeg	white meat only – 1
⅛ teaspoon of pepper	pound (450 g) raw
12 ounces (330 g) of thinly sliced cooked chicken,	1 ounce (28 g) of grated Parmesan cheese

Cut broccoli into flowerets. Put 12 fluid ounces (330 ml) of cold water in the bottom of a steamer and heat to boiling. Steam broccoli until just tender. Drain and save the juice. Arrange broccoli in an 8-inch-(20-cm-) square baking dish.

In a saucepan, heat the broccoli juice, adding, if necessary, enough additional cold water to make 11 fluid ounces (300 ml) of juice. Stir in cornflour. Add milk, sherry, bouillon cubes, nutmeg and pepper, stirring until thickened. Pour half the sauce over the broccoli. Layer chicken slices on top, then pour on remaining sauce. Sprinkle with cheese and paprika.

Bake, uncovered, at 350°F (Gas Mark 4/180°C) for 20 minutes.

Makes 6 servings at 166 calories per serving.

CHICKEN OAHU

4 boneless, skinned chicken breasts	1 sweet red pepper, chopped
1 8-ounce (225-g) tin of unsweetened pineapple chunks, undrained	3 tablespoons of lemon juice
1 onion, sliced thin	3 tablespoons of orange juice

Combine all ingredients in a large casserole. Marinate, covered and refrigerated, for 2 hours, stirring occasionally. Place casserole in preheated oven at 325°F (Gas Mark 3/170°C) for 1 hour, or until chicken is tender.

Makes 4 servings at 161 calories per serving.

CHICKEN PAPRIKA

1 teaspoon of butter	white meat only – 1
12 ounces (330 g) of cooked chicken pieces,	pound (450 g) raw
	1 teaspoon of paprika

⅛ teaspoon of rosemary,   Dash of black pepper
   crushed   Garlic powder to taste
   Dash of salt

Melt butter in a small saucepan. Toss in chicken, coating with butter. Stir in seasonings. Serve warm or cold.
   Makes 2 to 4 servings; 3 ounces (80 g) will contain 138 calories, and 6 ounces (170 g) will contain 276 calories.

CHICKEN SESAME

3 pounds (2 kg) of   marjoram and salt
   chicken pieces, skinned ½ teaspoon of dried
2 ounces (56 g) of   parsley
   breadcrumbs   ½ teaspoon of dry
⅛ cup of ground sesame   mustard
   seeds   ⅛ teaspoon of black
1 clove of garlic, chopped   pepper
   fine   1 small egg, lightly
¼ teaspoon each of onion   beaten
   powder, thyme,

Combine dry ingredients and seasonings; mix well. Place a layer of chicken pieces in the bottom of a large casserole dish. Brush the chicken with the beaten egg. Sprinkle with some of the sesame mixture. Continue layering chicken, egg and sesame mixture until all ingredients are used up.
   Bake, covered, at 300°F (Gas Mark 2/150°C) for 1½ to 2 hours, or until chicken is tender.
   Makes 8 servings at approximately 210 calories per serving.

CHICKEN TERIYAKI

4 chicken breasts,   1 large clove of garlic,
   skinned   crushed
1 dessertspoon of   1 dessertspoon of fresh
   vegetable oil   ginger, grated
2 dessertspoons of soy
   sauce

217

Combine all ingredients except the chicken in a large bowl, and mix well. Add the chicken and marinate at least 4 hours in the refrigerator, stirring occasionally. Line a baking pan with foil and arrange chicken pieces on it. Baste each piece with the marinade. Bake at 350°F (Gas Mark 4/180°C) for 45 minutes, or until chicken is tender, basting frequently with the marinade.

Makes 4 servings at 154 calories per serving.

HALIBUT STEAK WITH VEGETABLES

2 pounds (1 kg) of halibut steak
Nonstick vegetable cooking spray
1 large onion, sliced thin
4 ounces (110 g) of fresh mushrooms, chopped
1 large or 2 small tomatoes, chopped
½ a green pepper, chopped
3 tablespoons of fresh parsley, chopped
2 tablespoons of chopped red pepper
4 tablespoons dry white wine
2 dessertspoons of lemon or lime juice
1 teaspoon salt
¼ teaspoon of dillweed
⅛ teaspoon of pepper
Lemon or lime wedges

Cut fish into 8 pieces. Spray baking dish with cooking spray. Line bottom of dish with onion. Place fish on top of onion. Combine tomato, green pepper, parsley and red pepper, and spread over fish. Blend wine, lemon or lime juice and seasonings, and pour over vegetables. Bake at 350°F (Gas Mark 4/180°C) for 25 minutes, or until fish flakes easily with a fork. Serve with lemon or lime wedges.

Makes 8 servings at 137 calories per serving.

LEAN AND PERFECT PIZZA

Topping

8 ounces (225 g) of extra-lean beef mince
1 clove of garlic, minced
1 small onion, chopped

218

1 16-ounce (450-g) tin of tomatoes, chopped
½ a green pepper, chopped
1 full teaspoon of oregano

1 scant teaspoon of basil
½ teaspoon of fennel seed
⅛ teaspoon of salt
1 cup shredded mozzarella cheese – 4 ounces (110 g)

Crust

4 ounces (110 g) of whole-wheat flour
½ a package of easy blend or fast action dry yeast
Dash salt

4 tablespoons of warm water
1½ teaspoons of vegetable oil
Nonstick vegetable cooking spray

Brown beef, garlic and onion in saucepan. Drain well. Stir in undrained tomatoes, green pepper, oregano, basil, fennel and salt. Bring to the boil. Then reduce heat and simmer gently, uncovered, for 30 minutes.

Meanwhile, combine ⅞ of the flour with the yeast and the salt. Add the warm water and oil. Beat at low speed with an electric mixer for 30 seconds, then beat at high speed for 3 minutes. Add as much of the remaining flour as you can stir in with a spoon. Turn out onto a floured board and knead in enough additional flour to make smooth, elastic dough (about 6 minutes). Cover dough and let stand in a warm place for 10 minutes. Roll dough into a 13 inch (32 cm) circle. Transfer to a pizza pan or a baking sheet sprayed with cooking spray. Turn up edges of the crust slightly. Bake at 425°F (Gas Mark 7/220°C) for 12 minutes, or until lightly browned.

Pour meat mixture onto crust, top with cheese, and bake for 15 more minutes, or until bubbly. Slice and serve.

Makes 4 servings at 354 calories per serving.

MEDLEY CASSEROLE

2 medium potatoes, cubed (leave skins on!)

1 medium carrot, sliced in ¼-inch (½-cm) rounds

1 stalk of celery, chopped
1 onion, sliced in ¼-inch
(½-cm) rounds
½ ounce (15 g) of butter
1 teaspoon of dillweed
1 teaspoon of basil
½ teaspoon of rosemary
¼ teaspoon of salt
¼ teaspoon of black
pepper

1 pound (450 g) of white
fish fillets
1 medium green pepper,
chopped fine
1 dessertspoon of lemon
juice
1 medium tomato,
chopped fine

Layer potatoes, carrot, celery and onion in an 8-inch-(20-cm-) square baking dish. Melt butter and combine with dill, basil, rosemary, salt and pepper. Spoon half of the seasoned butter over the vegetables. Cover and bake at 425°F (Gas Mark 7/220°C) for 25 minutes.

Arrange fish fillets on top of the vegetables and sprinkle with lemon juice. Spoon the remaining seasoned butter over the fish. Top with chopped green pepper. Cover and bake for 15 more minutes or until fish flakes easily with a fork. Uncover and add chopped tomato. Bake 5 minutes more, or until tomato is hot and vegetables are tender.

Makes 4 servings at 201 calories per serving.

ORIENTAL STIR-FRY

12 ounces (350 g) of
topside beef
4 fluid ounces (110 g) of
water
2 cups of broccoli
flowerets
2 medium carrots, sliced
1 teaspoon of cornflour
¼ teaspoon of sugar

2 dessertspoons of soy
sauce
2 dessertspoons of dry
sherry
2 dessertspoons of
cooking oil
1 medium onion, cut into
thin wedges

Slice beef across the grain into thin, bite-sized pieces. Set aside. Bring water to the boil and steam broccoli and carrots over hot water for 3 minutes. In a small bowl or measuring cup, combine cornflour, sugar, soy sauce and sherry, and reserve.

Preheat a wok or large frying pan over high heat for 1 minute. Add 1 dessertspoon of the oil. Add vegetables, including onion, and stir-fry for several minutes, until just tender. Remove vegetables. Add remaining oil. Add beef and brown, stirring constantly. Add soy mixture, still stirring constantly, and stir until sauce thickens. Return vegetables to pan, cover and cook 1 minute more.

Makes 4 servings at 292 calories per serving.

PAPRIKA PORK GOULASH

1 pound (450 g) of pork tenderloin	8 fluid ounces (225 ml) of plain yogurt
Nonstick vegetable cooking spray	3 tablespoons of fresh parsley
1 large onion, chopped	2½ cups of cooked whole-wheat noodles (5 ounces/150 g uncooked)
6 fluid ounces (175 ml) of bouillon	
1 dessertspoon of paprika	
1 dessertspoon of cornflour	

Trim all visible fat from pork. Slice pork diagonally into ¼-inch (½-cm) slices. Spray a frying pan with cooking spray and heat over medium heat. Brown meat, stirring occasionally. Remove meat from pan. Place onions in pan and cook lightly until clear. (You may add some of the bouillon if there isn't enough fat to cook the onions.)

Return meat to pan. Add bouillon and paprika. Cover and let simmer 15 to 20 minutes, until pork is tender. Take 4 tablespoons of bouillon out of pan and reserve in small container in refrigerator.

Blend cornflour into yogurt in a small bowl. Take the reserved bouillon out of the refrigerator and stir into the yogurt mixture, 1 tablespoon at a time. Add yogurt mixture to pan and heat through. Stir in parsley and serve over hot noodles.

Makes 5 servings at 296 calories per serving.

PEPPER BEEF BURGERS

3 tablespoons of fine dry breadcrumbs

2 dessertspoons of low-fat dry milk

½ teaspoon of basil

½ teaspoon of oregano

½ teaspoon of garlic powder

⅛ teaspoon of salt

⅛ teaspoon of black pepper

12 ounces (350 g) of best quality mince

2 medium onions, sliced thin

6 fluid ounces (180 ml) of tomato sauce

3 tablespoons of red wine

1 large green pepper, cut into julienne strips

Combine breadcrumbs, milk and seasonings in bowl. Add meat and mix well. Shape into four patties, ¾ inch (1½ cm) thick. Brown patties on both sides in a shallow pan. Drain off fat. Add onions to pan. Blend together tomato sauce and wine, and pour into pan. Cover and cook on low heat for about 10 minutes. Top with green pepper, cover, and cook 10 minutes more.

Makes 4 servings at 219 calories per serving.

TOMATO SAUCE

1 15-ounce (425-g) tin tomatoes

3 fluid ounces (75 ml) tomato paste

1 dessertspoon grated onion

Bring to the boil and simmer gently for 15 to 20 minutes, mashing with a wooden spoon.

QUICK PORK FRY

2 cups (about 12 ounces/350 g) of lean roasted pork, cut into 1-inch (2-cm) cubes

2 dessertspoons of water

3 tablespoons of unsweetened pineapple juice

2 onions, cut into chunks
2 dessertspoons of soy
  sauce
12 ounces (350 g) of fresh
  asparagus, cut into
  1 inch (2 cm) lengths
1 ounce (28 g) of fresh

mushrooms, sliced
3 tomatoes, cubed
1 scant teaspoon of
  cornflour
3 tablespoons of white
  wine or vinegar

Combine pork, onions, soy sauce and water in a shallow pan. Cook on high heat for 1 or 2 minutes. Add juice, asparagus and mushrooms and cook 6 minutes more. Add tomato. Dissolve cornflour in wine and stir into meat mixture. Stirring constantly, cook for 2 or 3 minutes more, until sauce thickens and vegetables are tender.

Makes 4 servings at 257 calories per serving.

ROLLED HAM AND VEGETABLES

2 inches (5 cm) of
  cucumber, chopped
1 large or 2 small
  tomatoes, chopped
1 ounce (28 g) of fresh
  mushrooms, sliced
2 dessertspoons of sliced
  ripe olives
2 dessertspoons of spring
  onions, chopped

3 tablespoons of
  low-calorie Italian salad
  dressing
4 large lettuce leaves,
  from outer part of head
1 6-ounce (150-g)
  package of sliced,
  cooked ham (8 slices)
3 ounces (80 g) of grated
  mozzarella cheese

Combine cucumber, tomato, mushrooms, olives, onion and salad dressing in a bowl. Chill, covered, for at least 2 hours. (You can keep this overnight in the refrigerator, if you wish.)

Top a lettuce leaf with two slices of ham. Drain the vegetables and place ¼ of the mixture in the centre of each with ¼ of the cheese on top. Roll up, turning the edges of the lettuce inward to seal the ends. Secure with a toothpick.

Makes 4 servings of one roll each at 205 calories per serving.

SAVOURY TURKEY ROLL

1¼ pounds (565 g) of
boned turkey breast in
one piece
¼ teaspoon of garlic
powder
⅛ teaspoon of black
pepper
3 tablespoons of chopped
onion
2 tablespoons of chopped
fresh parsley

2 ounces (56 g) of
Cheddar cheese (4
half-ounce slices)
8 fluid ounces (225 ml) of
tomato juice
2 teaspoons of
Worcestershire sauce
Dash of Tabasco sauce

Preheat oven to 350°F (Gas Mark 4/180°C). Sprinkle turkey meat with garlic, pepper, onion and parsley. Top with cheese slices. Roll up and place in small baking dish. Secure with toothpicks or skewers if necessary. Combine remaining ingredients and pour over turkey roll. Bake covered for 2 hours, basting occasionally. Uncover and bake another hour. Slice and serve.

Makes 4 servings at 209 calories per serving.

SESAME SCALLOPS

1 pound (450 g) of large
fresh scallops
2 tablespoons of sherry
2 dessertspoons of
cooking oil
1 dessertspoon of sesame
seeds, crushed
2 teaspoons of grated
onion
1 clove of garlic, crushed

¼ teaspoon of salt
⅛ teaspoon of pepper
1 green pepper, cut into
chunks
1 sweet red pepper, cut
into chunks
1 8-ounce (225-g) tin of
unsweetened pineapple
chunks, drained
12 cherry tomatoes

Combine sherry, oil, sesame seeds, onion, garlic, salt and pepper in a large plastic bowl. Add scallops and pepper chunks, and marinate in refrigerator for 3 or 4 hours, stirring occasionally. Thread scallops, peppers and pineapple on 6 skewers. Place skewers in baking pan and pour in marinade. Bake at 425°F (Gas Mark 7/220°C) for 10 minutes, or until scallops are tender, turning skewers occasionally. Place two tomatoes on the end of each skewer, and return to oven for 5 more minutes.

Makes 6 servings at about 174 calories per serving.

SHRIMP JAMBALAYA

8 spring onions, chopped
½ green pepper, chopped
1 clove of garlic, minced
⅔ ounce (20 g) of butter
2 dessertspoons of whole-wheat flour
1 16-ounce (450-g) tin of tomatoes, undrained
6 ounces (175 g) cooked, cubed ham
4 fluid ounces (110 ml) of water
2 bay leaves
½ teaspoon of thyme
½ teaspoon of basil
¼ teaspoon of dillweed
¼ teaspoon of crushed red pepper
¼ teaspoon of salt
⅛ teaspoon of black pepper
Dash of Tabasco sauce
8 fluid ounce (225 ml) measure of uncooked brown rice, washed and drained
1 pound (450 g) of shelled shrimps

Melt butter in saucepan and soften onion, green pepper and garlic until tender. Blend in all remaining ingredients except the shrimps. Bring to a boil, then reduce heat and simmer for about 30 minutes, stirring frequently. Add shrimps and cook 15 minutes more, or until rice and shrimps are cooked.

Makes 6 servings at 283 calories per serving.

SLIM SOUTHERN-STYLE FRIED CHICKEN

4 pounds (1 kg 800 g) of chicken pieces, skinned
Water
2 ounces (60 g) of breadcrumbs
½ teaspoon of paprika
¼ teaspoon of salt
¼ teaspoon of thyme
¼ teaspoon of marjoram
¼ teaspoon of celery seed
⅛ teaspoon of black pepper

Brush chicken pieces with water to moisten. Combine

225

remaining ingredients in a large bowl. Dredge chicken in the coating, and arrange on a nonstick baking sheet. Bake at 375°F (Gas Mark 5/190°C) for 45 minutes, or until crisp on the outside and tender inside.

Makes 8 servings at about 186 calories per serving.

SPICY ORANGE PORK

6 pork chops, ½ inch (1 cm) thick
Nonstick vegetable spray
¼ teaspoon of salt
¼ teaspoon of pepper
3 tablespoons of unsweetened orange juice
2 medium oranges

8 fluid ounces (225 ml) of water
2 scant teaspoons of sugar
1 dessertspoon of cornflour
8 fluid ounces (225 ml) of unsweetened orange juice
¼ teaspoon of allspice

Trim pork chops of all visible fat. Spray a shallow pan with nonstick vegetable spray and heat over medium heat. Brown chops on both sides. Sprinkle with salt and pepper and add the 3 tablespoons of orange juice. Cover and let simmer 25 minutes or until tender.

Meanwhile, remove a thin layer of peel from one orange, and slice the peel into julienne strips. Simmer strips in water for 15 minutes, drain, and set aside. Peel and section both oranges, and cut the sections into ½-inch (1-cm) chunks.

Combine sugar, cornflour, and 8 fluid ounces of orange juice in another saucepan, stirring constantly over medium heat until thickened. Add the julienned orange peel, orange chunks, and allspice. Simmer 1 or 2 minutes longer, stirring occasionally. Remove chops to serving dish, and top with sauce.

Makes 6 servings at 205 calories per serving.

VEAL IN MUSHROOM SAUCE

12 ounces (350 g) of boneless veal-leg round steak

2 teaspoons of butter
1¼ teaspoons of Worcestershire sauce

226

1 clove of garlic, chopped fine

1 medium onion, sliced into rings

3 ounces (80 g) of sliced fresh mushrooms

3 fluid ounces (70 ml) of beef bouillon

1 dessertspoon of lemon or lime juice

2 teaspoons of cornflour

3 tablespoons of cold water

2 cups of cooked whole-wheat noodles

Lemon or lime wedges (5 ounces/150 g raw)

Trim visible fat from veal and cut into 4 pieces. Pound meat with a mallet to ¼-inch (½-cm) thickness.

Melt butter in shallow pan. Add Worcestershire sauce, garlic and onion. Cook over medium heat until onion is clear. Add veal and brown on both sides. Pour mushrooms over veal and add bouillon and lemon or lime juice. Reduce heat to low, cover, and simmer for about 5 minutes, until meat is cooked.

Combine cornflour and water, and stir onto meat. Heat and stir until bubbly and thick. Serve over hot noodles, garnished with lemon or lime wedges.

Makes 4 servings at approximately 290 calories per serving.

VEAL STEW

1¼ pounds (800 g) of lean boneless veal, cut into 1-inch (2-cm) cubes

2 small cloves of garlic, minced

½ medium onion, chopped

2 teaspoons of butter

14 fluid ounces (385 ml) of bouillon

2 tablespoons of white wine

2 medium potatoes, cubed

2 medium carrots, sliced

1 cup of frozen or fresh peas

3 ounces (80 g) of fresh mushrooms, halved

2 dessertspoons of fresh parsley, chopped

1 teaspoon of marjoram

2 dessertspoons of water

1 dessertspoon of cornflour

In a large pan brown the meat, garlic and onions in butter. Add bouillon and wine, and bring to the boil. Reduce heat, cover and simmer for 30 minutes. Add remaining vegetables and seasonings. Cover and cook another 30 minutes, or until meat is cooked and vegetables are tender. Skim any visible fat off the top. Combine the 2 dessertspoons of water and the cornflour; add to the stew and stir until thickened.

Makes 6 servings at 311 calories per serving.

Vegetables

CARROTS ALOHA

2 medium carrots
3 tablespoons of water
1 dessertspoon of fresh
  orange juice

2 teaspoons of fresh
  lemon juice
2 lemon slices
4 orange slices

Cut carrots in quarters lengthwise, then cut into 1-inch strips. Bring water to a boil in saucepan. Place carrots in water, reduce heat, cover and cook until just tender. Add juices and stir. Place sliced lemon and orange rounds on top of carrots, cover and cook 2 or 3 minutes more.

Makes one serving of 52 calories.

CHINESE FRIED RICE

8-fluid-ounce (225-ml)
  measure of brown rice
16 fluid ounces (450 ml) of
  water
  Nonstick vegetable
  cooking spray
2 eggs, beaten
2 large onions, chopped
2 teaspoons of vegetable
  oil

3 tablespoons of water
2 stalks of celery,
  chopped
½ green pepper,
  chopped
1 clove of garlic, minced
3 spring onions, chopped

Bring 16 fluid ounces of water to the boil, add rice and reduce heat. Let simmer for 40 to 45 minutes, until tender. Set aside.

228

Spray a large frying pan with cooking spray. Add eggs and cook over low heat without stirring. When eggs are set, remove from pan, crumble with a fork, and reserve. Brown onions in pan with the oil. Add remaining ingredients and heat to boiling. Add cooked rice. Reduce heat and simmer 1 minute. Stir in egg. Remove from heat, cover and let stand 5 minutes.

Makes 8 servings at 92 calories per serving.

HERB AND GARLIC BRUSSELS SPROUTS

12 ounces (350 g) of fresh or frozen brussels sprouts
1 small onion, sliced thin
1 clove of garlic, minced
⅓ ounce (10 g) of butter

¼ teaspoon of thyme
¼ teaspoon of oregano
⅛ teaspoon of salt
⅛ teaspoon of black pepper

Steam brussels sprouts and onions over boiling water for about 20 minutes, or until tender.

Melt butter in saucepan, add garlic and sauté until browned. Add steamed vegetables and seasonings. Cook 4 minutes, or until vegetables are heated through, stirring occasionally.

Makes 4 servings at about 70 calories per serving.

ISLAND RICE

8-fluid-ounce (225-ml) measure of brown rice
16 fluid ounces (450 ml) of bouillon

½ medium onion, sliced thin
1 dessertspoon of toasted, shredded coconut

Wash rice, draining off excess liquid. Bring bouillon and onion to a boil in a saucepan. Add rice and reduce heat to low. Simmer for 40 to 50 minutes, or until rice is tender. Top with toasted coconut.

Makes 4 servings of ½ cup each, at 106 calories per serving.

OVEN-FRIED POTATOES

4 medium potatoes, skins
  on
1 dessertspoon of oil
⅛ teaspoon of garlic
  powder

⅛ teaspoon of onion
  powder
1 to 1½ teaspoons of
  paprika (to taste)
Salt and pepper to taste

Slice potatoes lengthwise into eighths.

Line a shallow baking pan with foil and put all ingredients into the pan, tossing well to coat the potatoes with the oil and seasonings.

Bake at 325°F (Gas Mark 3/170°C) for 1 hour, or at a higher temperature for less time if you wish. Adjust seasonings if necessary.

Makes 4 servings at 115 calories per serving.

PEAS AND PODS

10½ ounces (315 g) of
  frozen peas
2 handfuls of fresh snow

or mange-tout peas
1 small onion, sliced thin
1 teaspoon of basil

Cook frozen peas according to directions on package. At the same time, steam snow peas and onions over hot water until tender. When cooked, add snow peas and onions to frozen peas. Add basil, stir, and serve.

Makes 4 half-cup servings at approximately 54 calories per serving.

SPICY GREEN BEANS

12 ounces (350 g) of fresh
  whole french beans
6 fluid ounces (180 ml) of
  unsalted tomato juice
2 dessertspoons of
  chopped onion
1 teaspoon of oregano

½ teaspoon of basil
¼ teaspoon of garlic
  powder
¼ teaspoon of salt
⅛ teaspoon of pepper
1 dessertspoon of grated
  hard cheese

Wash and trim beans and cut into 1-inch (2-cm) lengths.

230

Combine beans and remaining ingredients in saucepan and bring to the boil. Reduce heat and simmer, covered, for 5 minutes. Uncover and continue to cook until beans are tender. Sprinkle with cheese.

Makes 3 servings at 47 calories per serving.

STOVETOP SPINACH CASSEROLE

12 ounces (350 g) of fresh spinach

4 fluid ounces (110 ml) of bouillon

2 dessertspoons of mayonnaise

2 tablespoons of fresh onion, chopped fine

Wash and trim spinach. Combine all ingredients in saucepan, and bring to the boil. Reduce heat immediately and simmer, uncovered, until most of the liquid has evaporated.

Makes 3 servings at 44 calories per serving.

Desserts

APPLE-NUT BRAN SQUARES

2 ounces (56 g) of Bran Flakes or Raisin Bran

4 rounded tablespoons of wheat germ

1½ ounces (40 g) of nonfat dry milk powder

½ teaspoon of baking powder

⅛ teaspoon of salt

2 beaten eggs

5 ounces (145 g) of soft brown sugar

1 apple, finely chopped, skin on

2 dessertspoons of vegetable oil

1 dessertspoon of dark molasses

1½ teaspoons of vanilla

2 ounces (55 g) of chopped walnuts

Nonstick vegetable cooking spray

Combine bran, wheat germ, milk, baking powder and salt in a large bowl. In a separate bowl, combine eggs, sugar, apples, oil, molasses and vanilla. Add egg mixture gradually to dry mixture, blending well. Add nuts. Spray a 9-inch (23-cm) square baking pan with cooking spray.

Turn batter into pan and bake at 350°F (Gas Mark 4/180°C) for 25 minutes. Cool and cut into 20 squares.

Makes 20 servings at approximately 85 calories per serving.

CHEWY RAISIN COOKIES

2 ounces (50 g) of butter	whole-wheat flour
2¼ ounces (60 g) of brown sugar	½ teaspoon of bicarbonate of soda
1 teaspoon of vanilla essence	¼ teaspoon of salt
1 egg	½ teaspoon of cinnamon
7 ounces (200 g) of	3 ounces (80 g) of raisins

Preheat oven to 375°F (Gas Mark 5/190°C). Beat together butter, sugar, vanilla and egg. Combine dry ingredients and add to butter mixture, blending well. Stir in raisins. Spoon out by level teaspoonfuls on to nonstick, ungreased baking sheets. Bake for 8 minutes, or until golden brown.

Makes 50 cookies at approximately 30 calories apiece.

HONEYDEW DE-LIGHT

1 medium honeydew or other melon	2 dessertspoons of lime or lemon juice
1 teaspoon of unflavoured gelatin	2 dessertspoons of honey
2 dessertspoons of water	Lime or lemon twists

Cut melon into cubes. Soften gelatin in water. Place jug or bowl containing gelatin in pan of water and heat until gelatin is dissolved, stirring constantly. Combine one quarter of the melon cubes, the lime or lemon juice, honey and gelatin mixture in a blender, and blend on high for 30 seconds. Add remaining melon and blend again until smooth. Pour into 8 inch (20 cm) square pan, and place in freezer.

232

When mixture is almost firm, remove from pan and place in chilled bowl. Beat with electric mixer at high speed until smooth. Return to freezer pan and freeze until firm (several hours). To serve, remove from freezer and let stand about 15 minutes at room temperature. Spoon into serving dishes. Garnish with lime or lemon twists.

Makes 6 servings at 61 calories per serving.

PINEAPPLE BREAD

10 ounces (300 g) of whole-wheat flour
1 ounce (30 g) of Bran Flakes or Raisin Bran
2 dessertspoons of wheat germ
1 teaspoon of bicarbonate of soda
1 teaspoon of baking powder
Pinch of salt
1 beaten egg
16 fluid ounces (450 ml) of pineapple yogurt
3 tablespoons of skim milk
2 dessertspoons of vegetable oil
2 dessertspoons of molasses
2 dessertspoons of honey
1 teaspoon of lime or lemon juice
6 ounces (170 g) of raisins
3 ounces (80 g) of chopped walnuts
3 ounces (80 g) of dates, chopped
Nonstick vegetable cooking spray

Combine flour, bran, wheat germ, soda, baking powder and salt in a large bowl. In another bowl, combine egg, yogurt, milk, oil, molasses, honey and lime or lemon juice. Stir into dry ingredients. Add raisins, nuts and dates. Spray 2 small loaf tins with cooking spray and turn batter into pans. Bake at 325°F (Gas Mark 3/170°C) for 1 hour, or until toothpick inserted in centre comes out clean. Cool for 15 minutes and remove from pans. Allow to cool completely on wire rack. Store overnight, wrapped well, before slicing.

Makes 30 servings at about 92 calories per serving.

TROPICAL COCONUT CRUST PIE

⅓ ounce (10 g) of butter
4 ounces (110 g) of flaked
  coconut
1 pound 4 ounces (565 g)
  tin of crushed
  unsweetened pineapple

Water
1 envelope of
  unflavoured gelatin
16 fluid ounces (450 ml) of
  orange yogurt

Preheat oven to 325°F (Gas Mark 3/170°C). Melt butter and toss with coconut in a 9-inch (23-cm) pie plate. Press onto the bottom and the sides of the plate. Bake for 15 minutes, or until golden. Cool on wire rack.

Meanwhile, drain pineapple, and reserve juice. Add water to juice, if necessary, to make 6 fluid ounces (180 ml) of liquid. Soften gelatin in liquid in a small saucepan. Cook over low heat until gelatin is dissolved, stirring constantly. Remove from heat and chill until partially set, to the consistency of unbeaten egg whites, then beat gelatin until fluffy. Fold in yogurt and pineapple and pour into cooled crust. Chill until firm.

Makes 8 servings at 139 calories per serving.

Crispbreads and Pancakes

GERMAN FRUIT PUFF

2 ounces (56 g) of plain
  flour
2 ounces (56 g) of
  whole-wheat flour
½ teaspoon of baking
  powder
½ teaspoon of salt
8 fluid ounces (225 ml) of
  skim milk

5 eggs
1½ teaspoons of
  vegetable oil
26-fluid-ounce (750-ml)
  measure of any variety
  of fresh fruit, sliced
  (about 1 pound 8
  ounces/680 g)

Preheat oven to 425°F (Gas Mark 7/220°C). Sift together flours, baking powder and salt in mixing bowl. Stir in milk. Beat eggs in, one at a time. Heat oil over medium heat in a large ovenproof pan. Pour in batter and let cook

234

1 minute. Place pan in oven and bake, uncovered, for 20 minutes, or until puff is golden brown. Top with fruit and slice into 6 wedges.

Makes 6 servings at 207 calories per serving.

TOASTED OAT THINS

2 ounces (56 g) of quick-cooking rolled oats or fine oatmeal

3 ounces (80 g) mixed plain and whole-wheat flour

3 rounded tablespoons of wheat germ

1 dessertspoon of sugar

1 dessertspoon of sesame seeds, crushed

½ teaspoon of garlic powder

⅛ teaspoon of salt

2 ounces (56 g) of butter

4 fluid ounces (110 ml) of cold water

Blend oats (if used) in a blender or food processor until evenly ground. Pour into mixing bowl. Add flours, wheat germ, sugar, sesame seed, garlic and salt. Cut in butter until mixture has consistency of coarse breadcrumbs. Gradually mix in cold water to form a dough. Shape the dough into a 9 inch (23 cm) long roll. Wrap in plastic wrap and chill for at least 3 hours. Slice into ⅛ inch (¼ cm) thick rounds and place on foil-lined, ungreased baking sheet. Flatten with tines of a fork until thin. Bake at 375°F (Gas Mark 5/190°C) for 12 minutes, or until edges are nicely browned. Cool on wire rack.

Makes 6 dozen crispbread at 19 calories each.

WHOLE-WHEAT BREAKFAST CAKES

5 ounces (145 g) of whole-wheat flour

2 teaspoons of baking powder

¼ teaspoon of salt

1 egg

10 fluid ounces (275 ml) of skim milk

Nonstick vegetable cooking spray

Combine flour, baking powder and salt in mixing bowl. Beat together egg and milk, and stir into flour mixture to form a batter. Spray a nonstick pan with cooking spray and heat over medium heat. Drop batter by spoonfuls onto pan to make 4-inch (10-cm) pancakes. Reduce heat to low and cook until bubbles begin to form on cakes. Turn and cook on the other side until golden brown.

This makes 8 cakes at about 87 calories each.

13

Epilogue

Do you remember those five little words – my magical cure for obesity?

EAT LESS FAT AND WALK

Use the Rotation Diet periodically if you have more weight to lose than you can take off in twenty-one days. Then practise the magical cure on a daily basis for ever after. Of course, if walking is not your thing, do whatever you like in the way of brisk physical activity. But always pay attention to my words about fat in your diet. *You can't get fat if you don't eat fat!*

And remember that I'd like to hear from you when you finish the Rotation Diet (see Appendix B). Write to me, telling me how the Rotation Diet worked for you and join our follow-up study. Joining might help you stay at desirable weight and it will help us in our research on the effectiveness of the Rotation Diet.

Here's to your success and I'm looking forward to hearing from you.

Appendix A

The Rotation Diet Quick Calorie Counter

Calorie Chart

FOOD	CALORIES
Apple, medium size with skin	80
Apple juice, unsweetened, 8 fluid ounces (225 ml)	59
Apples, stewed, unsweetened, 8 fluid ounces (225 ml)	50
Apricots, dried, 4 large halves	59
Apricots, raw, without stones (3)	55
Artichoke, globe, fresh, boiled	40
Artichoke hearts, frozen or water packed, 3 ounces/80 g (5)	20
Artichoke, Jerusalem, ½ cup	25
Asparagus, fresh or frozen, 3 stalks	9
Aubergine, 1 medium	92
Avocado, ½ medium	185
Bacon, 1 thin slice cooked crisp and dry	30
Baking powder, 1 teaspoon	5
Banana, ½ small	41
Barley, 8 fluid ounce (225 ml) measure, uncooked	700
Bean sprouts, ½ cup	19
Beans, baby broad, 2 ounces (56 g)	70
Beans, black-eyed peas, dry, cooked, 1 cup	190
Beans, navy, dry, cooked, 1 cup	225
Beans, red kidney, tinned, 1 cup	230
Beef, lean, 3 ounces (80 g)	165

Calorie Chart *(Continued)*

FOOD	CALORIES
Beef broth (bouillon), 8 fluid ounces (225 ml)	23
Beetroot, ½ cup	27
Blackberries, fresh, 1 cup	85
Blueberries, fresh, ½ cup	45
Bran cereal, pure, ½ cup	95
Breadcrumbs, dry, 4 ounces (110 g)	390
Bread, white, 1 slice	65
Bread, whole-wheat, 1 slice	65
Broccoli, cooked, ½ cup	30
Brussels sprouts, ½ cup	28
Butter, ⅓ ounce (10 g)	102
Buttermilk, skim, 8 fluid ounces (225 ml)	88
Cabbage, ½ cup	11
Cabbage, Chinese, ½ cup	6
Cantaloupe, ½ medium	60
Carrots, ½ cup	23
Cauliflower, ½ cup	13
Caviar, 1 ounce (28 g)	75
Celery, ½ cup	9
Cheese, blue, 1 ounce (28 g)	100
Cheese, Cheddar, 1-inch (2-cm) cube	68
Cheese, Gruyère, 1 ounce (28 g)	115
Cheese, Mozzarella, part skim, 1 ounce (28 g)	80
Cheese, Parmesan, grated, 1 dessertspoon	23
Cheese, Ricotta, part skim, 1 cup	340
Cheese, Roquefort, 1 ounce	111
Cherries, fresh, ½ cup	41
Chicken, cooked, 1 ounce of meat, no skin	43
Chutney, 1 dessertspoon	53
Cocoa, dry, 1 dessertspoon	14
Cod, fresh, 4 ounces (110 g) cooked	89
Coffee, 1 cup	2
Coffee, decaffeinated, 1 cup	3
Cottage cheese, low fat, 4 ounces (110 g)	90
Cream substitute (Coffee-Mate), 1 scant teaspoon	11
Corn kernels, ½ cup	69
Corn on the cob, 1 medium	74
Corned beef, 2 ounces (56 g)	200
Cornflour, 1 dessertspoon	30
Courgette, ½ cup sliced thin	9
Crabmeat, 4 ounces (110 g) cooked	116
Cream, half and half, 1 dessertspoon	20
Cream, whipping, 1 dessertspoon	45
Cream, sour, 1 dessertspoon	29

Calorie Chart *(Continued)*

FOOD	CALORIES
Cream cheese, 1 ounce (28 g)	106
Crispbread, whole-wheat	16
Cucumber, ½ cup	8
Curry powder, 1 dessertspoon	12
Dandelion greens, cooked, drained, 1 cup	35
Egg, 1 medium	72
Egg white, 1 medium	15
Egg yolk, 1 medium	52
Enchilada, 1 average	185
Endive, raw, 1 cup	10
Fat, vegetable, ⅓ ounce (10 g)	111
Figs, fresh, 1 small	30
Flounder, 5 ounces (145 g) cooked	118
Flour, bread, 1 ounce (28 g)	108
Flour, soybean, 1 ounce (28 g)	90
Flour, cake, 1 ounce (28 g)	102
Flour, self-raising, 1 ounce (28 g)	99
Frankfurter, 1, all beef, 1½ ounces (40 g)	142
French beans, ½ cup	18
Garlic, 1 ounce (28 g)	39
Gelatin, 1 dessertspoon	23
Ginger root, skinned, 1 ounce (28 g)	14
Grapes, 3 ounces/80 g (10 to 20)	34
Grape juice, sweetened, 4 fluid ounces (110 ml)	104
Grape juice, unsweetened, 4 fluid ounces (110 ml)	80
Grapefruit, ½	55
Grapefruit sections, 8 fluid ounces (225 ml)	80
Greens, cooked, 1 cup	30
Halibut, 4 ounces (110 g) cooked	114
Ham, 2 ounces (56 g)	106
Honey, 1 dessertspoon	64
Honeydew melon, ⅛	50
Ice cream, rich, 4 fluid ounces (110 ml), 2 scoops	164
Kale, cooked, 1 cup	45
Lamb, lean, cooked, 2 ounces (56 g)	105
Leeks, sliced, 2 ounces (56 g)	30
Lemon, 1 medium	20
Lemon juice, 1 dessertspoon	4
Lettuce, soft, 1 head	23
Lettuce, iceberg, 8 ounces (220 g)	30
Lettuce, iceberg, chopped, 1 cup	10
Lettuce, cos, chopped, 1 cup	8
Lime, 1	19

Calorie Chart *(Continued)*

FOOD	CALORIES
Liver, calf, raw, 2 ounces (56 g)	80
Liver, chicken, raw, 2 ounces (56 g)	73
Lobster, 2 ounces (56 g) cooked	52
Macaroni, cooked, ½ cup (2 ounces/56 g raw)	78
Mandarin oranges, tinned, unsweetened, ½ cup	31
Mango, ½ cup	56
Maple syrup, 1 dessertspoon	50
Margarine, ⅓ ounce (10 g)	102
Mayonnaise, 1 dessertspoon	101
Melba toast, 1 slice	15
Milk, goat, 8 fluid ounces (225 ml)	163
Milk, skim, 8 fluid ounces (225 ml)	80
Milk, 2% fat, 8 fluid ounces (225 ml)	120
Milk, cow's, whole, 8 fluid ounces (225 ml)	160
Muffin	140
Mushrooms, tinned, sliced, ½ cup	17
Mushrooms, fresh, sliced, ½ cup	13
Nectarine, ½ cup	70
Nuts, almonds, chopped, 1 cup (5 ounces/145 g)	775
Nuts, Brazil, 6–8 large	185
Nuts, cashews, roasted in oil, 1 cup	785
Nuts, coconut, shredded, 4 ounces (110 g)	275
Nuts, hazelnuts, chopped, 1 cup (5 ounces/145 g)	730
Nuts, peanuts, raw, shelled, 1 ounce (28 g)	155
Nuts, peanuts, roasted in oil, 1 cup	840
Nuts, peanuts, dry roasted, 1 ounce (28 g)	170
Nuts, Macadamia, 1 ounce (28 g)	218
Nuts, pecans or walnuts, shelled, halves, ½ cup (4 ounces/110 g)	370
Nuts, pistachio, 1 dessertspoon	46
Nuts, walnuts, chopped, 1 cup (5 ounces/145 g)	785
Oil, vegetable, 1 dessertspoon	120
Okra, 8 medium	24
Olives, 1 large	10
Onion, ½ cup	22
Onions, spring, 3 small	14
Orange, 1	71
Orange juice, 4 fluid ounces (110 ml)	41
Orange sections, ½ cup	42
Oysters, raw, 1 medium	7
Papaya, ½	60
Parsley, 1 dessertspoon	1
Parsnip, ½ cup	51
Peach, fresh, 1 average	38

Calorie Chart *(Continued)*

FOOD	CALORIES
Peanut butter, 1 dessertspoon	94
Pear, 1 fresh, 6 ounces (175 g)	80
Pear, tinned, water-packed, 4 fluid ounces (110 ml)	40
Peas, cooked, ½ cup	57
Peas, mangetout or snow, ½ cup	50
Pepper, green, 1 medium	16
Pepper, red, 1 medium	23
Persimmon, ½ cup	144
Pickles, dill, 1	3
Pie crust, 9-inch (23-cm) 1	675
Pie crust, ⅙	112
Pigeon, meat only, 4 ounces (110 g) cooked	161
Pineapple, ½ cup diced, fresh (about 1 slice, ¾ inch/1½ cm thick)	41
Pineapple, tinned, water-packed, 4 fluid ounces (110 ml)	39
Plum, damson, 1 raw	33
Popcorn, oil and salt, 1 cup	64
Pork, roasted, 4 ounces (110 g)	277
Pork, shoulder, lean, 4 ounces (110 g) cooked	220
Pork sausagemeat, 1 ounce (28 g)	142
Potato, 1 medium	88
Potato chips, 10	113
Pound cake, 1 slice	150
Pretzels, 1 small	4
Prunes, cooked without sugar, 5 medium	119
Prune juice, 4 fluid ounces (110 ml)	88
Radish, 4 small	6
Raisins, 1 dessertspoon	26
Raspberries, fresh, ½ cup	35
Raspberries, frozen, ½ cup	122
Rice, brown, ½ cup cooked	89
Rice, white, ½ cup cooked	82
Rice, blend of long grain and wild, ½ cup cooked	111
Ritz crackers, 1	15
Runner beans, ½ cup	18
Rutabaga, diced, ½ cup	30
Salami, 1 slice (1 ounce/28 g)	90
Salmon, 2 ounces (56 g) cooked	104
Salmon, smoked, 1 ounce (28 g)	50
Salsify, tinned, ½ cup	79
Salt, any quantity	0
Sardines, in oil, a 3¾ ounce (106 g) tin (6–8 small sardines)	167
Sauerkraut, ½ cup	21
Scallops, raw, ½ cup	92

Calorie Chart *(Continued)*

FOOD	CALORIES
Sesame seeds, 1 ounce/28 g (2 dessertspoons)	165
Shallots, 1 ounce (28 g)	14
Shrimps, shelled, about 3½ ounces (90 g)	91
Soft drinks, colas, 12 fluid ounces (330 ml)	145
Soft drinks, ginger ale, 12 fluid ounces (330 ml)	115
Soft drinks, root beer, 12 fluid ounces (330 ml)	150
Sole, 4 ounces (110 g) cooked	90
Spinach, trimmed, raw, 1 cup	14
Sugar, brown, 1 dessertspoon	49
Sugar, icing, 1 dessertspoon	31
Sugar, granulated, 1 dessertspoon	46
Sunflower seeds, dry, hulled, 1 cup	810
Sweetbreads, calf, 4 ounces (110 g) cooked	188
Sweet potato, 1 medium	152
Tangerine, 1 medium	40
Tea, 1 bag	1
Tomato, 1 medium	26
Tomatoes, tinned, 4 fluid ounces (110 ml)	25
Tomato juice, 4 fluid ounces (110 ml)	23
Tongue, pickled, 1 ounce (28 g)	76
Tortilla, 1	64
Trout, boned, 4 ounces (110 g) cooked	125
Tuna, water- or brine-packed, 6½ ounce (185 g) tin	240
Turkey, roasted, 2 ounces (56 g) sliced	108
Turnip, diced, ½ cup	18
Turnip greens, cooked, ½ cup	14
Turtle meat, 2 ounces (56 g), cooked	60
Vanilla extract, 1 teaspoon	8
Veal chop, 4 ounces (110 g) lean, cooked	220
Veal loin, roasted, 2 ounces (56 g)	135
Vinegar, 1 dessertspoon	2
Waffles, 7-inch (18-cm) diameter, 1	210
Walnuts, ½ cup shelled (2 ounces/56 g)	326
Water chestnuts, 2 ounces (56 g)	36
Watercress, ½ cup	3
Watermelon, ½ cup	21
Wheat germ, 1 ounce (28 g)	103
Yeast, compressed, 1 ounce (28 g)	25
Yeast, dry, 1 dessertspoon	23
Yogurt, skim, plain, 4 fluid ounces (110 ml)	62
Beer, 12 fluid ounces (330 ml)	150
Brandy, flavoured, 1 fluid ounce (28 ml)	75

Calorie Chart *(Continued)*

FOOD	CALORIES
Champagne, 3 fluid ounces (80 ml)	75
Distilled liquors, regular proof, 1 fluid ounce (28 ml)	65
Distilled liquors, extra proof, 1 fluid ounce (28 ml)	82
Wines, dessert, 3 fluid ounces (80 ml)	120
Wines, dry red, 3 fluid ounces (80 ml)	88
Wines, dry white, 3 fluid ounces (80 ml)	75

Appendix B

Instructions for Participating in the Rotation Diet Follow-up Study

You can participate in the Rotation Diet follow-up study by writing to:

The Rotation Diet
c/o The Vanderbilt Weight Management Program
134 Wesley Hall
Vanderbilt University
Nashville, TN 37240

Please indicate specifically that you want to participate in the Rotation Diet follow-up study, *and be sure to include your name and address and international reply coupons to the value of £1.10 in your letter.* You will hear from us periodically, at which time we will want to know how you are doing in managing your weight. We will ask you to fill out a very short questionnaire each time we write to you.

There is no charge for participating in this follow-up study and you will receive no solicitation for anything but information about how well you are doing in managing your weight.

HOW TO OBTAIN MORE INFORMATION ABOUT THE VANDERBILT WEIGHT MANAGEMENT PROGRAM

The Vanderbilt Weight Management Program offers consultation via mail and telephone on weight-management problems.

If you would like to receive information about the consultation services and other weight-management materials that are available at a modest cost from the programme, *please send a self-addressed envelope with 55p in international reply coupons requesting this information to:*

Ms Summer Davis
Associate Director
Vanderbilt Weight Management Program
134 Wesley Hall
Vanderbilt University
Nashville, TN 37240

You will not receive any of this information unless you specifically request it. Please write to obtain this information before calling the Weight Management Program on the telephone.

The Rotation Diet Pocket Edition for Women

You can average a weight loss of up to a pound a day for twenty-one days if you follow the menus exactly as they are laid out on the following pages. Best results are obtained *with no substitutions*. However, if a particular food does not agree with you, please read Chapter 6 concerning allowable substitutions.

Recipes and other suggestions for food preparation are found in Chapter 6. I have not given the names of specific recipes here, as I did in the Chapter 6 menus, but those foods with an asterisk have recipes in Chapter 6.

In order to be sure that everyone can follow the Rotation Diet and never feel hungry, I have designed an insurance policy that will enable you to overcome temptations and still achieve close-to-optimum results. It has two clauses. The first is called *free vegetables*. Should any temptations to deviate from the diet arise during the next twenty-one days, you may eat unlimited quantities of free vegetables with any meal and at any time of the day as snacks (see page 255 of this Pocket Edition). Free vegetables contain almost no calories. In addition, you may choose a *safe fruit* (see page 255 of this Pocket Edition). The safe fruit (remember to choose only one) will be additional insurance against ever being hungry. It will also be used as a source of quick energy whenever you need it.

You may photocopy the Pocket Edition of the Rotation Diet so that you can carry it with you for ready reference. In case a photocopier is not available to you, you may cut out the following pages without damaging the other contents of the book.

COUPLES CAN USE THE ROTATION DIET TOGETHER – see the text at the beginning of the menus for women (Weeks 1 and 2), or see page 52 of Chapter 6.

If you show the Rotation Diet to your friends and they wish to use it, please ask them to read Chapters 1, 6 and 7 before they start. (Be sure to read these chapters yourself before you start.)

THE COMPLETE ROTATION DIET PLAN MENUS FOR WOMEN

The Rotation Diet is designed to be used with the special recipes that are available for items marked with an asterisk (see Chapter 6 menus for specific names of recipes, or leaf through recipes). However, you can prepare everything in your own way provided you do not use any fat in preparation except where indicated. Also, you can use the portion sizes below as a guide when eating out during this period. *Weights below are all cooked weights.* See Chapter 6 for information on shrinkage to be expected during cooking. No-cal salad dressings can be used at any time, so they are not always indicated. Note: tablespoon and dessertspoon measures are level measures and teaspoons, ½ teaspoons, etc. should be scant.

Week 1

For couples who wish to use the Rotation Diet together, men may use the basic Week 1 diet plan for women with the addition of all of the following each day:

2 more grain servings (bread, cereal, or crisp-bread)
50 per cent larger portions of meat, fish, or poultry
1 dessertspoon of butter, oil or regular salad dressing
3 safe fruits

The calorie goal for men is 1200 calories for the first three days, and 1500 calories for the next four. Additional information on serving sizes, *with calorie values*, will be found with the recipes in Chapter 6.

DAY 1

Breakfast: ½ grapefruit, 1 slice of whole-wheat bread,* 1 ounce (28 g) of cheese,* no-cal beverage

Lunch: 2 ounces (56 g) of salmon* (canned in water), unlimited free vegetables, 5 whole-wheat crispbread, no-cal beverage

Dinner: 3 ounces (80 g) of baked chicken,* 1 cup of cauliflower,* ½ cup of beetroot,* 1 apple, no-cal beverage

DAY 2

Breakfast: ½ banana, 1 ounce (28 g) of high-fibre cereal,* 8 fluid ounces (225 ml) of skim or low-fat milk, no-cal beverage

Lunch: 4 ounces (110 g) of low-fat cottage

cheese,* unlimited free vegetables, 1 slice of whole-wheat bread,* no-cal beverage

Dinner: 3 ounces (80 g) of poached fish fillets,* 1 cup of broccoli,* ½ cup of carrots,* ½ grapefruit, no-cal beverage

DAY 3

Breakfast: 1 slice of whole-wheat bread,* 1 dessertspoon of peanut butter, 1 apple, no-cal beverage

Lunch: 2 ounces (56 g) of water-packed tuna* or 3 sardines,* 5 whole-wheat crackers, unlimited free vegetables, no-cal beverage

Dinner: 3 ounces (80 g) of beefsteak* or hamburger patty,* 6 stalks of asparagus,* 1 cup of dinner salad,* 1 ounce (28 g) of cheese, 1 orange, no-cal beverage

DAY 4

Breakfast: ½ banana, 1 ounce (28 g) of high-fibre cereal,* 8 fluid ounces (225 ml) of skim or low-fat milk, no-cal beverage

Lunch: Tuna salad* (2 ounces (56 g) of water-packed tuna), unlimited free vegetables, 2 slices of whole-wheat bread,* 1 teaspoon of mayonnaise or lo-cal dressing,* ½ grapefruit, no-cal beverage

Dinner: 3 ounces (80 g) of baked chicken,* ½ cup of carrots,* 1 cup of dinner salad,* 1 ounce (28 g) of cheese, 1 apple, no-cal beverage

DAY 5

Breakfast: 1 cup of berries, 4 ounces (110 g) of

low-fat cottage cheese,* 5
whole-wheat crispbread, no-cal
beverage

Lunch: 3 sardines* or 2 ounces (56 g) of
water-packed tuna,* unlimited free
vegetables, 2 slices of whole-wheat
bread,* 1 teaspoon of mayonnaise or
lo-cal dressing,* ½ grapefruit, no-cal
beverage

Dinner: 3 ounces (80 g) of beefsteak* or
hamburger patty,* ½ cup of french or
runner beans,* 1 cup of broccoli,* 1
ounce (28 g) of cheese, 1 apple, no-cal
beverauge

DAY 6

Breakfast: ½ cantaloupe, 1 ounce (28 g) of
cheese,* 1 slice of whole-wheat
bread,* no-cal beverage

Lunch: 1 hard-boiled egg,* unlimited free
vegetables, 2 slices of whole-wheat
bread,* 1 teaspoon of mayonnaise or
low-cal salad dressing,* ½ grapefruit,
no-cal beverage

Dinner: 3 ounces (80 g) of fish fillets,* 1 cup of
asparagus,* ½ cup of peas,* 1 apple,
no-cal beverage

DAY 7

Breakfast: ½ banana, 1 ounce (28 g) of high-fibre
cereal,* 8 fluid ounces (225 ml) skim or
low-fat milk, no-cal beverage

Lunch: 1 cup of berries, 4 ounces (110 g) of
low-fat cottage cheese,* 2 slices of
whole-wheat bread,* no-cal beverage

Dinner: 3 ounces (80 g) of baked chicken,* 1
cup of cauliflower,* ½ cup of carrots,*
1 apple, no-cal beverage

251

Week 2

In Week 2 you may add a mid-morning, a mid-afternoon, and an evening snack, intentionally incorporating three servings of your *safe fruit.* It is not obligatory to include all of these snacks in addition to the menus below, but they are permitted within the 1200-calorie limits for this week. You may also add 1 dessertspoon of oil or regular salad dressing or ⅓ ounce (10 g) butter or margarine to your diet each day. Use it for cooking or as a spread.

For couples, men should add all of the following each day to the daily menus of the Rotation Diet for women, below.

2 more grain servings (bread, cereal or crispbread)
50 per cent larger servings of vegetables and main courses

Optional for men: another dessertspoon of fat for spread or seasoning. The calorie goal for males is 1800 per day throughout Week 2. Additional information on serving sizes, *with calorie values,* will be found with the recipes in Chapter 6.

DAY 8

Breakfast: ½ grapefruit, 1 slice of whole-wheat bread,* 1 dessertspoon of peanut butter, 8 fluid ounces (225 ml) of skim or low-fat milk, no-cal beverage

Lunch: large fruit salad (16 fluid ounces/ 450 ml),* 1 ounce (28 g) of cheese, 5 whole-wheat crispbread, no-cal beverage

Dinner: salmon steak* (4½ ounces/125 g), ½ cup of peas and baby onions,* 1 cup of dinner salad,* no-cal beverage

DAY 9

Breakfast: ½ banana, 1 ounce (28 g) of high-fibre

252

cereal,* 8 fluid ounces (225 ml) of skim
or low-fat milk, no-cal beverage

Lunch: large chef salad* (1 ounce/28 g of
turkey and 1 ounce/28 g of cheese,
plus salad vegetables), 5 whole-wheat
crispbread, lo-cal dressing,* no-cal
beverage

Dinner: 4½ ounces (125 g) of baked chicken,*
1 small (3½-ounce/90-g) baked potato,
1 cup of green beans,* 1 ounce (28 g)
of cheese, 1 apple, no-cal beverage

DAY 10

Breakfast: 1 cup of sliced fruit, 4 ounces (110 g) of
low-fat cottage cheese,* 1 slice of
whole-wheat bread,* no-cal beverage

Lunch: sandwich* (2 ounces/56 g of meat or
cheese), unlimited free vegetables, 1
orange, no-cal beverage

Dinner: 2 cups of stir-fry vegetables,* ½ cup
cooked brown or wild rice,* 2
dessertspoons of grated cheese, 1
apple, no-cal beverage

DAY 11

Breakfast: 2 slices of fresh pineapple (or 2 pieces
other fresh fruit), 1 ounce (28 g) of
cheese, 1 slice of whole-wheat bread,*
no-cal beverage

Lunch: large (2–3 cups) spinach salad,* lo-cal
dressing,* 1 apple or pear, 1 ounce
(28 g) of cheese, no-cal beverage

Dinner: 6 ounces (175 g) of steak,* 1 small (3½-
ounce/90-g) baked potato, 1 cup of
braised carrots and celery,* ½
grapefruit, no-cal beverage

DAY 12

Breakfast: ½ cup of sliced fruit for cereal, 1 ounce

(28 g) of high-fibre cereal,* 8 fluid
ounces (225 ml) of skim or low-fat
milk, no-cal beverage

Lunch: tuna or sardine salad* (3 ounces/80 g
of water-packed tuna, 4–5 small
sardines), unlimited free vegetables
plus sliced tomato and green peppers,
lo-cal dressing,* 1 slice of
whole-wheat bread,* no-cal beverage

Dinner: 6 ounces (175 g) of lean pork chop* (or
other lean meat), serving baked
marrow or courgette,* 1 cup of
broccoli,* ½ grapefruit, no-cal
beverage

DAY 13

Breakfast: ½ melon, 1 hard- or soft-boiled egg,* 1
slice of whole-wheat bread,* no-cal
beverage

Lunch: 4½-ounce (125-g) ground-beef patty,*
4 ounces (110 g) of low-fat cottage
cheese,* sliced tomato and unlimited
free vegetables, lo-cal dressing,*
no-cal beverage

Dinner: 1 cup of pasta* (plus sauce*), 2
dessertspoons of Parmesan cheese, 1
cup of dinner salad,* choice of 1 fresh
fruit for dessert, no-cal beverage

DAY 14

Breakfast: ½ grapefruit, 1 cup of porridge, 2
dessertspoons of raisins, dash of
cinnamon, 4 fluid ounces (110 ml) of
skim or low-fat milk, no-cal beverage

Lunch: toasted open-faced sandwich* or
regular sandwich* (2 ounces/56 g of
meat or cheese), unlimited free
vegetables, 1 cup of assorted sliced
fresh fruit, no-cal beverage

254

Dinner: Pot roast of beef* (4 ounces/110 g of meat, plus vegetables), 1 cup of dinner salad,* lo-cal dressing,* 1 ounce (28 g) of cheese, 1 apple, no-cal beverage

Week 3

Repeat the menus of Week 1, or use the Alternative Menus in Chapter 12 for the 600- and 900-calorie rotations.

> When you finish your twenty-one days on the Rotation Diet, BE VERY SURE THAT YOU FOLLOW MY DIRECTIONS FOR MAKING A TRANSITION TO MAINTE-NANCE IN WEEK 4 (CHAPTER 8).

Unlimited Free Vegetable List

You may eat all you want of the vegetables on this list at any time. They provide many vitamins and minerals, together with beneficial amounts of fibre, with virtually no calories. Eat them plain or use only no-cal salad dressings (your choice, or see page 83 of the Rotation Diet).

asparagus	celery	chicory
Chinese cabbage	courgette	cucumber
endive	lettuce	parsley
radishes	spinach (raw)	watercress

Safe Fruit List

Choose *one* fruit from this list (or any other fresh fruit that is easily available to you) as your *safe fruit*. Eat up to three servings a day in addition to whatever is called for in the menus of the Rotation Diet when you need a lift, feel intolerably hungry or are tempted to deviate from your diet for any reason. Carry one with you at all times as a snack.

255

> *Whenever you are tempted to deviate from the Rotation Diet make a safe-fruit substitution instead. This ensures that you will achieve close to the maximum possible weight loss.*

apple	berries	grapefruit
melon	orange	peach
pineapple	tangerine	

Beverages

Drink eight 8-fluid-ounce (225-ml)-glasses of water a day. Use only no-calorie beverages except when milk is called for. You may drink up to 2 cups of coffee or tea each day, plus herb teas and low-sodium bouillons.

The Rotation Diet
Pocket Edition
for Men

You can average a weight loss of up to a pound a day for twenty-one days if you follow the menus exactly as they are laid out on the following pages. Best results are obtained *with no substitutions*. However, if a particular food does not agree with you, please read Chapter 6 concerning allowable substitutions.

Recipes and other suggestions for food preparation are found in Chapter 6. I have not given the names of specific recipes here, as I did in the Chapter 6 menus, but those foods with an asterisk have recipes in Chapter 6.

In order to be sure that everyone can follow the Rotation Diet and never feel hungry, I have designed an insurance policy that will enable you to overcome temptations and still achieve close-to-optimum results. It has two clauses. The first is called *free vegetables*. Should any temptations to deviate from the diet arise during the next twenty-one days, you may eat unlimited quantities of free vegetables with any meal and at any time of the day as snacks (see page 265 of this Pocket Edition). Free vegetables contain almost no calories. In addition, you may choose a *safe fruit* (see page 265 of this Pocket Edition). The safe fruit (remember to choose only one) will be another insurance against ever being hungry. It will also be used as a source of quick energy whenever you need it.

You may photocopy the Pocket Edition of the Rotation Diet so that you can carry it with you for ready reference. In case a photocopier is not available to you, you may cut out the following pages without damaging the other contents of the book.

COUPLES CAN USE THE ROTATION DIET TOGETHER – see the text at the beginning of the menus for women (Weeks 1 and 2), or see page 52 of Chapter 6.

If you show the Rotation Diet to your friends and they wish to use it, please ask them to read Chapters 1, 6 and 7 before they start. (Be sure to read these chapters yourself before you start.)

THE COMPLETE ROTATION DIET PLAN MENUS FOR MEN

The Rotation Diet is designed to be used with the special recipes that are available for items marked with an asterisk (see Chapter 6 menus for specific names of recipes, or leaf through recipes). However, you can prepare everything in your own way provided you do not use any fat in preparation except where indicated. Also, you can use the portion sizes below as a guide when eating out during this period. *Weights below are all cooked weights.* See Chapter 6 for information on shrinkage to be expected during cooking.

Men may add 1 dessertspoon of regular salad

dressing or ⅓ ounce (10 g) of butter or margarine to each day's menu and remain within the calorie limits. No-cal salad dressings can be used at any time, so they are not always indicated.

Men may also plan on having three *safe fruit* snacks each day, in addition to the items on the following menus. You do not have to eat them all, but they are available, within the calorie limits. Note: tablespoon and dessertspoon measures are level measures and teaspoons, ½ teaspoons, etc. should be scant.

Week 1

DAY 1

Breakfast: ½ banana, 1 ounce (28 g) of high-fibre cereal,* 8 fluid ounces (225 ml) of skim or low-fat milk, no-cal beverage

Lunch: large chef salad* (1 ounce/28 g each of cheese and turkey, plus any salad vegetables), lo-cal dressing,* 5 whole-wheat crispbread, no-cal beverage

Dinner: 4½ ounces (125 g) of baked chicken,* 1 small (3½-ounce/90-g) baked potato, 1 cup of french or runner beans,* 1 apple, 1 ounce (28 g) of cheese, no-cal beverage

DAY 2

Breakfast: ½ grapefruit, 1 slice of whole-wheat bread,* 1 dessertspoon of peanut butter, 8 fluid ounces (225 ml) of skim or low-fat milk, no-cal beverage

Lunch: large fruit salad* (2 cups), 1 ounce (28 g) of cheese, 5 whole-wheat crispbread, no-cal beverage

Dinner: 6 ounces (175 g) of fish fillets,* ½ cup of peas and baby onions,* 1 cup of

259

dinner salad,* lo-cal dressing,* no-cal
beverage

DAY 3

Breakfast: 1 cup of sliced fruit (your choice), 4
ounces (110 g) of low-fat cottage
cheese,* 1 slice of whole-wheat
bread,* no-cal beverage
Lunch: combination sandwich* (2 ounces/56 g
of meat or cheese), unlimited free
vegetables, 1 orange, no-cal beverage
Dinner: 2 cups of stir-fry vegetables,* ½ cup of
cooked brown or wild rice,* 2
dessertspoons of grated cheese, 1
apple, no-cal beverage

DAY 4

Breakfast: 1 cup of berries, 1½ ounces (40 g) of
high-fibre cereal,* 8 fluid ounces
(225 ml) of skim or low-fat milk, 1 slice
of whole-wheat bread,* 1 teaspoon of
jam or marmalade, no-cal beverage
Lunch: large (2–3 cups) spinach salad,* lo-cal
dressing,* 5 whole-wheat crispbread,
1 apple or pear, no-cal beverage
Dinner: ½ grapefruit, 6 ounces (175 g) of
steak,* 1 small (3½-ounce/90-g) baked
potato, 1 cup of braised carrots and
celery,* no-cal beverage

DAY 5

Breakfast: ½ melon, 1 hard- or soft-boiled egg, 2
slices of whole-wheat bread,* 1
teaspoon of jam or marmalade, no-cal
beverage
Lunch: 4½-ounce (125-g) ground-beef patty,*
4 ounces (110 g) of low-fat cottage
cheese,* unlimited free vegetables, 1

slice of whole-wheat bread,* 1 serving of fruit (your choice), no-cal beverage

Dinner: 1 cup of pasta* (plus sauce*), 3 tablespoons of Parmesan cheese, 1 cup of dinner salad,* lo-cal dressing,* ½ grapefruit, no-cal beverage

DAY 6

Breakfast: 1 cup of sliced fruit for cereal, 1½ ounces (40 g) of high-fibre cereal,* 1 slice of whole-wheat bread,* 8 fluid ounces (225 ml) of skim or low-fat milk, no-cal beverage

Lunch: sardine or tuna salad* (4–5 small sardines or 3 ounces/80 g of water-packed tuna), unlimited free vegetables plus sliced tomato and green pepper, lo-cal dressing,* 2 slices of whole-wheat bread,* no-cal beverage

Dinner: 6 ounces (175 g) of lean pork chop* (or other lean meat*), serving of baked marrow or courgette,* 1 cup of broccoli,* 1 slice of whole-wheat bread,* ½ grapefruit, no-cal beverage

DAY 7

Breakfast: ½ grapefruit, 1 cup of porridge, 2 dessertspoons of raisins, dash of cinnamon, 4 fluid ounces (110 ml) of skim or low-fat milk, no-cal beverage

Lunch: open-faced sandwich* (2 portions, see Mexican Bean Spread, with 1 ounce (28 g) of cheese and sliced tomato, or see lunch sandwich Day 3), unlimited free vegetables, lo-cal dressing,* 1 cup of assorted fresh fruit, no-cal beverage

Dinner: 4 ounces (110 g) of pot roast* (including vegetables), 1 cup of dinner

salad,* lo-cal dressing,* 1 apple,
no-cal beverage

Week 2

During Week 2 you can add 1 dessertspoon of
regular salad dressing or ⅓ ounce (10 g) of butter or
margarine to each day's menu, as well as the three
safe fruits, and remain within the calorie limits.

DAY 8

Breakfast: ½ melon, 2 slices of whole-wheat
bread,* 2 ounces (56 g) of cheese,
no-cal beverage

Lunch: tuna-salad sandwich* (3 ounces/80 g
of water-packed tuna), unlimited free
vegetables, 1 serving of fruit (your
choice), no-cal beverage

Dinner: 6 ounces (175 g) of baked chicken,* ½
cup of spinach and broccoli casserole*
(or 1 cup of broccoli*), serving of
baked marrow or courgette,* 1 apple,
1 ounce (28 g) of cheese (if casserole
recipe is not used), no-cal beverage

DAY 9

Breakfast: 1 cup of porridge, 2 dessertspoons of
raisins, dash of cinnamon, 4 fluid
ounces (110 ml) of skim or low-fat
milk, 1 slice of whole-wheat bread,* 1
teaspoon of jam or marmalade, no-cal
beverage

Lunch: large fruit salad* (2 cups), 4 ounces
(110 g) of low-fat cottage cheese,* 5
whole-wheat crispbread, no-cal
beverage

Dinner: 6 ounces (175 g) of fish fillets,* ½

baked tomato,* 1 small (3½-
ounce/90-g) baked potato, 1 cup of
dinner salad,* 1 ounce (28 g) of
cheese, 1 apple, no-cal beverage

DAY 10

Breakfast: 1 orange, 2 slices of whole-wheat
bread,* 2 ounces (56 g) of cheese,
no-cal beverage

Lunch: tuna salad* (3 ounces/80 g of
water-packed tuna) on salad greens
with sliced tomatoes and green
pepper, plus unlimited free
vegetables, lo-cal dressing,* no-cal
beverage

Dinner: 6 ounces (175 g) of steak,* 1 cup of
stir-fry spinach,* 1 small (3½-
ounce/90-g) baked potato with cottage
cheese dressing* (or 2 dessertspoons
of sour cream), choice of 1 fruit, no-cal
beverage

DAY 11

Breakfast: ½ melon, 4 ounces (110 g) of low-fat
cottage cheese,* 1 slice of
whole-wheat bread,* 1 teaspoon of
jam or marmalade, no-cal beverage

Lunch: sandwich* (2 ounces/56 g of meat or
cheese), unlimited free vegetables,
lo-cal dressing,* no-cal beverage

Dinner: 6 ounces (175 g) of baked salmon,* ½
cup of peas and baby onions,* 1 cup of
dinner salad,* lo-cal dressing,* choice
of 1 fruit, 1 ounce (28 g) of cheese,
no-cal beverage

DAY 12

Breakfast: ½ grapefruit, 2 slices of whole-wheat
bread,* 1 dessertspoon of peanut

263

butter, 1 teaspoon of jam or
marmalade, no-cal beverage

Lunch: 8 fluid ounces (225 ml) of soup
(commercial or see Soups*), 10
whole-wheat crispbread, 2 ounces
(56 g) of cheese, unlimited free
vegetables, lo-cal dressing,* no-cal
beverage

Dinner: veal loaf* (or 6-ounce/175-g serving of
lean meat of your choice*), ½ cup of
carrots,* 1 cup of dinner salad,* lo-cal
dressing,* 1 apple, no-cal beverage

DAY 13

Breakfast: 1 cup of berries, 1½ ounces (40 g) of
high-fibre cereal,* 1 slice of
whole-wheat bread,* 1 teaspoon of
jam or marmalade, 8 fluid ounces
(225 ml) of skim or low-fat milk, no-cal
beverage

Lunch: large chef salad* (1 ounce/28 g each of
turkey and cheese, plus salad
vegetables), lo-cal dressing,* 5
whole-wheat crispbread, no-cal
beverage

Dinner: 6 ounces (175 g) of baked chicken,* ½
cup of cooked brown or wild rice,* 1
cup of broccoli,* 1 ounce (28 g) of
cheese, 1 apple, no-cal beverage

DAY 14

Breakfast: 1 cup of sliced fruit, 4 ounces (110 g) of
low-fat cottage cheese,* 1 slice of
whole-wheat bread,* 1 teaspoon of
jam or marmalade, no-cal beverage

Lunch: sandwich* (2 ounces/56 g of meat or
cheese), unlimited free vegetables,
lo-cal dressing,* ½ grapefruit, no-cal
beverage

Dinner: 6 ounces (175 g) of baked or broiled
fish,* ½ baked tomato,* 1 cup of green
beans with chives,* 1 slice of
whole-wheat bread,* 1 ounce (28 g) of
cheese, 1 fruit of your choice, no-cal
beverage

Week 3

Repeat the menus of Week 1, or use the Alternative
Menus in Chapter 12 for the 1200- and 1500-calorie
rotations.

> When you finish your twenty-one days on
> the Rotation Diet, BE VERY SURE THAT
> YOU FOLLOW MY DIRECTIONS FOR
> MAKING A TRANSITION TO MAINTE-
> NANCE IN WEEK 4 (CHAPTER 8).

Unlimited Free Vegetable List

You may eat all you want of the vegetables on this
list at any time. They provide many vitamins and
minerals, together with beneficial amounts of fibre,
with virtually no calories. Eat them plain or use only
no-cal salad dressings (your choice, or see page 83
of the Rotation Diet).

asparagus	celery	chicory
Chinese cabbage	courgette	cucumber
endive	lettuce	parsley
radishes	spinach (raw)	watercress

Safe Fruit List

Choose *one* fruit from this list (or any other fresh fruit
that is easily available to you) as your *safe fruit*. Eat
up to three servings a day in addition to whatever is
called for in the menus of the Rotation Diet when you
need a lift, feel intolerably hungry, or are tempted to

deviate from your diet for any reason. Carry one with you at all times as a snack.

> Whenever you are tempted to deviate from the Rotation Diet make a safe-fruit substitution instead. This ensures that you will achieve close to the maximum possible weight loss.

apple	berries	grapefruit
melon	orange	peach
pineapple	tangerine	

Beverages

Drink eight 8-fluid-ounce (225-ml)-glasses of water a day. Use only no-calorie beverages except when milk is called for. You may drink up to 2 cups of coffee or tea each day, plus herb teas and low-sodium bouillons.

Index

267